"It has been said that teachers affect eternity, having no id( exactly their influence stops. If you are a teacher or a parent or simply a human being, read The Playful Classroom. And watch your influence, not only with the children around you, but with the adults, too, ripple toward eternity. Prepare to be inspired!"

**Dr. Anthony DeBenedet, Medical doctor and author of**
***Playful Intelligence***

"Jed Dearybury and Julie Jones take readers on a fun, engaging, and creative journey into the pedagogy of play! This must-read resource is perfect for all ages of learners and provides a wealth of ideas teachers can turn key straight away. Fantastic!"

**Dyane Smokorowski, 2013 Kansas Teacher of the Year, 2019 National Teacher Hall of Fame Inductee**

"The Playful Classroom is essential for every educator. During a time where education reform is a MUST, this book helps educators place value back to the relationship between the student and the educator as well as being creative and flexible throughout the learning process. I have gifted all my teachers with this FABULOUS book!"

**Ann Marie Taylor, Executive Director, Horse Creek Elementary Aiken, South Carolina, 2008 SC Teacher of the Year**

"With practical and readily applicable classroom strategies, Jed and Julie invite us into the wonderful world of play through laughter and creativity! I laughed a lot and learned even more. From early learning through secondary education, all educators can find golden nuggets throughout this text!"

**Dr. Jemelleh Coes, EDU Professor, UGA, 2014 Georgia Teacher of the Year**

"Playful learning isn't a reward. It's required! If you want deep, satisfied, inquisitive learning, the ideas inside The Playful Classroom will inspire and equip you."

**Matt Miller, Author, *Ditch That Textbook, Don't Ditch That Tech*, and**
***Ditch That Homework***

"Fittingly, The Playful Classroom finds ways to help teachers elevate learning and boost engagement, while also creating a sense of joy and whimsy for readers. Dearybury and Jones provide educators with the practical strategies and excellent examples they need to infuse the critical element of play into any classroom."

**Mike Soskil, Author *Teaching in the Fourth Industrial Revolution: Standing at the Precipice*, Top 10 finalist for the Global Teacher Prize, 2017**

# The Playful Classroom

# The Playful Classroom

## THE POWER OF PLAY FOR ALL AGES

**Jed Dearybury**

**Julie Jones, PhD**

**JB JOSSEY-BASS™**
A Wiley Brand

Published by Jossey-Bass
A Wiley Brand
111 River Street, Hoboken NJ 07030
www.josseybass.com

Jossey-Bass books and products are available through most bookstores. To contact Jossey-Bass directly, call our Customer Care Department within the US at 800-956-7739, outside the US at 317-572-3986, or fax 317-572-4002.

Wiley also publishes its books in a variety of electronic formats and by print-on-demand. Some material included with standard print versions of this book may not be included in e-books or in print-on-demand. For more information about Wiley products, visit www.wiley.com.

**Library of Congress Cataloging-in-Publication Data**

Names: Dearybury, Jed, 1978- author. | Jones, Julie, 1977- author.
Title: The playful classroom : the power of play for all ages / Jed
    Dearybury, Julie Jones.
Description: Hoboken, NJ : Wiley, 2020. | Includes index.
Identifiers: LCCN 2020010794 (print) | LCCN 2020010795 (ebook) | ISBN
    9781119674399 (paperback) | ISBN 9781119674467 (adobe pdf) | ISBN
    9781119674481 (epub)
Subjects: LCSH: Play. | Child development. | Classroom environment.
Classification: LCC LB1137 .D43 2020  (print) | LCC LB1137  (ebook) | DDC
    649/.5—dc23
LC record available at https://lccn.loc.gov/2020010794
LC ebook record available at https://lccn.loc.gov/2020010795

Cover Artwork & Design: New York Times bestselling author Peter H. Reynolds

Printed in the United States of America

First Edition

PB Printing SKY10035103_071122

*To our students—past, present, and future.*

# CONTENTS

In order for the PLAYFUL Classroom to become a reality,
there are some foundational beliefs that always matter.

## Section 1   The Case for Play
Play designs the future. Trains, planes, and automobiles of today
were the kids' cardboard creations of yesterday.

## Section 2   Play Inspires Creativity
### Creativity Inspires Play

Remember when you needed a tent, but had no tent? You found chairs and blankets and made one. You played and solved a problem through critical thinking using the materials you had.

## Section 3   Play Builds Trust
### *Trust Builds Opportunities for Play*

. . . in ourselves, students, parents, colleagues, and administration.
If we constantly doubt one another's abilities, motives, judgments,
and qualifications, how can we move forward together?

# Section 4   Play Builds Relationships
### *Relationships Are Strengthened Through Play*
Our students are humans before they get to us, and they're still humans when they leave. It will do us well to remember that fact more than their test scores, data, and grades.

## 24  The Theme Park Experience  146

## 25  Learning with Them, Alongside Them  149

# Section 5  Play Builds Community

*Communities Are Strengthened When We Play*
We live and interact with others—locally, regionally, and globally.
Play helps us shape a mindset of advocacy, awareness,
sensitivity, and compassion for all.

## 26  Relevance and the Four-Legged Stool  157

## 27  Fostering a Sense of Belonging  163

## 28  Getting to Know Students Personally  167

## 29  Supporting Academic Success  172

## Section 7   Get Out There and Play!

"She could never go back and make some of the details pretty. All she could do was move forward and make the whole beautiful." —Terri St. Cloud

# FOREWORD

This is a landmark book. The joyful southernisms suffused throughout allow the essential vitality of the authors' playful natures to transcend what might otherwise be dull, pedantic, linear prose that would miscarry the essence of play itself. (For those inexperienced with Southern idioms, there is a glossary to get you through.)

Even though I have been studying play behaviors and play science for most of my life, don't just take my word for it.

Read it!

While play behavior itself eludes clear definition, one concrete characteristic of authentic play is that it produces positive emotions; and a traverse through this book ensures that the reader will have the *experience* of remembering the emotions of their own play (and non-play). That recollection will enable them to "grok" the nature and importance of play, both cognitively and emotionally. Applying that experience to the classroom is the expertise of the authors.

Frankly, it is this union of cognition and emotion that fixes memory and learning in a positive, optimistic, and progressively more intricate scaffolding that has the student-player searching for more. Thus, play and learning are . . . almost synonymous. Intrinsic, play-sourced motivation is a major dynamic, within the developing brain, that produces learning.

Parents of young children and professional educators will discover—along with an "aha" about their own play—the guidance to *apply* the accessible play science in this book to the uniquely individual patterns of play-based learning that await activation in their children and students. And the union of play and learning will strengthen and sustain the foundation for their charges to become more fully alive, more fully human. This book also encourages teachers to become comfortable with their own play nature and incorporate that into the classroom climate, providing permission for teacher and student to embrace their play natures. . ..

Wow!

After much formal training in medicine, psychiatry, and clinical research, I have been enjoying studying play behaviors for 50 years. I have learned that the benefits of play are available for all of us for all of our lives, and the consequences of not playing, particularly early in life, are devastating. I have observed the unfettered play of wild animals in African fields; I have interviewed homicidal men in prisons, finding that play was absent in their lives; and I have spoken with scientists at Harvard and Stanford, and other scientists doing the objective scientific research to identify the biology of play. I've learned that play has existed for millions of years, evolving uniquely in each playful species, particularly us homo sapiens.

These varied life experiences have allowed me to see play for what it is, and what it is not; I've concluded that is a necessity for the long-term survival for all of us.

Jed and Julie have successfully distilled the core of play knowledge and honed their professionalism in applying it to the classroom.

Wow again!

I particularly like Chapter 23 on individual Play Personalities; there is so much potential benefit to recognizing an individual's play personality, and its inherent contributions to ongoing curiosity and engagement in the process of learning.

Imagine that through your entire preschool, primary elementary, middle and secondary education, you experienced your parents, teachers, and friends reinforcing what you naturally love; they encouraged you to pursue activities within necessary curriculum that spontaneously engaged you, activities that helped you experience from within your authentic self. If that had happened, your education would have been crafted to fit who you really are, and you would be a more self-secure, competent adult.

Over time, as the concept of Play Personalities enters the mainstream, aware parents will know to notice—from their child's earliest days—the activities and behaviors that cause their child to be gleeful, to be thrilled; they will be able to discern and nourish the Play Personality of their children. With that awareness they (and subsequently, teachers and other caretakers) can guide the child's development and education to better custom fit the innate capabilities of each young person.

Given the current norms for parenting and educating our youth, the focus on individual play personality as a teacher priority is not significant. However, the play science that is emerging, specifically that education based on the deeply engaging, natural curiosities of each child, may be perceived as idealistic and impractical.

It is not.

But, that is the wonder of this book. Jed and Julie are showing us how to do better than current test-driven educational norms. They have recognized and are using the growing flood of science that shows that combining play with learning is an optimal means for maximizing our human capacity for competency—for developing in kids their progressive ability to deal with the challenges of our rapidly changing work and home lives.

Yes, we have a long way to go from current norms, but we have evolutionary biology, human nature, science, and the pursuit of joy on our side.

Everyone likes to play. Science has shown that play-suffused curricular engagement is how humans learn best. All teachers want their students to learn quickly and well. Parents are dedicated to their kids' overall fulfillment and happiness. Given those facts, the logical conclusion is that *play*—as Jed and Julie demonstrate it—belongs front and center in the classroom. They are showing us the way out of the entrapment of failing mainstream educational practices.

One major obstacle is the belief that work and play are opposites —if you are playing, enjoying what you are doing, you are not working. A normal belief is that the classroom must be a place where one works, memorizing "facts," studying for tests, grinding out the grades. This landmark book, *The Playful Classroom,* not only refutes this, it provides in captivatingly fun cadences the truth that PLAY = LEARNING. It brings to light the latest research, which indicates the key to unlocking sustained learning in the classroom is playful engagement. The evidence from scientific research on learning is that a playful learner and a playful teacher form an extraordinarily effective learning system. Add to this the clear understanding of research scientists: the opposite of play is not work, it is depression. Depression results from serious lack of play. Further, national data is showing that the occurrence of depression and suicide among our youth is growing. Our current approaches to developing and educating our youth are too often shutting them down, stifling their abilities versus guiding them to bloom into stable, competent adults.

This book needs to reach beyond classrooms to policymakers and parents nationwide. Policymakers already acknowledge that teaching to standardized tests is not working as hoped, and recognize that educational science can explain why it's not working. Teachers cannot be playful when driven by reams of testing standards; students are often joyless where the essence of learning is fun. Parents must recognize that choosing their children's playdates (versus the children choosing) and setting expectations for extra-curricular activities, music lessons, tutors—fully scheduling their kids—perhaps in the well-intentioned pursuit of an Ivy League college is not the best path for their beloved child.

Dr. Stuart Brown

# ABOUT THE AUTHORS

**Jed Dearybury** began his education career in 2001. During his 13-year early childhood classroom tenure, Jed received numerous awards. He was featured in *GQ Magazine* as Male Leader of the Year, met President Obama as the South Carolina winner of the Presidential Award for Excellence in Math and Science Teaching, and was named as a top 5 finalist for South Carolina Teacher of the Year. Since 2015, he has been leading professional development across the country, as well as training the next generation of educators through his work in higher ed. As of August 2019, he is the Director of Creativity and Innovation at http://mrdearybury.com LLC. His mission: Equip, Encourage, Empower the teaching profession using creativity, laughter, and hands-on fun! Connect with him online, Twitter @mrdearybury or www.mrdearybury.com.

Since starting her career in 1999, **Dr. Julie Jones** has had an exceptional journey in education. Previously, she has taught 4th, 5th, 7th, 8th, and 9–12 grades in both general and special education, as well as higher ed at the University of South Carolina Upstate. Currently, she is the Director of Student Teaching and Director of Early Childhood in Converse College's School of Education and Graduate Studies. She maintains an active research agenda with interests including instructional technology and pedagogy, always with a mix of creativity and play. She is the editor of the *Teacher Education Journal of South Carolina*, and past-president of the South Carolina Association of Teacher Educators. Follow her on Twitter @JuliePJones, and view her full curriculum vitae at www.juliepjones.com.

# ACKNOWLEDGMENTS

First of all, we must thank the coffee and the tea. Without thy substance, we shan't have accomplished much. The scones and pimento cheese biscuits, especially Friday's flavor—you know who you are. And, that one day at Bond Street Wines where Jeff House provided complimentary midday inspiration. For that, we are grateful.

Gratitude to the gang at Little River Coffee Bar, Pharmacy Coffee, Hub City Bookshop, and Downtown Deli and Donuts. Mmm, those muffins. Mmm, that dressing. And we mustn't forget the strawberry tea and free donut on our first trip. Smack ya lips!

We are so inspired for the playful creatives who share their talents and make the world a more beautiful and connected place:

- Peter Reynolds, you have long been a hero of ours, but we never dreamed that your artwork would grace the cover of this work. We are so thankful for our connected dots.
- Stuart Brown, who dances to the Spider-Man theme song as if it's an everyday occurrence. Play is in your bones, and we're thrilled to have met you and work with you.

We are so grateful for the educators who inspire us every day. You know who you are because we tell you—every time we see you. We would be remiss if we didn't mention the specific contributions of both Matt Johnson and Gina Ruffcorn here. You two filled our heads with new ideas and challenged our antiquated ones. Dr. Melissa Walker, of @heydaycoaching, thank you for coaching us through the rough bits; Lord knows we love to argue, and you kept us on track in spite of ourselves.

To our family and friends who have supported us in this journey— so much patience, so much love, so many eye-rolls that we've already forgiven you for.

Also, special thanks to Jackie B for the secret room in which the muse must apparently spend its winter break. Sorry for the smudge; it was chocolate. We swear.

To the Wiley team: thank you for choosing our work and for being just as excited about sharing this message with the world as we are.

# INTRODUCTION

Dear Teacher,

Are your ears burnin'? In the deep South, that means someone's been talkin' 'bout ya. It's us. We love y'all! We think you are
the bee's knees, the best thing since sliced bread, the butter on
the biscuit, and as fine as frog hair! If y'all *cain't* tell it, we are as
Southern as it comes, and there may be a need for a translator
as you read our work. Feel free to tweet us if you need help, but
we think the context clues will fill you in. If you get stuck, there's a
glossary in the back.

Speaking of clues . . . Do you have any clue how incredible
you are for reading this book? You picked it up to strengthen your
work, to be stronger for the profession, to be better for your students. You already have a teaching degree, you most likely have
spent countless hours in professional development, and now here
you are continuing to seek growth as an educator by reading our
words. You want to have a playful classroom, where students are
fully engaged in authentic hands-on learning that is meaningful
and fun.

We wrote this book because we have a message that will
hopefully help you with that growth. We're fired up. We're 'bout
to boil over. Not in a mad way of fire and boiling. Don't misun-
derstand that. What we mean is that we are filled with zeal and
excitement about the work we do with students and we want
you to be too. Julie says this whole topic really cranks her tractor.
That just means she is really excited. We digress. You see, for the
true Southerner, we let these little bits of southern speak fly when
we're really fired up. Here's the rule: even the rudest thought is forgiven if it's followed by "bless his heart," even more so if said with
a shake of the head.

It is incredible to us that you have chosen this path for your
life's work. It's not easy. In fact, it is one of the hardest jobs on the
planet, and some of the things we are going to ask of you in this
text will make it even harder. We are gonna ask you to dig deep,
to challenge yourself, to question yourself (and us), and to focus
clearly on the heart of teaching . . . the children. Without them
we have no job, we have no profession, we have no calling.

Many days after school, tears have probably run down your
cheeks because you felt defeated. If they haven't yet, don't

worry . . . tears are coming. Both of us have stories where we just sat in our classrooms and fell apart. There were so many tears, you'd think it was comin' a gully washer. Could we do it? Could we reach students? Could we make learning relevant, engaging, and fun? How do we make learning meaningful for our students? How do we connect the content to their lives?

We bet that many days you might have closed the door to your classroom, looked at the walls, and questioned everything you did that day. We did. Many days after that faculty meeting, you have probably been so mad at your admins and coworkers that you felt like quitting. We did. Many days you have likely felt as lonely as a pine tree in a parking lot. We did. Many days your kids have probably run around like chickens with their heads cut off. Ours did. But trust us, the journey is worth it. The calling is stronger than the hardships.

> Learning must be meaningful.
>
> Learning must be relevant.
>
> Learning must be fun.

We know that many family members may have tried to talk you out of teaching. *Why would you wanna do that?*

We know you won't make a lot of money. *We made more waiting tables.*

We know that you will be looked down on because you don't work a full year like every other profession. *OFF EVERY SUMMER!*

We know that you may be ridiculed for your career choice. *You could do anything you want!*

You must ignore those naysayers. Tune them out.

Find something new to listen to.
Listen to the voices of students you've taught and will teach.
Listen to them begging for your attention.
Listen to them crying out for learning that is meaningful and inspiring.
Listen to them needing your love, compassion, and understanding.

When you focus on their voices, there's nothing you won't do to help them. You will want for nothing less in your career than a classroom where learning is relevant, meaningful, and fun.

You won't care about the Negative Nellies who tried to keep you from real teaching.

You won't worry about the days you cussed and cried after school.

You won't worry about how angry you were with your coworkers who don't get it like you do.

Why? Because the voices of students who begged, cried, and needed you will drown them out in your pursuit of creating a playful classroom.

Wait . . . "What do you mean playful classroom?" We hear you, you there in the back. We're not talking about a school where recess lasts all day. We don't mean a place where it's all fluff and no meat. The playful classroom is a place where the teacher embraces something beyond the ordinary, mundane, traditional boredom of school to reach students who are desperately crying out for something more.

A place where the learning is more than "activities" to cut, paste, and hang on a bulletin board.

A place where learning is more than worksheets upon worksheets upon worksheets with none of them "growing dendrites."

A place where learning is never "ugh . . . back to school" after a long break.

The playful classroom is a place where learning is meaningful, relevant, and fun. Unlike that PD you just attended—you know, the one with the slide show presentation that was read to you—the ideas in this book will equip, encourage, and empower you to make this classroom dream a reality. These cow horns'll hook. This dog'll hunt. We promise.

In order for the PLAYFUL Classroom to become a reality, there are some foundational beliefs that must always matter.

- THE CASE FOR **PLAY**. Play designs the future. Trains, planes, and automobiles of today were the kids' cardboard creations of yesterday.
- PLAY INSPIRES **CREATIVITY**. Remember when you needed a tent, but had no tent? You found chairs and blankets and made one. You played and solved a problem through critical thinking using the materials you had.
- PLAY BUILDS **TRUST** in students, parents, colleagues, administration, and ourselves. If we constantly doubt one another's abilities, motives, judgments, and qualifications, how can we move forward together?
- PLAY STRENGTHENS **RELATIONSHIPS**. Our students are humans before they get to us, and they're still humans when they leave. It will do us well to remember that fact more than their test scores, data, and grades.

- PLAY CULTIVATES **COMMUNITY**. We live and interact with others—locally, regionally, and globally. Play helps us shape a mindset of advocacy, awareness, sensitivity, and compassion for all.
- PLAY NURTURES **GROWTH**. We can always be better. Play helps us to grow.

The core beliefs of the playful classroom transcend the history and future of education. They have always been present and always will. Whether we have a large classroom budget or none at all, we can have a playful classroom. We're here to paint a picture of why. When we understand the why and the what, the how will come naturally.

When we look for playful moments.
When we provide ourselves and students with time, space, and opportunity to play.
When we aren't afraid to play, mess up, learn, repeat.
When we keep in mind that the more we play, the more playful we become.
When we remember that playfulness makes us happy, and happy people play.

We have given you a peek into the fun. Now, pull up a chair, and sit a spell. Good Lord willin' and the creek don't rise, we're fixin' to get you all kinds of fired up!

Y'all play purdy now,
Jed and Julie

# The Playful Classroom

# SECTION 1

# The Case for Play

*Why we must get on the floor with kids, ask questions, be curious; new ideas won't come from regurgitating facts. Play designs the future. Trains, planes, and automobiles of today were the kids' cardboard creations of yesterday.*

# CHAPTER 1

# Hey y'all! (yes, all y'all)

Hey y'all. We see you there, wondering how we're going to devote a whole book to those 15–20 minutes of recess. Are you afraid we're going to tell you to get out there on the monkey bars with your students? Well, you should, but that's not the purpose of this book. You see, when I (Julie) started thinking about the concept of play, I did so with a snarky look on my face.

(Yes, she did.)

Give me a little grace, Jed. My children were still in diapers and I was teaching in a very Direct Instruction–based middle school that was praised for high test scores. What did I know about play? Nothing.

Ok, that's a lie. Growing up, play for me was swinging on a metal swingset inside a chain-link-fenced yard outside my Papa's plumbing store. Yes, I swang and sang—at the top of my lungs.

Play for me was challenging my Barbies to put on all-weather gear and climb their Everest—the white crochet blanket hanging off the side of Nana's bed.

Play was hula hoops.
Play was paint and cardboard.
Play was channeling my inner E. B. White on my (new!) Canon typewriter.
Play was roller skating on our indoor/outdoor carpeting of our basement.
Play was my carefully curated collection of the Babysitters Club and Nancy Drew in order, on my shelf, just so.
But, play was always separate from *school*.

Then, along comes my friend, Jed. He's an early childhood educator at heart, but don't go getting all "*oh, that's cute*" on us. He teaches adults now, and the concepts behind his (now, our) methods are much the same. We're like sweet potatoes and yams when it comes to instruction. We're close—'bout the same. Not *Waffle House–sittin'* close, but the good kind.

So here's how it's going down in this section: First, we're going to crank your tractor on the concept of play. Yeah, get excited. It's happening. Then, for you high-brow, scientific folks we're going to give you the research behind play, including why kids—not just the littles, but even the teenagers (*and us teachers*)—should be doing more of it. Then, we're going to take you on a journey, reframing the classroom in a world of play. You'll be more effective as a teacher and as a human. And you'll love it. You'll love it because it's fun and entertaining.

You will love it a bushel and a peck and a hug around the neck!

Kinda like when you get off the "It's a Small World" ride at Disney—you'll be singing this song all day.

## Defining PLAY

We have all played at some point, hopefully. While our play histories may not be identical because of various socioeconomic, cultural, and societal norms, most of us know what playing feels like. It's those moments where our spirit lets go of time constraints, our minds get lost in the moment, and we seemingly lose ourselves in the experience. There is a name for that, and we will discuss it more in depth in a bit. But, when it gets down to defining play, we get silly headed—especially academic folk. In the halls of academia, from third grade all the way to higher education especially, it seems that the idea of playing while learning/learning while playing has gotten a bad rap. No one seems to be able to agree on anything but its ambiguity.

> We had quite the playful moment right in the middle of the Marriott lobby deciding if the correct word there was "wrap" or "rap." Trust us, neither of us will ever forget which one is the correct word because of the hilarity of the playfulness that transpired. The learning stuck because we played.

Getting this train back on its tracks here . . . Let's consider these historically academic definitions for play:

- Play is a "paradox" because it both *is* and is *not* what it appears to be. —Geoffrey Bateson, biologist (1955)
- Play is "liminol" or "liminoid" (occupies a space between reality and unreality). —Victor Turner, anthropologist (1969)
- Play is "amphibolous" (goes in two directions at once). —Michael Spariosu, classical scholar (1989)

We could go on, but you get the point. Let's get some things straight. Mama would say, "Let's have a word of prayer." Play isn't what you're thinking it is. Take a look at the next image. We sketched it for you, but the real worksheet is floating around out there and was recently texted to us from a fellow teacher buddy. Do you see the problem? No? Don't worry, you will soon. In reality, play is so much more than the perception presented here.

When most people hear play, they think of the behavior. They think of monkey bars and swings. Hide and go seek and Red Rover. Red light, green light, and Simon says.

Four square.
Freeze tag.
Mother may I?
A tisket, a tasket.

Sardines.

Pickle.

Yes, they're right. But let's expand this concept: there's *play*; then there's *playful*. One describes a behavior, the other a mindset. We're going to talk about both.

Play is throwing a frisbee in the yard (air currents and wind power) or painting what you see (scientific method of observation) or reading for pleasure (imagination and visualization of text). Playfulness is the inclination to smile or laugh during all of these activities. Playfulness is the way we see the world. Playfulness is skipping and frolicking instead of walking. Playfulness is a mindset—an approach to each situation with intentional fun. The playful mindset includes having an awareness of our world, being intentional about our choices, honoring the process until it becomes a habit, and using results as a catalyst for more creativity.

According to our friend Anthony DeBenedet, MD, playfulness is not a radical new form of intelligence. Rather, it's an extension of both intrapersonal and interpersonal intelligences (you know, all that work by Howard Gardner).

(Jed: Do we all know it? I don't . . . Googlin' now!)

While these two are separate concepts, both are needed and reap maximum benefits. Read on.

# CHAPTER 2

# Play as a Behavior

Let's dive into the first notion: play as a behavior. Yes, children play every day. But it's not just the 20 minutes after lunch when teachers chat on the sidewalk and scan the playground for potential dangers or risk-taking before injuries occur. That is play. But that's just one kind: free play. We could go off here on how much love we show for our students when we play with them—on the swings, with the football, foot races, etc. But, granny said there's a time and a place for everything; just know that sermon is a comin'. Through free play, children learn to cooperate, follow rules, expand imaginations, strengthen their mind and body, and take failure in stride (Pang, 2016). Games of chance and simple video games are also in this category.

Another kind of play, not so well known, is deep play. The term was made popular by Clifford Geertz (1973), an anthropologist writing about Balinese cockfighting. Cockfighting in Bali is more than free play. In the United States, cockfighting is illegal, mean, and wrong, and we are in no way condoning this practice; however, in Bali it's a show of wealth and social status. It's competition between villages with high symbolic stakes. It's also personal and provides people with a satisfaction that has lasting benefits of the kind free play doesn't.

In her book, *Deep Play* (2000), Diane Ackerman explains, "Deep play is the ecstatic form of play. In its thrall, all the play elements are visible, but they're taken to intense and transcendent heights. Thus, deep play should really be classified by mood, not activity." When we are using the phrase *deep play*, we are really talking about the process—the *how* of what's going on. *What's* happening isn't as important as *how*. Just because we're playing cards doesn't mean we're engaged in deep play, but we could be if we're in the strategizing, competitive zone. Ackerman shares, "Some activities are prone to it: art, religion, risk-taking, and some sports—especially those that take place in relatively remote, silent, and risky environments, such as scuba diving, parachuting, hang gliding, mountain climbing."

So, what is the qualifier that separates free play from deep play? Well, there are four. And, only one of them has to be present to consider a behavior deep play.

An experience becomes deep play when it . . .

1. . . . is mentally absorbing, offering challenges and problems to solve.
2. . . . offers players a new context for using the same skills as work.
3. . . . offers the same satisfaction as work, but different because the rewards are more clear.
4. . . . offers a connection to the players' past (childhood memories, home, etc.) (Pang, 2016).

Read those again. Go ahead. We'll wait. You see that? We have opportunities to have deep play in the classroom every day. All day long. We don't want deep play all day, though; we want a mixture of deep play and free play (also known as *rest*, or *non-work*) in the course of our time with students. The brain needs periods of focus and relaxation (Carey, 2015). It's why authors take time from their work to go on a walk, and scientists stop experimentation to play racquetball. Our brains are like a wave—with a crest and a trough. You can't have one without the other. There is balance. In this balance we find inspiration. With a balance of work, deep play, and rest, our brain can stimulate and sustain creativity. It's why Google intentionally organizes its physical spaces for playful thinking. We may not have the funding in public schools for office putting greens, vintage subway cars, and revolving bookcases. But there are aspects of playful thinking in cultures across the world that we could incorporate. Let's explore some ideas with a little imaginative play:

- Imagine if schools adopted the cultural phenomenon known as the *siesta*. The siesta as we know it, originated in Spain and is derived from the Latin *hora sexta*, meaning the sixth hour. Traditionally, the day's hours began at dawn, so the sixth hour would be noon—a great time to recharge via rest. For schooling, siesta could be considered generally resting, be it physically, mentally, or otherwise. Imagine being encouraged to slow down, have conversations, and just be.
- Imagine if all educators espoused the Hygge lifestyle popular in Denmark. All spaces would be designed with coziness

and comfort in mind. Talk about flexible seating! Classrooms would include couches or puffy chairs for curling up with a good book. Pleasant scents would permeate the hallways, and lighting would be natural and easy on the eyes. Rather than looking at phones while lunching, all students would enjoy their meals with friends, conversation, and eye contact. Oh, and that teacher's lounge? It could actually be used for lounging.

• Imagine if we offered recess for 15 minutes every hour. Yes, that's recess and free play at least seven times in a traditional school day. Do you think we're making this up? This is the cultural norm in Finland. Students play outside with a rare teacher interruption for 15 minutes each hour. Some schools in Texas have adopted this structure, and the early results are amazing! We'll talk more about this later, but if you're curious, search the Internet for the LiiNK Project at Texas Christian University.

"I think 99 times and find nothing. I stop thinking, swim in silence, and the TRUTH comes to me."

—Albert Einstein

Do you see what we did there? We took a brain break from the discussion of deep play to be playful and dream. Now, our musical bridge has concluded and we're back. Many of you may be thinking that one 20-minute recess will provide the balance between deep play and free play. You take the class out, you let them run and wiggle, then you bring them in and get back to work. But that's 20 minutes out of a 6- to 7-hour school day. How many breaks have you taken since starting this book? Have you gotten up to use the bathroom? Did you change positions from sitting at a table to a chair with a soft throw blanket? Have you turned to have a conversation with a friend or significant other? We know you probably want a formula for the classroom—X amount of play + X amount of rest—but, in reality, these two should be combined throughout the day to develop a whole class full of students and teachers with a playful mindset.

# CHAPTER 3

# Play as a Mindset

In *Playful Intelligence*, DeBenedet identifies five qualities of influence on overall happiness and well-being: *imagination*, *sociability*, *humor*, *spontaneity*, and *wonder*. Through observation, study, and hundreds of interviews, DeBenedet found those who personify these skills seem to live lighter and smarter—bringing enjoyment to their daily lives.

Don't we all want that for our lives?
Don't we want that for our classroom?
Don't we want our students to *imagine* the *wonder* of it all?

As we break these qualities down for you, we hope you reflect like we did: (i) How are we modeling these qualities for our students?, and (ii) How are we encouraging our students to embrace these aspects of playfulness?

## Imagination

You might expect imagination to be associated here with artistic or musical expression. DeBenedet did, too, but that's not where he found it showing up in the interviews. In his work, the quality of imagination in healthy adults manifested in the ability to psychologically reframe difficult situations. Not escaping our struggles, but rather viewing them differently—using imagination to problem-solve and cope. Imagination, when practiced through deep play and daydreaming, increases our capacity for empathy. *Empathy*. That's the word to focus on here. It's the seed from which positive global change can occur.

Surely you've heard the name Greta Thunberg. She's a 16-year-old from Sweden who is lending her voice to the #climatechange efforts. On September 18, 2019, Thunberg spoke to the US Congress urging them to take action. When applauded, she responded, "Please save your praise. We don't want it; don't invite us here to just tell us how inspiring we are without actually doing anything about it, because it doesn't lead to anything" (I want you to take action, 2019).

How many of our students know the varying perspectives on the topic of climate change? It is number 13 of the 17 Sustainable Development Goals (SDGs) (see Figure 3.1): an urgent call to action by the United Nations for cultivating and healing the world in which we live. We could focus our instruction on the (SDGs) every day, and what a wonderful way to provide rich learning experiences—talk about developing empathy!

Imagination is also a quality that helps us transform our mindset. For example, take a moment to Google "the Einstellung Effect." This study, which focused on identifying solution bias, showed participants solving a problem based on previous experience even when a better solution exists. Their mindsets were *fixed* based on the experiences they had been provided.

Right now, as you're reading, pause. Think of a clown in your head. You might even want to doodle it in the margin. Does your clown have red hair? See, that's what we're talking about! Think about how McDonald's and Bozo have taught us all that a clown has to have red hair. There are all kinds of cool clown hair color variations, but dog-it if we aren't fixed on red (no offense, Annie).

FIGURE 3.1 Sustainable development goals.

Once, I was trying to teach a class of first graders how to write a letter. I modeled on the anchor chart:

Dear mama,

    etc. etc. etc. (insert content here)

Love, Jed.

Can y'all guess how many first graders wrote "Love, Jed" at the bottom of their letters?

If we rely too much on our past experiences to solve a problem, we allow these neural connections to strengthen, thus limiting our ability to think creatively. We use our thought-defaults and get stuck. When we exercise our imaginations, we reframe problems, open our minds, and look at the world in a new way.

Think about the impact of reframing for students. Just the other day, I (Julie) was challenging my students to read like a historian. This was a class of preservice teachers who in less than a year would have a class of their own. Imagine here your middle schoolers, your high schoolers, the faculty at your school. They have much the same learning trajectory. Students in my class have a choice of assignments; they propose ways to showcase their knowledge using the ISTE standards for educators. The student's question went something like this: *How do you want us to do X? How long should it be? Do you want images?*

These questions come every semester. It's the reframing of educational mindset I have to coach them through. My response? It's not what *I* want. What do *you* want to create that will showcase you have this understanding or this skill? Who will benefit from the product you create? These are college students. When they finally do cross the bridge from receiving content passively to acting in the role of leaders—that. That is learning reframed.

How many times do we *do it the way it's always been done* because it worked one time in the past? We don't know about you, but every class we teach is unique and requires specialized strategies from us as educators. Teachers with a strong imagination are able to recognize opportunities to follow paths to new outcomes instead of relying on the same ol' same ol'.

## Sociability

Playful sociability includes the ability to reject a *THEM* vs. *US* mentality. Those with the quality of playful sociability see only WE. Those who embody this trait have a strong sense of egalitarianism, built by the approach to social situations with humility and powerlessness. These people have a way of making everyone around them feel valued. They interact with authenticity, seeing others as humans rather than labels. Teachers who personify playful sociability reject stereotypes, loving their students first and teaching them second.

To truly educate, those with the trait of playful sociability block labels and listen to student stories. We must hear them. We must listen. These nuggets of authenticity are clues to their needs. Do they need remediation? Do they need challenge? Do they need the connection of friendship? Do they crave leadership roles? In the medical field, listening is key to diagnosis. In the field of education, listening is key to meeting the needs of our students. In the end, we are all working on the diagnosis of how to be a better human.

In our path to diagnosis, we must beware of the trap of anchoring bias. When we place too much value on initial information (think data, test scores, grades, last year's teacher, first impressions), our brain starts anchoring. Once this occurs, it's hard to adjust our thinking. Don't try to act like y'all don't know about this. Mrs. Smith, the second grade teacher, runs down the hall at the beginning of every year to tell all the third grade teachers about the new batch of "sweethearts" coming up. Sadly, she never has much sweet to say because she just wants to *discuss* all the ones she didn't like.

Y'all . . . Shut that down. Remember, the goal here is to develop playful classrooms, and doing that starts with strong playful minds. There ain't nothing playful about a gossiping teacher.

## Humor

Because we recognize humor as laughter, it is the easiest characteristic of DeBenedet's (2018) playful mindset to spot. However, we have to be careful in our analysis of it, according to E. B. White, not to kill it in the process. *Caution:* What you're about to read is a little heady.

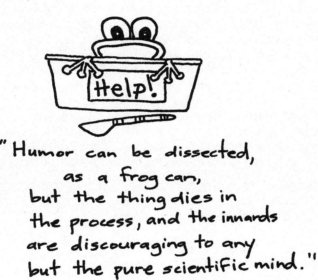

"Humor can be dissected, as a frog can, but the thing dies in the process, and the innards are discouraging to any but the pure scientific mind."

— E.B. White

The area of the brain that controls laughter is the subcortex—the same area that controls breathing and muscle reflexes. The areas of the brain that light up when we experience joy are known as the ventral tegmental area. So, basically we're looking at the bottom and the back of the brain. When we experience joy or laughter, the "pleasure chemical" dopamine pushes from those areas toward the front of the brain (the part responsible for judgment, creativity, and problem solving). Here's the key. Are you ready? Joy, pleasure, creativity, and critical thinking are connected. That's not all. Our brain's connective, dendrite-firing awesomeness pairs an emotion with each learning experience. Educators have a choice. We have students potentially shut down from frustration (it's just too painful!) or we build strong connections by associating learning with positive emotions (Berridge & Kringelbach, 2015; Jenson, 2005). DeBenedet calls this effect *resiliency,* one of the main benefits of humor.

Another benefit of humor is human connection. The right kind of humor "says to others that it's safe to explore, play, and nurture a relationship together" (DeBenedet, 2018). Think about the last time you went out with a group of friends. Not just random people, but those who you are close to, comfortable with, and connected to. Those in your inner circle where you don't have to be "on" like when you're at school. Maybe y'all went to dinner at your favorite spot, saw a movie, then had drinks after. All along the way you were cuttin' up. There's no doubt that what you're doing is playing. You may not call it that, because you're grown-ups, but that's what it is. You most certainly laughed, shared funny stories, and had moments of playful banter. That's exactly what we are talking about here. When we use *affiliative humor* (the kind that puts others at ease, amuses, and improves relationships), we allow ourselves to drop personal walls and engage openly in conversations (Martin, 2006). We already know that education is first about relationships, so now you can see how humor is an essential element to successful classroom communities. According to our friend, Dr. Lee Hurren, author of *Humor in School Is Serious Business* (2010), there are seven benefits of laughter:

1. Decreases stress hormones.
2. Increases immune cells.
3. Triggers the release of endorphins.
4. Can temporarily relieve pain.
5. Provides a natural workout.
6. Increases memory and intelligence.
7. Enhances creativity

With all these benefits, combined with the fact that it's just plain fun, why would we not be giggling and cracking puns all day?

## Spontaneity

Spontaneity is the trait exhibited when we do unplanned things, outside of routine. The art of teaching includes the use of spontaneity when we teach in the moment, when we use student questions to follow curiosities to their *aha* moments. Some of our most favorite memories from the classroom are the days when our lesson plan books were rendered useless as we became so enthralled in the moment of learning that we followed paths to places we never dreamed of in accordance with the district's scope and sequence because we embraced the spontaneity of being led by children and their curiosities rather than a prescribed plan created by someone miles away with no knowledge of our students. As my friend Teri would say, those people are as far away as where Jesus lost his slipper. We don't even know what that means, but we trust that his slipper is far, far away.

Students trust us to let them explore, and spontaneity allows exploration to take the lead in classrooms. There's a science to spontaneity as well; it manifests itself in our day-to-day lives as psychological flexibility—the mental response to the unplanned and unpredictable. Although you do not know this, we experienced spontaneity at the exact moment we were writing this passage. The whole story about the slipper and its whereabouts came up in a discussion about a teacher many states away from us, and we had no plans of adding that into this work. But, after rereading this section, we wanted you to have a little giggle here to remind you that we like to be playful and spontaneous.

Let's get a little closer to home: you know those folks who get all bent out of sorts when they get a new student? When they are given a new paperwork task? When their carefully planned lesson goes off the rails? Those folks might need a little practice in rolling with it—in spontaneity. We don't want to be all haughty here—we have most certainly gotten all bent out of shape and gone off the rails, but the times where we've let things roll off us like water on a duck's back are most definitely the times where life has been much more enjoyable and memorable.

We'd like to say we're the kind of teacher who eases through disruptions, but in reality we feel a little scattered. It's not that we don't ease through; it's that we can't remember where we were before the phone rang, the visitor came, or where our dog-gone clipboard went. It's like that old saying about making lemonade out of lemons; if we have the mindset of psychological flexibility, we don't get rattled. Our students won't worry what will set us off. We won't take away recess because we've HAD IT! We won't throw silent lunch around like glitter. We breathe. We smile. We reassess, and we roll through.

How do we encourage spontaneity in our students? We can start by giving them opportunities to problem solve. Did someone in the back say PBL? Yeah, we heard you. Yes. Any kind of learning situation, project-based or otherwise, that's messy and unpredictable (yes, like real life) will do it.

Think about how often we ask students to imagine alternate solutions or reframe problems. In personality science, this is called "openness to experience." If we're open, we'll be spontaneous. If we're spontaneous, we have flexibility. If we're flexible, we give ourselves permission to create, have bold ideas, and craft new solutions. Guess what? You're playing. And what a nifty cycle.

As we mentioned "alternate solutions or reframe problems" just now, my brain went immediately to teaching second graders how to do two-digit addition and subtraction with regrouping. At the time we taught this concept, there was lots of talk in the world about "new math." People, mainly parents, could just not wrap their brains around the possibility of solving two-digit add and subtract equations with a method other than the old "borrow or carry" options. We borrow in subtraction; we carry in addition (OK, now we regroup); that's the way parents had learned it. That was the only way. There was no other way. Even if their precious little Timmy thought his way was easier, they were just not gonna stand for it. He must learn to borrow or carry.

Ironically, the very idea of "new math" is a misnomer. People around the world have been solving equations for centuries using the methods we were now teaching. What made them new was that it was the first time this group of adults had ever encountered various solutions to a problem. They were all suffering from the Einstellung effect. Even though there was an easier way for some students, it wasn't what had been fixed, constructed, cemented into their parent's learning—therefore, they insisted these new methods weren't right. WRONG . . . they were right, but the parents' method were, too. Being spontaneous in our thinking can sometimes allow us both to be right because we can get to the same outcome. As granny would say, there's more than one way to skin a cat . . . Although we still aren't sure why anyone should be skinnin' a cat.

## Wonder

You might read this section title and think *wonder* is the same as *curiosity*. While these two can be interchangeable as synonyms, the mindset for wonder here is different. Curiosity spurs action, but the kind of wonder Dr. DeBenedet is referring to is the kind that stops you in your tracks. It's awe. It's that moment when time freezes and you appreciate the raw emotion in a moment. Kids experience wonder all the time. They'll pause to watch a woolly worm make its way up a tree. They'll turn their heads to the side, mouth falling open as they experience the push and pull of magnetic forces. The wonder can be seen on their faces. We know it because their eyes light up. There may be a grin. There may be scrunched up eyebrows. But there's always a pause. The pause is when the emotional experience occurs; it's our brain allowing time to regroup and reflect.

Wonder, on a neuropsychological level, is an emotion. We know what you're thinking here: "Yes! This is great. I'm going to hook all my learners though wonder-ful experiences." And we do want you to do just that, but if you start making lists of more hooks for tomorrow's plans, you'll be going about this *wonder* thing all wrong. Wonder is not the *what* of the experience; it's the *how*. The playful quality of wonder is more about focusing on *how* we perceive our environment than in *what* we're seeing. If we keep going bigger and better, allowing our students to experience wonder through the grand and majestic, we'll cause wonder inflation. Students may begin to depend on the "extra," and their wonder threshold gets higher and higher.

So what do we do? Easy. We model for our students how we find wonder in the small things. Each experience, each lesson has an opportunity for wonder. Find it, whisper it to them. Your eyes are wide, your voice is low. They're leaning in . . . do you see it? Wonder is contagious.

## CHAPTER 4

# Benefits of PLAY

The purpose of this chapter is to help reframe your thinking about play. For you academics in the crowd (Julie, put your hand down), this chapter is for you. Some of you need these nuggets, these juicy research bits, to support a change of thinking. Like that dollop of mayo in your cornbread recipe, this part makes the experience rich and tasty for you. You'll see a mix here of some classic (early) research and some more recent publications. As you can see, science supports classroom play well beyond early childhood, and the evidence grows every day.

## Brain Benefits

- Play and exploration trigger the secretion of brain-derived neurotrophic factor (BDNF) a substance essential for the growth of brain cells (Greenough & Black, 1992; Gordan et al. 2003; Dewer, 2014), read more on BDNF in Chapter 14.
- Movement fuels the brain with oxygen, but it also feeds it neurotrophins, which increase the number of connections between neurons (Jenson, 2005).
- Play and movement may increase catecholamines (brain chemicals such as norepinephrine and dopamine), which generally serve to energize and elevate mood (Chaouloff, 1989; Jenson, 2005).

## Academic Benefits

- We pay attention to academic tasks when given frequent, brief opportunities for free play (Kesslak, Patrick, So, Cotman, & Gomez-Pinilla, 1998; Bjorkland & Pelligrini, 2000; Pelligrini & Holmes, 2006; Stevenson & Lee, 1990).

- There is a link between play and the development of language skills, particularly if the play is symbolic, pretend play such as theater (Fisher, 1992; Lewis et al., 2000).
- Many early cognitive researchers ignored play, assuming it disconnected from intellectual growth. They were wrong. In reality, play and play-oriented movements improve cognition (Silverman, 1993).
- Play allows us to make mistakes without high-stakes consequences, thus enhancing learning (Fordyce & Wehner, 1993).
- The resting brain automatically switches to a default-mode network (DMN), a series of interconnected sections that activate when we stop focusing on external tasks, shifting the outward focus to inward. The DMNs of creatives differ from those of the average person (Pang, 2016).
  - Why is this important? The complexity of the default mode shapes our capacity for
    - Self-awareness
    - Memory
    - Ability to imagine the future (predictions)
    - Empathy
    - Moral judgment
  - Children with greater DMNs have
    - Superior reading skills
    - Better memory
    - Higher intelligence and attention scores
    - Greater empathy
    - Higher abilities to see from another's point of view

## Creative Benefits

- Play promotes creative problem solving (Pepler & Ross, 1981; Wyver & Spence, 1999).
- Play builds imagination, which is necessary for empathy (DeBenedet, 2018; Frank, 1978).
- Exercising your imagination through daydreaming increases your capacity for empathy (DeBenedet, 2018; Frank, 1978).

## Social Benefits

- Playfully intelligent people seldom form strong first impressions; therefore, they approach social situations with a strong sense of egalitarianism (DeBenedet, 2018; Kahenman, 2013; Tversky & Kahneman, 1974).

- Play enhances social skills, emotional intelligence, and conflict resolution ability (Jenson, 2005).
- Free play allows children to practice decision-making skills, learn to work in groups, share, resolve conflicts, and advocate for themselves. It also allows them to discover what they enjoy at their own pace (Ginsburg, 2007).

If you're like Jed, all that research may have felt a tad heavy. He will admittedly tell you he skimmed over the bullets. Not because he doesn't value the research or want it to be in his repertoire of knowledge, but because it gets all jumbled in his brain. He needs real-world, concrete explanations of each one so that his brain can be full of BDNF and his DMN gets stronger. Do you need the simple nuggets? Do you need to see a real-world connection for playful benefits? Check out this list of authentic lessons we compiled from friends via our social media. See "Things we learned from playing" on page 23.

We took some of our favorites from this list and made y'all a little poster for your classroom. You can download it for free from theplayfulclassroom.com. We would love to see pics of it hanging about so feel free to take a playful pic and post it to the interwebs. Don't forget the hashtag #theplayfulclassroom.

In educator preparation programs, one rarely has classes in the role of constructivist methods outside of early childhood educator programs (grades pK–3). Sadly, even most elementary programs (grades 2–6) begin to shift more toward content and B. F. Skinner (think: model . . . lead . . . test) than play and Piaget. Why do we continue to do that when we obviously learn so much through play? For those of you who are years removed from your last learning theory course, here's an overview: In a nutshell, constructivism is willfully seeking the answers to one's own questions. Teachers who set up situations where students ask their own questions and seek their own answers are increasing in number, but still, we need more. These kinds of learning experiences—asking questions (imagination), seeking answers (with wonder)—are playful!

Let's review, when we say *play*, we are not just talking about recess. Sure, recess is great, the need for activity in schools is supported throughout the literature. But that's not the purpose of these pages. We're talking about the kind of play that can sharpen our minds—the kind of play that makes us more creative.

Let's reflect on how our classrooms inspire students to think. When is the last time a student came to you with an idea? How did you respond? Teachers like a plan. We know we do. It's why we bullet journal; we like the checkboxes. We like the order. So,

## Things we learned from playing:

- How to share
- How to make equal groups
- How to solve problems
- How to use the materials I have
- How to work with someone with different ideas
- How to handle conflict
- How to use my imagination
- How to read body language
- How to be fair
- How to take a joke
- How to be patient
- How to entertain myself
- How to engage in life with other people
- How to be alone
- How to organize things
- How to try new things
- How to love old doohickies
- Number skills
- What I like
- What I don't like
- How to use time wisely
- How to make friends
- How to handle enemies
- How to speak up
- When to be quiet
- Sequencing
- Following directions

- Empathy
- Determination/tenacity
- Life isn't fair
- Gravity always wins
- It's OK to get dirty
- The mess is worth it
- Healthy competition is a good thing
- Sometimes I win
- Sometimes I lose
- Everyone isn't good at the same thing
- Some people are better than me at things
- I am not always the best
- Sometimes you get hurt
- Sometimes you need a plan
- Sometimes you just go with the flow
- Sometimes you don't get what you want
- Roosters fight back
- Climbing is difficult, but the view is worth it
- That yellow stuff inside acorns isn't really cheese
- Dog food isn't that bad
- Mud pies really do taste like mud
- Sometimes the kickball wins
- We all make mistakes
- Tag is more than a game!

for those teachers like us, here's a framework for how to cultivate thinkers amidst the perceived chaos.

Consider the following mindset. Though the text makes it appear to be a linear model, it is more like a game of Frogger. You can't have an idea unless you have the time, space, and opportunity to play with concepts. It is through play that we can be creative. Anytime we have been creative, it feels like play. It feels good. We get lost in the moment. And none of this can authentically exist unless we play. We must adopt play as a mindset.

# The Playful Mindset

1.  **Look for playful moments. They are all around us. (awareness)**
    This is ideation. Getting an idea. How does an idea happen? By reading, writing, doodling, chatting, playing, collaborating.
2.  **Provide ourselves and students with time, space, and opportunity. Make a plan to invite playfulness in. (intentionality)**
    This intentional use of time allows creativity to happen. Allowing students the time and freedom to make an idea become their own. It's 20% time. It's genius hour. It's project-based learning.
3.  **Don't be afraid to play, mess up, learn, repeat. Embrace the perceived chaos as part of the learning experience. (process)**
    Creativity is an idea in motion. It's ideas doing something. Here's the kicker. This step is the magic that occurs between the first two. At some point, the work becomes unique. It becomes singular. Your students have something unlike everyone else's. This is where innovation can occur. This is an opportunity.
4.  **Keep in mind that the more we play, the more playful we become. On average, it only takes 3–6 weeks to create a routine. (habit)**
    This step combines awareness, intentionality, and process. Keep seeking. Keep allowing time. Keep doing.
5.  **Never forget how playfulness makes us happy. Happy people play. (results)**
    Is this the last step? No! It could be the first. In fact, it is threaded throughout. We must be intentional about communicating the joy that comes with the work. Without it, how does one move forward? We must remember that in the doing and in the joy, we must provide our students with the opportunity for *audience*. If a student's work has an audience of one (the teacher), we have failed them. Greatness is meant to be shared. It is meant to inspire. It is meant to impact others.

# CHAPTER 5

# Excuses

OK, so by now, you might be listening with two ears. While we have you, let's go ahead and debunk some of those reasons you might talk yourself (or let someone else talk you) out of shifting your pedagogy. In all the keynotes and workshops we've given across the United States, here are some common replies from teachers when we suggest integrating more play into the curriculum:

1. It's not part of my standards.
2. Administrators won't allow it.
3. I don't have time.
4. Play isn't on "the test."
5. Life isn't always fun.

Let's take a moment to unpack each of these excuses and really take a look at why they aren't valid in a field that hopes to inspire the next generation of humans.

## Excuse 1: It's Not Part of My Standards

This one probably ruffles my (Jed's) feathers more than any of them. I used to work with a grade-level team that constantly, and by *constantly* I mean *all the time*, reminded me how many standards that we had to teach.

**180 standards.**

Yes . . . they counted them. Seriously, how can a great teacher have time to do that? I digress. Every day at lunch and recess I heard about them. At faculty meetings, they reminded the whole school how much they had to teach. In the hallway, in the work room, in the faculty lounge, in schoolwide emails, even once when I walked out of the restroom, I overheard them talking about it. They were obsessed with them. Don't get me wrong—I knew my standards and what was expected of me, but I didn't belabor the fact that they were there, and they certainly didn't come before student needs. I always took into account the likes and dislikes of my students first, then figured out creative ways to weave those into the mandated curriculum. That said, however, in South Carolina we have a great document called "The Profile of the South Carolina Graduate" (SCDOE, 2019). The document was created by the South Carolina Association of School Administrators with the purpose of inviting various nonstandard skills like creativity, collaboration, communication, and critical thinking, as well as integrity, self-direction, global perspective, and more into the classroom. The document (scan the code to see it online; Figure 5.1) was approved by

- the South Carolina Association of School Administrators
- the Superintendent's Roundtable
- the South Carolina Chamber of Commerce
- the State Board of Education

While you may be reading this in another state, or dare I say another country, the ideals here should be similar. Doesn't this graphic paint a fantastic picture of what we want in a well-rounded citizen of Earth?

I am sure many of you may be asking why I chose to mention this in a section about play. The naysayers will be quick to say that play isn't a "rigorous standard in language arts or math" that will make students college and career ready. I beg to differ, though. Look at those "Cs" under World Class Skills. Those are vital, crucial, imperative (all the synonyms) to being a successful leader anywhere you work, regardless of what field. Please, tell me a time when you were playing with blocks, shooting a game of Horse, or

**FIGURE 5.1** Link to the Profile of the South Carolina graduate.

playing Red Rover that you didn't practice all of those skills. Let's break one down just for the fun.

Picture it . . . 1986 . . . the school playground (yep, that was a *Golden Girls* reference. I am channeling my inner Sophia here). The class has been divided into two teams without any arguing (collaboration). A rousing game of Red Rover has commenced. The other team loudly requests that you "Send Jimmy right over" (communication). Jimmy immediately starts planning his attack (critical-thinking). Jimmy is running straight for the other side. He hopes to break through and bring back a new team member. At the last minute, the opposing team members lock arms in a new secret ninja warrior grip that they planned for weeks (creativity). Bam! In just two minutes, world-class skills are in full effect, and the kids had no idea they were doing it. Ahhh . . . the beauty of play.

I realize that Red Rover has been banned in many places due to safety concerns of the game, but I found it useful in illustrating my point. Please note that I did say it was 1986. That was before we all knew better—when we rode bikes without helmets and lay in the back of the stationwagon *unbuckled!* I was just in second grade. Nonetheless, the point can be made that play invites learning in a way that textbooks, novels, worksheets, and technology can never deliver. Lean in close. Listen carefully. I value the work that we all do, and admit that sometimes all of those things have had a place in my classroom.

I am not saying I never used a worksheet. But, I am saying if I used that type of practice in a way that invited play into my classroom, it was way more effective than telling everyone to sit down, be quiet, and work independently. Yes, I agree there are times that students must work on their own, but if your entire classroom is structured around independent work done quietly in nice neat rows while students drift in and out of consciousness, then you are missing out on the joy of teaching.

I will never forget one experience I had while working toward certification. I was working with a fourth-grade class and I planned this really fun lesson about adjectives using a pumpkin. I planned to divide the students into groups (the cooperating teacher had them in military-style rows), give each group a pumpkin, and for five minutes they could just play with the pumpkin. Of course, I planned to bring in the adjective part of the lesson as soon as possible, but based on the needs of the students in the class, I felt five minutes of free play with the pumpkins would be good for them. Some kids in the room had never touched a pumpkin. In the fourth GRADE! Most of us do not even remember the first time we touched a pumpkin because we have always had that experience year after year as Halloween approaches. This fueled my drive for the five minutes of pumpkin play.

As the students began, the cooperating teacher pulled me aside and asked, "What standard are you covering by allowing this?" As a preservice teacher, I began to tremble. This woman was fierce, taller than me, and spoke with a tone that would cause Satan to tremble. She was scary. I always felt bad for the students when I had to leave them with her. I had no idea how to respond to her. I was petrified she was gonna call my advisor and have me removed from her class. I replied, "There's not a standard about playing with pumpkins." Her hammer, axe, and every sharp object she could find came crashing down. "Your lessons must be standards-based!" Sheepishly, I replied, "I don't think standards should drive all of my instruction." Her face reddened. Her eyes grew wide. I swear I saw steam burst out of her ears. She looked like a cartoon when it's about to blow up. "Shouldn't lessons be fun and engaging?" I asked. She replied, "Playing with pumpkins won't be on the test at the end of the year. You better learn that early on in the profession. Standards drive everything, not fun!"

This present-day, nationally known, award-winning, 18-year veteran educator would love just another brief moment with this teacher.

**I would tell her that the best moments I ever had with students had nothing to do with "standards."**

**I would tell her that I didn't join the world's most noble profession to teach to a test.**

**I would tell her that I love my students too much to reduce them to a score and a grade.**

I would tell her that I grieve for the students who passed through her classroom and missed out on what could've been a great year of learning had she just opened her eyes to their needs more than what the state said she was required to force into them through her antiquated teaching practices. I would also point out to her that inviting play into the classroom is indeed part of her standards. The inquiry, communication, and critical thinking involved in play is so vital to all aspects of learning. Try conducting a science experiment without inquiry skills. Try delivering a speech to your class without communication skills. Try diagramming a sentence without critical-thinking skills. The *play is not part of my standards* excuse just doesn't work.

# Excuse 2: Administrators Won't Allow It

My last administrator before I (Jed) left the classroom was incredible when it came to supporting my vision of what learning should look like. She was, without a doubt, one of my biggest cheerleaders. She was always leaving encouraging notes in my mailbox after an observation. She handed out jean-day passes like candy for all of my extra work. She nominated me for lots of awards. She once wrote my mom a letter to tell her what a good job I was doing as a teacher. Needless to say, I was super proud of that. She affirmed my work further by bringing visitors by my classroom to observe. When the door would open and the guests would pile in, the students were not studiously working from their seats. They were not laboriously working through the even/odd problems on page 272 in the math textbook. They were not robotically copying definitions from the end of the chapters. They were not silently reading the chapter on animal adaptations in the science text. More often than not, students were laying in the floor constructing models with math manipulatives. They were sitting on beanbags with their legs over their heads as they were reading a book they chose. They were covered in paint as they created their latest masterpiece. They were up to their elbows in mess from the latest science experiment. They were gathered around the class piano singing our newest parody or just being silly as we sang "She'll Be Coming Around the Mountain."

The atmosphere in my classroom was one that invited play at every moment. This happened because of the freedom, encouragement, and support I felt from my administrator. I realize that many of you reading this do not have that. In my role as a director of creativity and innovation, I have seen and heard a lot from teachers across the country regarding lack of administrative support. I know it's tough. Tougher than a $2 steak. I used to work for a "less than supportive" admin as well. There are administrators out there who "don't get it," just like there are teachers out there who don't always implement best practice. You feel stifled. You feel afraid. You feel like the hammer could come down on you at any moment.

All fears aside, however, we have to do what is best for children. As you read a few pages ago, the science is there to support the work of play in your classroom. Use this work to show your admins about the power of play in learning. Play actually helps the brain to grow in ways that will strengthen every other part of your curriculum. Even with documented research connecting brain growth and play, there are still articles out there about schools cutting recess or limiting time in gym class that make the educator in us scream and say lots of bad words. School boards filled with people who just don't understand are infuriating, but the short and skinny of it is this: We must provide students with quality, relevant education or, simply put, "it's on you." The excuse of *blame the administrator* just isn't a valid one because . . .

- It is your name on the degree and the teaching certificate.
- The students will have your name in their legacy of teachers forever, not the admin.
- If the admins really don't support the work of innovative teaching, including play in your curriculum, then why stay there?

We realize that not everyone reading this book has the option to change your setting; if not, why not *show them the research here?!* Did you really go through four years of college to take a job that you don't enjoy, working for someone who doesn't support you as a professional? We hope not. Life is too short for that. You deserve better, and your students most assuredly do. Every day in the classroom should be fun! Yes, there are hard days, difficult days, days that will leave you exhausted and sometimes filled with tears; but we can honestly say that you can and should love every moment with your students.

The moments where we gathered around the piano for no other reason than to sing to the top of our lungs; the moments where we ran around the playground and sped down the slide; the moments where we held impromptu puppet shows; the moments where we laughed 'til we cried because of the crazy bullfrog outside of the window; the moments where we pretended to be scared of pigs as we learned about mammals; the moments we decorated gingerbread houses, baked cakes, drew for the love of drawing, and danced for the love of moving taught me as much as they taught the children. What did I learn? Learning is fun, and it has to be if we want it to stick. It has to be engaging and meaningful. It has to be emotional and connect with our humanity. Worksheets, textbooks, copying notes from a projector screen, and hour-long lectures delivered in monotone voices don't do that. Play does.

## Excuse 3: I Don't Have Time

At my former school, the day began with students for me at 7:25 a.m. That's the time they were released from the cafeteria and made their way down to the classrooms. I ain't gonna lie about it. That time in the cafeteria was the worst. Kids were supposed to eat breakfast and then move along to their assigned waiting spots before class time began, but like most humans, they wanted to be social and talk to their friends. You can imagine that this talking so early in the morning only led to lots of "shushing" and hushing. It really started the day off on a horrible foot for many students.

The administrator who I mentioned previously knew this, and she came up with a plan. She called it "Can Do." It consisted of those big tin cans you find in the cafeteria trash every day after the sweet lunch workers had prepared the food. Tons of those were going to waste, so she rescued a few and repurposed them to become the centerpiece of her new project. She filled the cans with flashcards and games to keep the kids busy during the morning wait time. While she had hoped that the "busy"ness would keep them quiet and focused on a task, it had the opposite effect. Kids were laughing and talking and having a great time all the while learning. Guess what they were doing . . . PLAYING! I loved it! I wanted cans all over the building at all times of the day. I made a few cans and kept them in my classroom for those moments when students finished early and needed something to fill their time until we moved on to the next thing. Of course, that invited the noise and chaos from the cafeteria into my classroom, but I didn't care. It was great! Not everyone was a fan, though, and soon the cans were phased out of the morning cafeteria and the shushing and hushing returned.

Why did I mention this here in this section? I did so in hopes that you would see two things. One, we do have time, we just gotta look for it. In the mornings, in between subjects, in transition times, after lunch, before lunch, before dismissal. I know. I have been there. There are all kinds of spots to bring in play. We like to call these the nooks and crannies. The thing is, we have time if we make time. We make time for what's important to us, and if we have a playful mindset and we value play in all its forms, we will make time for play. These moments are out there waiting to be filled with engaging bits of learning through playful experiences that will ignite minds and fuel passions that will spill over into other areas of the curriculum.

Ah yes . . . There it is. The Curriculum. That is the second point I hoped you'd see here. The cans we mentioned were filled with curriculum. Standards-based items. The whole time the students were playing, they were engaged in learning all the "stuff" they needed, and they were doing it while having fun. This kind of play, while not the same kind of play as recess and "free time," encourages brain growth in the same manner.

This has been a big discussion for Julie and me. I am all about free play and letting students chart the course for their learning. Julie likes a little more structure with content connections. The beauty of play is that both of these are valid forms of student engagement and have enormous potential to bring students to learning in unique ways. According to Dr. Stuart Brown (2010), there are 124 different types of play. We won't list them all here, but just know that we are sure all 124 of them have a place in the classroom. Well . . . maybe not the rough and tumble play. I don't want anyone getting hurt. The best part about all of them, how-ever, is that they are all supported by countless medical doctors and brain research.

## Excuse 4: Play Isn't on "the Test"

Finally, an excuse with some validity. Play isn't on the test. You are all exactly right. Play isn't and probably never will be a part of the state testing that we gripe about on a yearly basis. Every public school in America is judged based on its test scores, and we understand the pressure you face. We have faced it ourselves, and quite frankly, it makes us nervous as a cat on a porch full of rocking chairs just talking about testing. We both can remember having those "data meetings" with our administrators to discuss our growth at the end of the year. Nothing is worse than hearing the judgment of 180 days of work that is born as a result of one day of assessment. Students and teachers both suffer from this type of critique, and it is damaging everything about education. All the more reason we need more play throughout the learning experiences of school. The science supports that play will in fact help students to be better focused, to be less stressed, to feel refreshed and energized, and more apt to learn new information because their mind is clear.

Remember when we were little and we would attend the pep rallies for the big state tests? Oh, you didn't attend one of those? Let me paint a picture for you. We've been a part of one of those test rallies not too long ago. Every kid in the school gathers in the cafeteria floor, and they're led in various cheers and chants by teachers in an effort to get them ready for their big day. "You can do it! You can do it! You can beat that test," are among the chants we remember most. A test isn't something you are supposed to beat. It is something that is supposed to help an instructor gain insight into what the students know so that they can help them know what they don't know. Confused yet? Us too. What in the world are we doing in education that makes these rallies seem beneficial but play isn't respected more than a 15- to 20-minute recess? Some would argue that the rally is a form of play, and in some aspect we would agree. But we would rather have an hour of fun and laughter not related to a test than a whole celebration in hopes of making the test scores better. Imagine how the children who bomb the test feel after the whole school screams and yells about how beating the test is the goal. Talk about hating school. Those students will never feel successful if all they ever perceive school to be is one big test machine.

These types of test rallies still exist. The whole time they are going on, the leaders of the rally are telling kids to be focused, to get a good night's rest so they aren't frazzled in hopes that they will feel refreshed and energized so their mind will be clear to do the best on their test. Sound familiar? Yep, you just read it a few lines ago. And the best way to get all of that for a student . . . PLAY!

Don't think one test can affect a student that much? Listen to this story. When I (Jed) was in second grade, all the students were screened for placement in the gifted and talented program. It was called "Climb." Every kid wanted to be in Climb. The class was so much fun! Students in there participated in all of these amazing learning experiences. They were out of "class" all day, they had a special lunch time which was sometimes in their Climb room, and they went on these incredible overnight field trips. Everyone knew that only the smart kids got into Climb, so you had to "beat the test" to get in.

The big day came and went. I did my best. Weeks later, the results arrived in our mailbox at home. I didn't make the cut. I wasn't smart enough. My cousins made it in. My best friends made it in. Even the kid I thought wasn't so bright made it in. I didn't. I was devastated. But tests tell the truth, and this one told me I wasn't smart. It affected me deeply from that moment on. I never felt smart enough all the way through school. I never signed up for Honors or AP classes. I always felt remedial. Still to this day, I struggle with feeling as smart as my peers. I am literally terrified of the EDU world reading this book and my secret of being "not smart" getting out, but I must share all this so you'll know why play, not a test, is so important. The impact of the test doesn't affect me quite as bad as it once did, but it still haunts and lingers. One test did this. One.

Of course, our words aren't gonna change the testing world. It has turned into a money-making machine fueled by more folks than we care to name in this book. But, we sure hope that we cause you to reflect on your approach to testing. We beg you to stop letting the excuse of "play isn't on the test" keep you from having a playful approach to learning and teaching.

When I hear teachers say that they don't have time to invite play into their classrooms, all I can hear is, "I don't have time to allow students to develop their collaboration, critical-thinking, communication, and creativity skills." True story. I secretly laugh in my head at every teacher who has ever told me that they are too busy teaching to bring play into their curriculum. Not laugh like I am making fun of them or that I think I am somehow more evolved as an educator. But, it is a laughter at how I know that no good teacher would ever say they don't have time for cultivating the skills we just listed. For some reason, however, the word *play* in the education world has been so far removed from our work that it has caused some educators to make such illogical statements as "I don't have time." Here is the best response I have come up with for those teachers: You don't have time not to! There is no way in the world that you can teach all 180 of your standards, build community, cultivate empathy, provide problem-solving opportunities, and develop authentic twenty-first-century thinkers without play. It is too valuable for you not to make time for it!

## Excuse 5: Life Isn't Always Fun

If there is one excuse we can get behind, it's this one. Life isn't always fun. As kids of the 1980s and teens of the 1990s, we were just short of the "everyone gets a trophy" era, and we had our fair share of chores and "come to Jesus" meetings. For those of other faiths, that basically means our moms made sure we understood how to mind our manners and the "consequences" of what would happen if we didn't. Sometimes the meetings involved a hickory switch of our choosing from the nearest tree. Trust us—neither the chores nor the meetings were fun.

I (Jed) remember several moments at school that weren't fun, either. Once in sixth grade, during a game of kickball, a PE teacher asked me when I was going to start playing like the rest of the boys. Once in seventh grade, I got docked in gym class for not wearing the right shoes . . . that I didn't even own. Another time when being bullied by a kid older than me, I was chased into the bathroom where I locked myself into a stall and prayed for safety. The bully crawled under the stall after me, and I escaped by crawling out the other side. I ran to the principal in the hallway. I told him all about what happened. His response, "I guess you better bring a ball bat and keep it in your locker. Use that instead of running next time." That was almost three decades ago, and I still remember how "unfun" it was.

These are just a few of the highlights of life not being fun for me. I didn't mention the first time I was called a homosexual slur in the fourth grade. I left out the part where my grandad passed away in ninth grade. Be glad I didn't share the story of what happened to me and one of my African American friends after school in the high school parking lot as a racist bully spewed his hate. It was the worst. No fun.

See why we need to make school a more playful place? I am not saying everyone's school years were filled with these kinds of horrible experiences, but everyone has moments in school that haunt them because as we all know, "That's life."

How's that excuse about "life isn't always fun" sittin' with you right now? We will never be able to keep all of our students from these "unfun" moments, but as educators, can't we load them up with incredible experiences—filled with playful moments so that their memories of school might be happy times? They have the rest of their lives to be beaten down by the world.

Playing at school, in *all* grades, should be required. Whether it's free play at recess or deep play while learning algebra, it's a must. Play is so important that it's even part of the United Nations Convention on the Rights of the Child (1989). Article 31 states that children have the right "to engage in play and recreational activities." As our friends at the US Play Coalition often state, "Play is a human right" (Play and Playground Encyclopedia, 2019).

# CHAPTER 6

# Reframing PLAY

To make all this fun come full circle for you, and most importantly for your students, we know that you, like us, need some next steps . . . some "OK, now what?" How does one take the information thus far and start reframing play in traditional education? You see, there are certain ideals, strategies, and cultural awareness that promote a playful classroom. Take a gander at the topics below, and assess where you are in response to the questions.

1. **How is a culture of reading cultivated in my classroom?** When we read fiction, we relate to the work as a *window* or a *mirror*. We enjoy it because we see ourselves in the characters and we value the journey as we relate to the plot complexities (mirror). The text shows a reflection of the reader's identity and experiences. Or, we enjoy the reading because it gives us a glimpse into a life unlike our own (window); the culture is different or the plot is unlike anything the reader has encountered. Books are often the only place in which readers meet people who are not like them, who offer alternative worldviews. Because fiction simulates social experiences, a culture of reading diverse fiction in classrooms is a key component to building empathy. This is the playful mindset of sociability at work. Please take note here . . . Diverse literature doesn't just mean you have books by authors of color, but also books with themes that represent various cultures, mindsets, religions, lifestyles, etc. No matter if you have someone in your classroom who practices a religion unlike your own, ALL students need to be aware that our world is a wonderful mix of cultures.

2. **How open is my pedagogy to the concept of make believe?** Yes, even in high school. Problem solving in most all subjects requires a whole heap-uh make-believe: visualizing how the Eskimos live, reading stories,

imagining a tale and putting pen to paper, pondering a math equation, and determining the next step as you seek a solution. History, geography, and literature are all make-believe. We learn them as conceptual constructions that we never experienced ourselves. So, if we're playing make-believe, why not make it magical while we're at it? Put on a costume and have fun with it! Maybe you don't have a degree in theatrical costume design, but don't let that stop you. Thrift shops and yard sales are great places to build your dress-up supplies. If that's not your cup of tea, swing by Target on the day after Halloween and load up on the 50% off costumes. Check out the resources on ThePlayfulClassroom .com to learn more about how to fill your classroom with playful materials.

3. **How often is a global perspective present in my classroom discourse?** Travel is a great way to exercise imagination. Traveling as a class is limited by time and budgets, so why not utilize the power of the Internet to simulate travel? Skype for Education is a great site for connecting with other classrooms to play games like Mystery Skype, Mystery Number Skype, Mystery Animal Skype, etc. Empatico, a relatively new platform as we type this, is a nonprofit group that specifically connects classrooms with the purpose of building empathy. Connecting with classrooms from other parts of the world opens our eyes to so many new and inspiring people. You will read later about the power of some of the virtual experiences we have made and how they have both strengthened the work and engaged our students.

One little tidbit of fun before we tell you more: Did you know that the average African elephant can create up to 300 pounds of dung each day? We were shocked to find that out, but we learned it while on a virtual field trip to an elephant sanctuary in Kenya. You know the day we learned that in a classroom full of middle schoolers sure was fun and playful! Our friends at Empatico explain the need for these kinds of connections like this: Imagine if children everywhere could discover what life is like for other children around the world. Millions of people do not have the opportunity to see new places, meet different types of people, or learn about other cultures. While technology has come a long way in connecting us, it can also stifle meaningful conversations and social interaction. By creating shared and engaging interactions for educators and students, we believe we can spark a global movement to spread kindness and empathy around the world (Empatico, n.d.).

4. **What is my view regarding the role of the teacher?** We know from Responsive Classroom concepts that having a morning meeting every day sets the tone (Kriete & Davis, 1999). Students are greeted by name and the day begins with an awareness of goals and intentions. Morning meeting is done with all participants on a level plane. The teacher sits amongst students, not standing over them. We challenge ourselves and you to notice where you are during class discussions. Are we *among* students physically showcasing a sense of egalitarianism? We need to be.

5. **Is my classroom a safe space for ALL students?** Classrooms are a "safe zone" for so many children. According to Brené Brown (2019):

   *We can't always ask our students to take off the armor at home, or even on their way to school, because their emotional and physical safety may require self-protection. But what we can do, and what we are ethically called to do, is create a space in our schools and classrooms where all students can walk in and, for that day or hour, take off the crushing weight of their armor, hang it on a rack, and open their heart to truly being seen.*

   As educators, we lead the processes of unlearning any hate that students bring with them from experiences outside school. Doing this can be as simple as the provision of diverse texts in the classroom or as elaborate as incorporating the UN's Sustainable Development Goals in our curriculum. Whatever your method, creating a safe space is the most important aspect of our role as educators.

6. **How do I allow students freedom for elaboration?** The inclusion of purposeful times during the school day for student choice in study is a form of play. These opportunities—such as Genius Hour, makerspace, 20% time, inquiry-based learning, or Socratic seminar—give students a chance to learn skills while also expanding and elaborating on them. These types of learning experiences require teachers to loosen their control with many traditional classroom procedures and expectations, and when given freedom to explore, plan, create, and implement their ideas without unnecessary constraints and judgment, students and adults alike flourish.

Jackson Pollack, a classically trained painter, invented his own way of painting through play, and is now a world-renowned artist because of the power of play (Elkind, 2007). How will we know if the next Jackson Pollack, Etta James, or Dave Thomas is sitting amongst us if we don't allow students the time to explore to satisfy their curiosities?

During my senior year of high school, I (Jed here) enrolled in a third year of Spanish class. I didn't have to take the course because I had already fulfilled the two-year requirement for my diploma. Choosing a language as an elective was a no-brainer for me, because I wanted to be able to travel and use the language around the world. Something magical happened to me as a learner that year. There was no need for the teacher to hook me, to reel me in, to convince me that I needed her information. I was all in from day one because of my choice.

The choices didn't stop with class selection. Señora Farr's class was filled with meaningful, playful options to pursue learning. For one particular assignment, we had to create an interactive vocabulary-building game that would be played by the class. That was basically all the directions she gave. We were free to determine the path and the outcome. (Read that again: we were *free to determine*. I hear angels singing.) Our only objective was game + vocabulary building + classmates playing said game. I couldn't believe the flexibility, the freedom . . . learning and showing off that learning as I saw fit. WOW! What a concept that was for 1995. Because I had also elected to participate in a Service Learning class as an apprentice to a local elementary teacher that year, I chose to synthesize the learning from both classes: I created my game on the bulletin board in the Spanish classroom. Señora Farr told me that no one had ever done that before, and she was intrigued to see my final product. The title of the game was called "Juanito Dice." (This is *dice*, pronounced *dee-say*; not the six-sided game cube!) My Spanish name was Juanito because my legal name is John and I'm the third John of the family. Juanito literally means "little John"; "Juanito Dice" means "Little John Says." The vocabulary theme of my board was animal vocabulary. I included *vaca, perro, pájaro, tortuga, serpiente, cerdo, caballo, oveja,* and *burro* just to name a few. No, I won't tell you what those mean, but I will trust your playful spirit to seek answers to your own curiosity.

I worked for hours and hours over several days on this project. The grade wasn't weighted that heavily toward the final, yet I was eager to dig into the work as often as I could. I remember feeling so proud as I created each piece of the game. I became more and more excited about classmates actually playing the game I created as the big presentation day got closer. I had never worked or cared about a project like this before and it was a weird feeling. The only thing I could deduce about this experience versus my other years of schooling was that it felt like I was playing and I had been given a choice. When the big day finally arrived, my game was a smashing success and everyone loved it. I can still see all of my animals hanging on that bulletin board as Miguelita, Jota Jota, and Mateo ran to label them before the timer ran out. Man, that was fun!

7. **What is the balance in my class between teacher and student action?** Direct instruction, while effective for learning *skills*, is not the bee's knees when it comes to cultivating intellectual curiosity or a socially adept citizenry. Children who complain of boredom at school or home are experiencing what David Elkind (2007) calls *intellectually burned*

*syndrome.* When teachers and parents subscribe to the "Watch me. I know what, when, and for how long you should be learning" ideology, we tell students their interests and passions are of little value. Instead, we must foster student voice and choice. Let them follow their interests: work alone or work together. When we allow time for students to appropriately adapt social skills to various learning situations, we foster a citizen's mentality—when to cooperate and when to speak up. What is the status quo? When should it be challenged?

Be prepared for this approach to be uncomfortable for both you and the student if you are just starting out with more student-focused strategies. Most students have been conditioned to wait for directions, produce the same products, wait for their grade, and move on. *You can see it: Every student's five-paragraph essay about a haunted house hangs beside the same-size pumpkin art in long, stapled lines along the school hallway.* Classrooms where students take the lead often are not linear, but spherical, in their processes. Student A may start at one point, while students B and C start at another (please refer to Chapter 4, where Frogger is discussed). What you perceive as the end of the learning experience may be your students' beginning, repeating itself over and over. The final products of their studies may all arrive at different times and appear in different ways. And . . . that's OK!

8. **How often do students move from their assigned seat?**
   With all the research to support movement and play on cognition and critical thinking, many educators dismiss the connection past second grade. Too many of us want to separate movement, emotion, and thinking into their respective compartments, and we need to stop. Research tells us these are integrated, not separate entities (see Section 3, Chapter 14 for more on this integrated concept). Students may feel awkward if they want to express emotions (practice drama, integrate the arts, create) when teachers want them to be still and think. So, let them get up. Let them sit down. Hello standing desk. Hello flexible seating. Hello learning.

So while we're playing, whether it's structured or unstructured, quiet or loud, let's be intentional about modeling a playful mindset. One last bit of neuroscience before you turn the page. We can't help it. This part is just too cool not to share.

In our brains, we have these special neurons called mirror neurons. Mirror neurons explain our ability to understand another's actions and behaviors. They're like your brain's own Stacy and Clinton—

*("Julie, who are Stacy and Clinton?"*

*"From the TV show* What Not to Wear?"

*"Oh. I don't know them. Oh wait, yes I do . . .")*

Ugh. Anyway . . . I imagine my brain's version of Stacy and Clinton wearing skinny jeans and a black tee . . . once we observe what we discern to be valuable, we imitate it. "I just love that imaginative spirit you have; where'd you get it?" Grin. When we imitate, our brains rewire to make the new behaviors more permanent (Winerman, 2015).

You know what this means don't you? Y'all best sit down for this one. You ready? (Julie, they're ready.) As long as we are intentionally living playful lives, teaching playfully, enjoying our students and our craft, we start a ripple effect in our circle. Others witness the benefits, and their mirror neurons take charge. Good news! It works for new teachers and for those of us who've been around for a while.

Playful classrooms believe ...

The effects of play are grounded in sound research.

Playing is connected to human nature—it's instinctive. It's who we are!

Playfulness is a vital attribute of an effective teacher.

All classrooms need playful learning experiences.

# Play Inspires Creativity
## Creativity Inspires Play

*Remember when you needed a tent, but had no tent? You found chairs and blankets and made one. You played and solved a problem through critical thinking using the materials you had. Play inspired your creativity.*

# CHAPTER 7

# Friday Afternoons and Monday Mornings

We met with a principal recently over coffee. He is starting a brand new school and wants it to be innovative from the ground up. The building, the classrooms, the teachers . . . everything. Our meeting was to discuss curriculum and ideas—our favorite topic. At least that's what we thought we were meeting about. He started our conversation with this: "OK guys, I need you to make me a list of teachers who *get it*. You know, the ones who are already teaching creatively. Or the ones you've trained to come out of college and hit the ground running—for kids." We asked if he wanted good teachers who might need a little training in innovative practices. His answer was no. "I don't have time for buy-in. I need their head in the game from day one."

Wow. We want our kids at that school. The school where something different is promised. Where "sit and get" and "stand and deliver" won't happen because the leadership took a year to scout around for the best teachers. Isn't that what college sports teams do? They send out recruiters years in advance to create the best teams and win national championships. Producers hold auditions months ahead of the airing of a pilot show to ensure its success. Elected officials begin their campaigns years before the election.

Imagine your own children in a place where new techniques are welcomed, tried, and tested for effectiveness. We aren't talking about where something new and fun is added to the end of the day on Friday once a month, although, lots of what happens at the end of the day on Fridays is great teaching. For some reason that is the moment of the week when teachers relax—when they create true relevant, meaningful, and fun experiences—and magic happens. Sadly, it rarely continues on Monday morning.

There is one particular Friday afternoon I can remember (Julie here) in which half of my fifth-grade class was taken out for some event; I can't remember the specific reason, but it was unplanned and long. The remaining half asked me what we were going to do with the two hours together.

It was one of those moments when the heavens open up and the light shines in on our circle of gray carpeting; I remember thinking, *what would I want to do if I was 10?* We made a list of topics students were curious about but hadn't yet had a chance to explore. They were to pick one, determine answers to their questions, and create a way to show us all they had learned. In my naïveté, I really thought this experience would be all tidy and done in the time allotted. It wasn't. So, we carried it into every moment we could find in the next week. From this one allowance of freedom came a beautiful showcase of how fashion changed across the decades from 1900 to present day. We also now had a bust of Dr. Martin Luther King Jr. to sit atop our classroom bookcase. The bust came with a monologue on achievements and societal impact. Mind you, these ideas fit our social studies standards perfectly, and they all came from student wonder and a playful spirit of learning. The children begged for a regular time in our schedule for this kind of work. I honored their voice and request, and we looked forward to this part of our day from then on. This event was around 2008; I like to think we helped pioneer the Genius Hour movement, before it was called such. And to think, all of this creativity started on a Friday afternoon.

## Taking Risks with a Full Toolbox

The playful classroom includes using time to take a risk and try something new in pedagogy (even if it's unstructured); that's where real creative teaching occurs, where traditional worksheets and workbooks are used for scrap paper instead of being the king of instruction. Where it's OK if your standard isn't posted because the kids are learning by choice and may be practicing in many areas at various levels and stages. According to Tanner Christensen (2014), creativity guru, "Play removes limits that otherwise constrain us to what we currently know to be possible. It's by removing those constraints and opening ourselves to diversity (through play) that creative insights become the *norm* of what we're doing." How badly do we need that mindset, that thinking, that freedom in education? In a world where standardization seems to drive every second of every day so that the scores will increase so that funding will increase, so that school report cards shine and communities thrive because of the illusion of strong schools—seriously, how badly do we need this?

Don't get us wrong: posting the learning focus on the board is good practice; even repetition of concepts (think flash cards) has its moment. There is an appropriate type of lesson for that kind of teaching. It takes a toolbox of instructional strategies to maintain the flow of a classroom. We need a *full* toolbox. (Jed says, "You can't screw with a hammer.") But . . . You cannot depend on the same tool every day for every child. It just doesn't work. Playfulness, however, can work with all types of students because there are all types of play that lead to incredible learning experiences.

## Creativity Is Not the Degree to Which You Can Create Art

Too often, creativity is relegated to artistic ability. It is this misconception that scares people away from the idea. So, what does creativity in the classroom look like? How can you implement it into your classroom? Don't go throwing a hissy fit; we're gettin' to that. First, we show you.

| Instead of . . . | Try . . . |
| --- | --- |
| pen and pencil practice | a game |
| raising a hand to answer | turn and talk to your neighbors |
| a paper exit ticket | a video reflection via Flipgrid |
| a five-question quiz | show learning with the arts |
| round-robin reading | interactive reading and costumes |
| flash cards to learn facts | write or sing a song with the facts |
| presenting facts with a digital slide show | go on a scavenger hunt to find the facts |
| completing the practice sheet on plot structure | build the setting with LEGOs, act out the plot with LEGO characters |
| doing the workbook pages on ecosystems | take a nature walk/do a biome scavenger hunt |
| watching the video clip on sea life | go underwater with Google Expeditions |
| discussing the setting of your read aloud | use Google Earth to take the class from where you are to the book's location |
| looking at pictures of sea turtles | visit a sea turtle hospital virtually |
| learning about latitude and longitude on paper alone | hide a box on the playground and make a geocache event of finding it |
| Looking at an anchor chart about Author's Craft | Tweet several authors and ask them questions about their writing process |

# Lookin' with Fresh Eyes

There's the secret. There's no magic pill. No rules like "don't wear white shoes after Labor Day." Creativity is simply taking something you encounter every day (person, situation, idea . . .) and looking at it with fresh eyes. Taking something ordinary and making it new, making it playful. The definition of creativity, according to http://dictionary.com, is "the ability to transcend traditional ideas, rules, patterns, relationships, or the like, and to create meaningful new ideas, forms, methods, interpretations, etc."

This makes no mention of art; but because the artistic community often transforms a blank canvas into something never before seen, they contort and twist the human body through dance in ways never witnessed, they sculpt a lump of clay or stone into a lasting masterpiece, they transcribe a tune only heard in their head onto paper so that symphonies bring it to life—because of all this we often give them credit for being the sole owners of creativity. Did you know that the musical *Hamilton* came to life because Lin-Manuel Miranda, on a beach vacation, read the 2014 biography of Alexander Hamilton by Ron Chernow? He said something like *That's a hip hop story!* and began to craft the musical. In an interview, he said, "I knew that he was on our $10 bill in the States, and I knew that he died in a duel. You know you learn that in high school and that was about it" (Gibbs & Bryer, 2017).

Imagine if we educators walked away from the traditional methods and dreamed big, bigger, biggest. Imagine if we said *no more to standardization* and facilitated learning in such a way that students learned without constraints—so that nothing seemed impossible. Imagine if we allowed our students to pursue learning in paths unique to them so that they could have creative moments like Lin-Manuel on the beach.

We cannot help but wonder whether, if we had been focused on playful classrooms the last 30 years like we've focused on testing classrooms, we would have a colony on Mars by now.

We need to look at education with fresh eyes. We need to give students room to try, to fail without judgment, and to learn. They need time, space, and opportunity to explore. We are always telling teachers to be creative, but no one is showing them what it looks like. Until now. You still feeling ornery about that afternoon of PowerPoint PD? Us too. Wherever you are reading this right now, put the book down and play. We don't care what you do. Take goofy selfies, draw silly doodles, make barnyard sounds, skip around your classroom and sing a song. Even for introverts like us, that beats a death-by-slideshow any day. If you think you hate that same ole same ol' learning, imagine how your students feel. We would love to see all schools, elementary, middle, high, and universities adopt a mindset of playfulness in the classroom to save all their students from the monotony and boredom of years of digital presentations that they could click through alone and probably gain the same learning. If our instruction is such that a student can click through it alone, for what do they need us? What value do we add?

If you really want an idea to help you and your students' eyes to look with new lenses, you should hear what Jed says in his professional development workshops about the "thinking outside the box," as many creatives often implore educators to do. He says this . . .

One day I was sitting in yet another meeting, bored to death, watching the clock, hoping to will the end of the meeting into existence, and doodling on my notepad to make it look like I was engaged in the meeting by taking notes. Once again, we were all being encouraged to "think outside the box" while creating our lessons. Ironically, we were sitting there doing nothing. We should have actually been collaborating to create said lessons, but . . . I digress.

"Lord, if I hear that one more time I might scream," was the thought my inner voice was shouting at me. "*Who determines if I'm inside or outside the box? Why is there even a box?*"

These were the questions rattling around in my head. I didn't dare ask them out loud, because you don't do that in an after-school faculty meeting. It prolongs the dismissal, and "ain't nobody got time for that." There shouldn't even be a box when it comes to our work with students. We should be able to get rid of the box all together and meet their needs. Do whatever it takes. Who cares if we get tired? Doctors get tired, too, but they're saving lives. It's worth it. It is also worth me working as hard as I can to do whatever it takes to help my students be successful.

> We must not think outside of the box.
>
> We must destroy the box.

The proverbial box has one agenda: It holds us back. Then, when we are finished thinking outside of it, the safety, security, familiarity, and ease of its traditional methods woo us back like the Sirens' song. If we really want to think outside the box, just get rid of it, and then we don't have a choice. I can hear the collective "ahhhs" of the tired teacher who has tried lots of new things but is ready to hop back in the box where the worksheets, textbooks, and slide shows are. If we really want to become outlets that inspire creativity, we must learn to destroy the box, get rid of it, never to climb back inside.

As a result of my thinking that day, I began to seek out ways to build more creative, "box destroying" thinking into my life and work. Truthfully, that's when I found the definition of creativity that I doodled here.

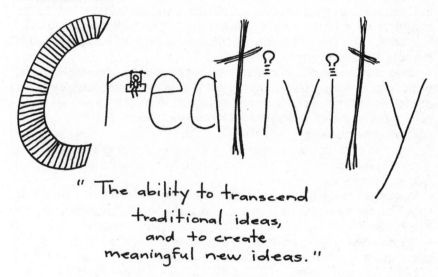

" The ability to transcend traditional ideas, and to create meaningful new ideas."

The definition changed my whole life. I had always thought being creative meant you were good at art. Every time I made a cool bulletin board outside my classroom, someone said, "Wow . . . You are so creative." They were talking about my artsy skills there—not my creativity.

Deep thought here: creativity isn't always artsy, but artsy is always creative. We'll explain using the definition in the doodle. Creativity means to transcend traditional ideas into new meaningful ones. Artists often take blank canvases, lumps of clay, their voices, or their bodies, and transcend the common, traditional, mundane to create something new and meaningful, something that has never been seen before. When a blank canvas is transformed from plain white into an image, that's creativity. The idea made its way from the artist's brain, down through their arms, into the paintbrush, and out into the world via the skill of the painter. It's easy to call that creative and associate all of creativity with art.

A square is always a rectangle, but a rectangle isn't a square; in the same way, art is always creativity, but creativity is not always art. Creativity is looking at a ruler and discovering 10 different purposes for it other than measurement and drawing straight lines. Creativity is learning to pack your clothes for a trip in a unique, more efficient way than other people. Creativity is seeing a crack in the concrete floor at your local coffee shop and imagining it is a river that flows through a tiny, unseen village that has a whole new species of creatures settling along its banks because they are learning to be hunters and gatherers after years of being fed solely by sunlight.

Destroying the box . . . that is creative. It is taking the box and looking at it with fresh eyes. What could it be other than a box? I (Jed) ran across the book *Not a Box* by Antoinette Portis during the middle of my box-destroying research and found a perfect companion for the ideal. It doesn't have to be a box as her book shares. It could be a rocket, a hot air balloon, or a race car. It could be whatever the mind said it could. There was no wrong answer.

I started leading "Destroy the Box" workshops about five years ago to help teachers kick down the walls around them. No, not literally, although most classrooms could be seen as concrete boxes. What I wanted for participants in my classes was to help them to, as author Tanner Christensen (2015) tells us, "not just change their thinking, but to change the way they thought about thinking." That's what creativity does. It gets in your brain, in the inner parts of you, and it makes you see the world differently. I often led teachers through creativity challenges found in Christensen's book *The Creativity Challenge* to help them see how stuck in the box they really are. Truthfully, we all are stuck. Even the most unstuck of us have areas where we need a box to be destroyed.

My favorite of Christensen's challenges is "Alternative Uses." I alluded to it with the ruler analogy above. To lead this challenge, I place a very common object in the center of a small group. I ask the group to then tell me its purpose. With a ruler, I always get two answers: measurement and drawing straight lines. Their task is to "destroy the box" of their traditional thinking and create a list of alternative uses for a ruler other than those perceived purposes. I play music while they do this, and I intentionally play two songs. The first song always provides the group with very practical answers: a door stop, a conductor's baton, a sword, etc. It is during the second song that their boxes are really destroyed. Without fail, the answers in the second song, where they have had more time, space, and opportunity to create, are always better. A ruler could be a bridge for ants to escape a flood. It could a tiny wooden leg for a miniature pirate. It could be a ramp for a toy car as it jumps the canyon to get away from the bad guy. It could be . . .

See the difference? See how the thinking changed and how the box was destroyed? The participants' own creativity helped them get rid of the box that the ruler manufacturers had put in their heads and they become thinkers, creative thinkers. Traditional thinking tells us that the only thing a ruler is good for is measurement and straight lines. After roughly six minutes of intentional creative thinking, most adult groups I work with generate hundreds of ideas. It is amazing what a little intentional time, space, and opportunity can do for creative thinking.

Many of the teachers I have worked with take this learning experience back to their classrooms. Some of my favorites—Brittany Sugg (Twitter: @Miss_Sugg1st), Sara Larkins (Twitter: @miss_larkins), and Brooke Daniel (Twitter: @Daniel1Teach)—have been leading their students in #DestroyTheBoxChallenge experiences for a few years now. They all have shared how their students have become more creative as a result of this practice in their classrooms. Because of their students' growth and my desire to see all students become strong, creative thinkers, I started creating Destroy the Box challenge videos each week with various items and dropping them on Twitter. No, you most certainly don't need my videos to do this, but it sure has been fun for me and the classrooms that I am connecting with. As of the writing of this book, there are 11 classrooms around the country who participate each week. Maybe more of y'all will join us soon! If you're ready to jump in with your class, just search the hashtag mentioned above and start. If the online world isn't your thing, we created Destroy the Box Challenge Cards that can be downloaded for free at theplayfulclassroom.com. Regardless of when and where you participate, we cannot wait to see how you start thinking outside . . . no . . . "Destroying the Box!"

# CHAPTER 8

# Begin with the Experience

Science classrooms are an easy place to invite creative, playful learning experiences. Dissections, model building, and experiments all manifest themselves into moments of play that students remember well into adulthood. Even just wearing safety goggles can launch students into role-playing scenes from their favorite mad-scientist movie. Everytime I (Jed) put on a pair, suddenly I am Doc Brown from *Back to the Future* building a DeLorean time machine!

Sadly, my science experience from eighth grade onward had ZERO, and I mean ZERO, playful moments. The eighth-grade life science teacher told us we were failures after every test. The ninth-grade earth science teacher was the head basketball coach, who couldn't have cared less if we learned anything. The tenth-grade biology teacher retired after my year with him. He spent most of the semester packing up his room. Eleventh-grade chemistry was delivered by a human attached to an overhead projector. I don't have one memory of any dissections, model building, or experiments. We did go to the lab once in chemistry, but it kind of flopped on the teacher's part, and we never went back.

As a classroom teacher I made it my personal goal to be a playful science teacher. Games galore, arts infusion, role playing, models, Skype calls with scientists, and yes, *every* kid had their own safety goggles that they wore whether they needed them or not. Sometimes, if the topic wasn't all that interesting, I would wear a lab coat and a mad scientist wig to present the information. Students would make up a different name for me each time, and it added to the excitement of an otherwise boring lesson. They never knew the moment I was going to jump into the role of the character they assigned me or when I would ask them to join me in the performance. Why did I do this? Because it was playful. It engaged the students and kept them hooked. Playful classrooms can inspire creativity in every nook and cranny of the school day, and we need more of then—as soon as possible.

Creatives (that group includes you) should be able to look at traditional methods and use their mind to come up with something new. Let's look around in our plan-books, in our filing cabinets, in our desktop files, in our unit bins, and see what needs a touch of playful creativity. We bet there are plenty of spots that could use a fresh wind. Creativity is a way of thinking . . . an approach to life that involves pursuing new ideas, methods, thoughts, and creations. It is looking at something you have seen or used every day for years and giving it a new purpose. It is taking those old lesson plans and breathing life into them instead of teaching the same tired way year after year. It is messing up those rows of desks and sitting in the floor. Creativity means creating ideas that don't fit into that perfect planning grid because of the mesh of subjects.

(Yes, we meant to say "sitting in the floor" even though the grammar check keeps telling us it's wrong. We said it a few times in section one and noticed the spelling/grammar check kept alerting us, so we added that to the list of Southernisms. It's just what we say here in the South.)

## Draw Your Own Lines. Insert Your Own Squiggle.

We get it. You might be frowning because you just bought your Emily Lay, your Erin Condren, or your (insert brand here) teacher planner and can't wait to put the math objective in the box you've labeled. Being playful in your teaching doesn't mean you can't use these pretty planners. Julie loves these planners; she has an Erin Condren bag with a Leuchtturm1917 A5 dot grid journal inside. We both enjoy journals and washi tape. But we need to use these as tools, not allowing ourselves to be limited by their rows and columns. Be bold. Be brave. Draw new lines. Insert your own squiggle.

So, how do we plan for maximum play? We're so glad you asked. Mind if we sit down? OK, so here's the deal. We're about to drop a big statement. Take a breath. Get ready. Here goes. Teacher preparation programs are coaching this incorrectly. We know this because we're both teaching college classes. We see it.

> You don't start with the standard.

Oooo, that intake of breath. Say that again? We *DON'T* start with standards? OK. Take a moment. Do you need to count to ten to calm yourself? Ready to move forward? **We did not say we don't need to know our standards.** We do. We need to know the standards we are to teach, including those that came before and those that come after. Once we are comfortable with the knowledge of them, we look to the experience first. What unique experiences do we want to provide for our students? What type of experiences are our students longing for? What have they never done in a regular school classroom while learning, but are common moments on the ball field, in dance class, on the playground, in the random field near their house where they had freedom to explore independently?

Picture it, a teacher has a required standard that says students must have a well-developed understanding of animal adaptations. The teacher finds the section on adaptations in the state-issued science textbook that no teacher in the whole district had input into selecting. There, students see a picture of a squirrel using its front claws to bury an acorn. Students are intrigued. They also see a picture of a hawk swooping down to grab a fish out of a pond. Ooohs and ahhs abound at the site of the picture. Students are engaged, intrigued, and curious. They are right where they should be. Cue the storm clouds. Rain begins to pitter-patter in our cinematic classroom. The teacher passes out the worksheet that accompanied the text, and students successfully fill in the blanks. The next day, students are introduced to the next standard in the list.

Why does this happen? Is it because of time? Is it that teachers feel student mastery has occurred with the adaptation standard by that one experience? Is it that they don't know what else to do because that's the way their teachers taught them and the way higher ed trained them?

All of these questions could be answered *yes* by most of us. It seems our own creativity has remained uninspired because of a lack of play. Imagine had we all been raised and trained in a world where play and learning were as valued as granny's secret family recipe.

Instead of looking at pictures in an irrelevant text and filling in blanks on a worksheet, why not walk outside the school building and go on an adaptation hunt. Find bugs under rocks, squirrels in trees, birds on nests, critters doing crittery things. Don't just read about them; experience them. Nature is all around us. Even in a big city where a tree isn't in sight, there are pigeons to observe and interact with for the purposes of learning adaptations. This is what a playful classroom teacher would do. This is what would impact student learning. This is what students would remember.

# CHAPTER 9

# Variations on Play in the Classroom

We found many references to play types during our research and knew it had to go in this chapter. It belongs here like Duke's Mayo on a mater-sammich. These 16 types of play, based on the work by B. Hughes (2002), could/should be in classrooms as much as possible. If we really want students to learn, we must connect the material with their memories so that it sticks. Play does that. Singing is a form of play. Just think how the ABCs stuck in your brain. Can you even say the alphabet without singing it? We can't, and yes we tried—right in the middle of the coffee shop. It was quite the public display of playfulness, and it helped us both overcome our after-lunch slump. Let's bring that type of experience into our classroom learning ASAP, right? Below, take a look at the list of how each type from the Types of Play poster could be dropped into your curriculum. We wrote each idea as if we were standing in front of students, explaining the experience they were about to have.

### Symbolic
Hey class! Today each partnership has a ruler at their table. Using that ruler, create a list of as many creative ways to use it as a part of an outfit you would see during the Renaissance Era.

### Rough and Tumble
Using the flag football kit from gym class, we will experience life cycles through a game of tag.

### Socio-Dramatic
Before you can operate the driver's ed car, you and a friend from class must act out the scene of getting in the car and readying it for driving.

# types of play

### imaginative
Play in which learners pretend that real things are otherwise. (Pretending it is raining inside)

### mastery
Play in which learners attempt to gain control of environments. (Marble mazes, Rube Goldbergs, DNA models)

### creative
Play that enables learners to explore, develop ideas and make things.

### exploratory
Play in which learners explore objects, spaces, etc. through the senses in order to find out information or explore possibilities.

### fantasy
Play in which learners take on roles that would not occur in real life. (Being a superhero)

### socio-dramatic
The enactment of real-life scenarios that are based on personal experiences. (Playing house, going shopping)

### communication
Play using words, songs, rhymes, poetry, etc.

### locomotor
Play which involves movement. (Hide and seek, animal mimicry, dance)

### rough tumble
When learners are in physical contact during play, but there is no violence. (energetic play)

### dramatic
Play that dramatizes events in which learners have not directly participated, as if in front of an audience.

### symbolic
Occurs when learners use an object to stand for another object. (A stick becomes a horse)

### recapitulative
Play in which learners might explore history, rituals and myths.

### role
Play in which learners take on a role beyond the personal or domestic roles associated with socio-dramatic play.

### social
Play during which rules for social interaction are constructed and employed. (Setting the table, creating a society, board games)

### deep
An ecstatic form of play that is intense and transcendent. Classified more by mood rather than activity.

### object
Play in which learners explore items using their senses. Basically, playing with stuff.

Ackerman, D. (2000). Deep Play. New York, NY: Vintage Publishing.
Hughes, B. 2002. A Playworker's Taxonomy of Play Types. 2nd ed. London: PlayLink.

### Creative
Using your imagination and some Play-Doh, create a pet you wish you could have. Name it, create its habitat, and develop as much information about it as possible.

### Social
Every Tuesday after lunch, we will be building community and strengthening cooperation and communication skills through board games. Be prepared to play, learn, and grow.

### Communication
Using the vocabulary words from our last biology unit, create a musical parody to show your understanding.

### Dramatic
Gather information about the Great Barrier Reef. After your research is complete, assign roles in your group, such as explorer, scuba diver, or scientist, and communicate your findings about the reef from their point of view.

### Locomotor
Alright friends, it's time for a body-break. Let's see how we can transform ourselves into animals. (Teacher reads page 1 of picture book with penguins as a focus.) OK . . . when I get to zero, you will transform into a penguin. When the lights flash, we're all going to freeze. 3,2,1, go!

### Imaginative
Today you become an animal cell. Gather a team to help you showcase the way you go from being one cell to two. In 10 minutes, our performances begin.

### Exploratory
I have placed items in brown paper bags that have a smell similar to items we read about in yesterday's assignment. Smell each bag and connect it back to the part of the book you remember.

### Fantasy
You are riding a dragon over a medieval village . . . describe what you see.

### Deep
"I know you don't want to stop building your cars for this afternoon's race, but if we don't, we'll miss lunch" (collective groans from students who are so lost in deep play, they would miss both lunch and recess).

### Mastery
Now that you have completed your amphibian research, construct a habitat using recyclable materials that would aid its survival.

**Object**

Using our Keva blocks today in your teams, build a contraption that shows the concepts of forces and motion, friction, and drag.

**Role**

After reading about sea turtles, take on the role of a marine biologist and explain to the naysayers why ocean conservation is important.

**Recapitulative**

As we complete the unit on the "Roaring 20s," plan a Gatsby party for the class.

## Recapitulative Disclaimer

Not all learning of ancestry, history, rituals, etc., can be playful. Role playing, games, and other playful experiences should be avoided at all cost when teaching historical topics such as the stealing of native lands, slavery, Jim Crow era, the Holocaust, as well as any lesson regarding genocide, racism, sexism, homophobia, etc. These should be handled with the utmost compassion and understanding. These are not playful topics, and should be treated as such.

You can find many more ideas for how to incorporate these types of play in your classroom on theplayfulclassroom.com.

# CHAPTER 10

# Creativity as Discovery and Invention

> We think of science as discovery, art as invention, but is there a "third world" . . . which is somehow mysteriously, both?
> Oliver Sacks, *On the Move*, 2015

Creativity is more than just saying we read Sark's *Creative Companion* or Elizabeth Gilbert's *Big Magic: Creative Living Beyond Fear*. Once you have read these fantastic works or books like them, what do you do with them? Do you put them back on the shelf like a trophy, or do you take their words and use them to take your plan book and curriculum to the next level? We cannot talk the talk while we close the door and deliver mediocrity. In the South, we call that a drugstore cowboy. These guys have shiny boots, but nothing to show for it. You know, all hat and no cattle.

What good is reading a book about living creatively, beyond fear, if we continue to live a limited life? How are we overcoming our fears to creatively implement the ideas we read about? Why retweet the profound wisdom of others without engaging in relevant and meaningful learning ourselves? In Gilbert's *Big Magic* (2016), she says, "Be brave. Without bravery you will never know the world as richly as it longs to be known. Without bravery, your life will remain small . . . far smaller than you probably wanted your life to be." We don't know about y'all, but we didn't become educators to have small lives. We wanted big lives, meaning big impact—big impact on the lives of our students and the profession. Can you fathom the world we would live in if every educator threw caution to the wind and invited the creative, playful mindset into their classroom? What a rich world would be known.

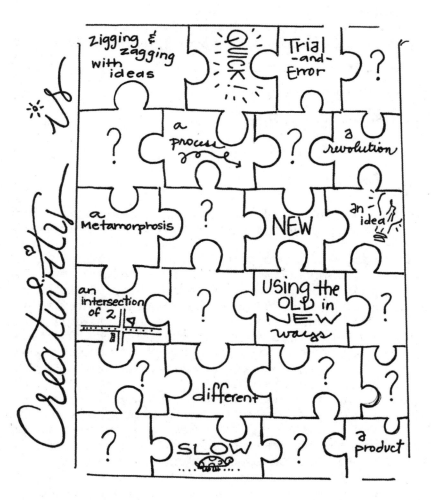

We know it's difficult. In fact, *very* difficult. But it can be done so simply. Instead of reading about the cycle of $H_2O$, make it happen live before your students with some water, a plastic baggie, and a hair dryer. Instead of looking at pictures of ecosystems, go outside and experience the one around you. Instead of having students complete a practice sheet about space, why not find an astronaut to Skype with or do a phone interview with a NASA employee? Could students not experience the Stamp Act rather than watch and listen to your well-prepared lecture on a Google Slide deck? Imagine it! Every piece of paper in your class is taxed—every letter, every book, every bookmark, even the playing cards for their favorite math game. Which will they remember?

Do you see? Creativity is in the *doing*. It's in the *thinking*. It's in the playful *experience*. It is both *discovery* and *invention*.

> PLAY INSPIRES **CREATIVITY**.
>
> CREATIVITY INSPIRES **PLAY**.

## Careful, Though

Just this week, I (Julie) watched a practice lesson on the regions of South Carolina using Play-Doh. How fun, right? Who doesn't love Play-Doh? In fact, we mentioned it a few pages back as we provided strategies for playful teaching. The smell takes us all back to our childhood. Ahhh . . . . Take a moment. Then why should you take caution, you ask? Because this particular experience lacked student thinking. A model was provided; students copied it. Students had no idea why they need to know these regions. They had no connection to the real world. They were given an assignment, and they were doing it. This kind of lesson is no better than a worksheet on the scientific method.

Lots of us, notice we said *us*, have done this exact thing. We fill our lesson plan books with "activities" instead of meaningful learning experiences. Activities are what people do on a cruise ship or in a nursing home. Playful classrooms must be both fun and meaningful. This Play-Doh example is an activity because it lacks the depth needed to make it meaningful to students. While those who participated appeared to be playing, the connection to the learning was lacking. We are educators; we provide learning experiences. No shame though; we have both done the *activity* in our early days of teaching, but reflective practice and conversation show us this kind of lesson isn't relevant for our students. It could have been. We just didn't make it so. Once we know better, we must strive to do better.

## Authenticity

We must stop relegating our work to something that could be done by anyone, and craft opportunities for authentic engagement coupled with a playful spirit in the learning process. *Authentic*, yes: another word educators toss around. What does it mean?

It means matching the content to the needs of each class, each student—because it's real for them in that moment.

Did we craft our lesson hook in a way that creates wonder?
Did we document student wonder for all to see?
Did we follow student curiosities to begin a journey of
    learning? ← That. That is creative, playful teaching.
It's not pom-poms and wiggly eyes.
It's not a pretty bulletin board.

It's engagement. It's kids who care about what they are doing; let's be specific here, though: it's caring for the sake of learning. Not caring to get the A. When students are fully invested in the learning experience you craft for them, they are emerged in the learning and achieve flow. Have you ever been there? Read on and see.

## Flow

In a 1996 *Wired Magazine* article, Mihaly Csikszentmihalyi (that's pronounced "Me High, Cheek Sent Me High") explained *flow* as . . .

> *being completely involved in an activity for its own sake. The ego falls away. Time flies. Every action, movement, and thought follows inevitably from the previous one, like playing jazz. Your whole being is involved, and you're using your skills to the utmost.*
>
> (Geirland, 1996)

Athletes call this state of flow being "in the zone"; a comedian might be "on a roll." Sadly, it's not as common among the general adult population. For us, this state of mind is cannibalized by schedules and responsibilities. We are very good at being busy, but not as good at being productive. Most of us are simply too busy to lose ourselves in what makes us truly happy. But you know who experiences flow the most—of course you do: children! Preschool and school-aged children are able to lose themselves in works of passion. Their passion almost always includes play. We suspect its freedom and limitless opportunity are a Siren song. Their attention is focused on building fairy houses outside, or model car tracks, or chalk drawings on the sidewalk. As awareness is brought to this phenomenon (or lack thereof), many adults are choosing to dedicate blocks of time on their schedule—set aside as an honored space—for this purpose. On our calendars, we block off time and call it "Cultivate" (that's a nod to Lara Casey and her #powersheets). Our friend artist Genevieve Strickland (Instagram @GenStricklandArt) sets apart time each day for her artwork and even leaves her materials out all the time so she will be more apt to continue in her scheduled practice. You'll want to check them out. Both Lara and Genevieve honor their creative time, scheduling it intentionally, and serve as models for us on how to get to work.

## A Question About Flow in Schools

If kids are so good at *flow*, and they love to be creative, and they long for play—even need it—then how often do we set aside time for it? In the typical elementary school schedule, we teach math, yes? Instead of a math drill, why not let two kids be frogs and two more kids (frogs) come hopping along. That's playful math, and it will make the learning stick. What say you, middle school educators? Yes, you can balance equations with frogs too. Just make sure the pond has an equal sign and no one sinks. See what we did there? Reading teachers, you ask? It's way more fun to practice reading while playing a part in a reader's theater or while exploring costumes in a dress-up center. High school teachers, costumes work in your grade level, too. Try dressing up in costumes as you read *A Separate Peace* or *The Scarlet Letter*. Your students will remember it forever!

In addition to being playful all day, purposeful play that is led by student voice and choice is vital to the playful classroom. We must intentionally block off time and dedicate it to student passion. Some call it g*enius hour*, some *passion projects*, some PBL (whether the *P* here is *project* or *problem-based learning*). No matter how we spin it, we need to allow for it because it invites play into the classroom on student terms and not just the teacher.

Think back to the social play suggestion a few chapters back. Why not schedule a once-a-week board game hour to develop and strengthen student communication and collaboration? Take the skills they practice during the play and apply them to other areas of learning in your curriculum. Once we start purposefully planning for play, not just in core subjects but all times of the day, we will begin to see its benefits and the mindset will transform our pedagogy—having a ripple effect across our schools. We get downright giddy as we think about the possibilities of positive effect on learning and the greater effect on the world at large.

# CHAPTER 11

# Make Time for What Matters

Between classes and PD workshops, we often meet at a local coffee shop to write and solve the world's problems. You should know, that's not an elitist statement; in the South, "solving the world's problems" is a phrase we use to mean having conversation, airing grievances, etc. While we are there, we almost always get into a flow. We dream up new ideas. We brainstorm answers to problems we cannot solve. We make list after list after list of things we want to do. We doodle in our journals.

Recently, while we were meeting, a teacher-friend of ours messaged us that she would love to have time to hang out at the coffee shop like we do. We chuckled at the thought . . . "have time." Neither us have time. I (Julie) teach a full load of course work at the college, am a wife, and the mother of two girls. I also recently joined a yoga teacher training class. Jed wears 14 hats and travels all over the state and country leaving sparkle wherever he goes—equipping, encouraging, and empowering the teacher profession. He's the coach we all need—in an awesome outfit.

The truth is, we don't have one second of time. Business (busy-ness) often consumes us both. What we do consistently, however, is make time. The time here fuels us, rejuvenates us, focuses us, sustains us. If we didn't make time to put ourselves in this space, none of our other work would happen quite so successfully. You wouldn't be holding this book! Why do we tell you this? Because as an educator, you must give yourself and your students opportunities for flow to happen. When we are "in the zone," we are where the magic happens. This time is where curiosity leads to new learning. It is where shared ideas become innovation. Oddly enough, when we spend this time together, we are playing—our best kind of work.

## Intermission: A Story

Let me (Jed) tell you about a teacher we know here in South Carolina, Stacy Crump. She teaches fourth grade and has recently been named Teacher of the Year at her school. This lady is the classic example of a creative teacher.

She isn't afraid to sit in the floor and get lost in flow with her students.

She isn't afraid to try new things.

She isn't afraid to think way outside the box to reach her students.

She isn't afraid to play . . . with students, at recess, during her grade level planning.

She isn't afraid to fail.

Recently, we visited her class to participate in a STEM lesson where students were challenged to construct a paper pedestal that could support the weight of a basketball. They were given unlimited paper and tape. Paper and tape . . . Not very creative, right? Not the latest and greatest in tech, right? After a quick Internet search, we learned that paper was invented somewhere around 100 BC and tape was created in the 1920s. Hardly new tools, yet the practice, methodology, thinking, and problem solving combined with those tools was very creative. These students were so engaged in the learning experience that they never asked, "How much longer do we have to do this?" They never said, "Are we done yet?" In fact, the experience ran over the allotted time and went all the way to the lunch hour. Normally, students cannot wait for lunch. On this day, they begged to work through lunch and continue with the pedestal building. These students were experiencing flow through the power of play at its finest. They were so into their learning that their desire was not food, but rather the task at hand. Who knew paper and tape could be so engaging or, dare we say, creative?

Honestly, it wasn't the paper or the tape—it was the teacher, who, with knowledge of her students and content, crafted a creative, playful learning experience for her students to discover the foundational skills needed to construct a building. She implemented math and science standards throughout the lesson, as well as fostered growth in collaboration, communication, and critical thinking. Sure, she could've downloaded a worksheet about the said math and science and had kids work in silence as they sat in rows facing the front, but her playful spirit wouldn't let her. Simply put, she made time for what mattered in her schedule and created a playful classroom. You can follow Mrs. Crump's creative classroom on Twitter: @crumpsclass

Imagine with us for a moment if we provided more opportunities like this for our students.

What inventions could be born?

What diseases could be cured?

What global problems could find solutions?

What change makers could students become?

If we truly want a playful class, we must strive for more opportunities for thinking, for creativity to infiltrate our classrooms.

## Plan, Do, Review

We have another fantabulous friend who teaches kindergarten, Stephanie Seay (@kimdersteph12). She was the 2005 South Carolina Teacher of the Year and is an amazing educator. Each day her class has a "Plan, Do, Review" time based on the model by High Scope. Her students decide on a project or task. For example, *I want to create an elephant out of construction paper*, or *I want to explore with the light box*, or *I want to read about sharks*. Then they *do* what they intended. Finally, they come together as a group and *review* how they used their time. These kinds of open, intentional opportunities for exploration have led her kindergarteners to learning the concepts of chromatography (with markers, coffee filters, and water), temperature (clothing for snowmen?), and gravity (when crafting marble tracks out of paper towel tubes). It's also a developmentally appropriate (and challenging) practice for 5- and 6-year-olds to decide on a task, stick with it, and reflect with their peers. Could we not plan-do-review in the third grade? In the ninth? In higher education? Of course we can. And we should. These skills transfer more fluidly into adulthood than bubbling in standardized tests will ever accomplish. What beautiful discoveries! Wouldn't you have longed for this time when you were sitting in the student chair? We would have.

## A Creativity Disclaimer

Creativity will look different in every classroom, every day, every year. We love pom-poms, wiggly eyes, and super-cute bulletin boards. They have their place in learning and shouldn't be avoided at all costs. However, teaching cannot be just those things. It has to be more than just cute and fun.

If you are a teacher of grades 6–12, you may chuckle at some of the creative ideas of preschool teachers, but sometimes cutting out the number 100 and gluing it down on the 100th day is in fact meaningful and relevant for a student of poverty who has never held scissors, never held glue, and just learned to count to 100. I overheard a colleague as we were discussing the topic of innovation, who said, "Cutting out and gluing the number 100 is not a deep learning activity." This person has a limited view of kindergarten pedagogy. She lacks understanding of early childhood development and the many faces that relevant learning can have. The cutting out of the number and using glue appropriately is mind boggling for students who have never done it.

*How does glue stick?*
*How do scissors cut?*
*Isn't it cool that the number 100 equals the same as 10, ten times?*

All of these are questions we have heard K5 students ask as they cut and glue the number 100. Fine motor development in itself is meaningful for a student with a disability. Imagine their pride when they finally master the cutting and gluing. We aren't here to judge your creativity. We are here to encourage you to dig deep and find it in every area of your classroom. That's how the playful classroom becomes a reality.

## Student Choice

Ok, so we know that *flow* is a goal for creativity in the playful classroom. We want students to be engaged daily in meaningful tasks. How do we inspire flow? I'm so glad you asked. It's not magical—in fact, the answer is simple. It starts with student choice.

Choice in what they'll do first.
Choice in the questions they ask.
Choice in the answers they seek.
Choice in who to work with.
Choice in where to sit.
Choice in how to show you they know it.
Choice in what to write about.

Choice in the audience for their writing.
Choice in what they read.
Choice in goal setting.
Choice in . . .

Some of you are getting anxious. We can sense it. We can feel your exhale and see those nervous side glances going on. You in the back—we saw that. We know you're feeling antsy because we've been there. We've felt it, too. You're thinking . . .

*That's crazy.*
*What in the world?*
*That's madness!*
*Where's the order?*
*Where's the control?*
*How do I know they learned something?*
*How will I assess this?*
*What grade will put in PowerSchool?*
*What will my admins think?*
*What about my standards?* (We didn't forget about the standards . . . remember our big bold print a few pages back?)

We hear your concerns and fears loud and clear. We worried over the same topics. It's true! But we weren't teaching like we wanted to, then. There was only a 90-minute block for ELA, and we struggled. If we were teaching writing well, we weren't leaving time for reading. And, then what about vocabulary? Heavens, there's no time for independent reading; we have skills to model and scaffold!

You see, teachers have been going about this all wrong. Don't worry, we're not pointing fingers here. In fact, we are standing beside you looking in the mirror. We too have been doubters. We have sat in the meeting on problem-based learning and been the naysayer. We can still see ourselves in that small grade-level meeting shaking our heads and saying no, explaining why we had to teach our students the skills first. We were emphatic that they could not tackle the questions without the skills. We are almost certain many of you are shaking your head even as you read. All we are asking here is, just like your mama begging you to try vegetables when you were 5 years old, try.

What we soon learned as we developed our art of teaching was that the skills didn't matter to students. We had to give them a problem and create disequilibrium (thank you, Piaget) for them to seek the skills. Until they were curious, the skills were just *school* to them. But this realization took some time. Once we found our playful spirits, we wanted everyone on board. That didn't happen like we wanted. Some folks want to bless our hearts; give 'em some time though. They'll come 'round.

## "Nothing Worth Doing Is Easy"

Jed's great-grandma Maudie used to say, "Nothing worth doing is easy." Truer words have never been spoken, except when Henri Matisse said, "Creativity takes courage." It most certainly does, and it most assuredly isn't easy. Fighting decades-old societal norms and traditions is quite the uphill task, but one that we are willing to tackle, and we hope you will join us. The first battle in the fight is to recognize the opponent. What is it that we are so desperate to change? Check out the list of educational traditions below; see which ones were part of your educational experience. No judgment here. Be honest. Do any of these invite play into the lives of our students? Maybe some of them could be made playful, but we'd gather to say most of these just suck the life right out of you like a tick on a dog's ear.

- ❏ worksheets
- ❏ paper/pencil tests
- ❏ standardized tests
- ❏ textbooks
- ❏ homework
- ❏ questions at the end of the chapter
- ❏ complete the odd/even problems
- ❏ scolded for not having signed paper
- ❏ reading logs
- ❏ rote practice
- ❏ timed math drills
- ❏ silent lunch
- ❏ no recess as a punitive measure
- ❏ copying definitions of vocabulary
- ❏ desks in rows
- ❏ name on the board for misbehaving
- ❏ identical art projects

OK. Confession time. It is, after all, good for the soul, right? At some point in our many years as K–12 educators, all of these things happened in our classroom. They didn't happen every day, but we were trained and learned to teach just like everyone else. We didn't start out running. It was more like a casual mosey on a Sunday afternoon. We are terribly embarrassed to admit it, especially after the words we have typed thus far, but in the spirit of open, honest transparency, and vulnerability (thanks Brené), we want you to know. This process, as mentioned previously, takes courage and is very difficult. Remember the words of Elizabeth Gilbert, "Be Brave!" We embrace the difficulty of that confession and move forward in this statement: We have evolved, greatly, and are on a mission to help others speed up their educator evolutionary process. Our current trajectories are leading us down new paths of exploration and creativity. We are eager to help all who wear the badge of honor that is *teacher* to see the magnitude of the work we do, and the urgency with which we must transcend traditional ideas to create meaningful new ones.

# CHAPTER 12

# Finding Balance

We talk of creativity like it's an out-of-body experience, but it's in all of us. Some just harness its powers more often than others. Hugh MacLeod (2009) tells a story regarding creativity and courage in his book *Ignore Everybody and 39 Other Keys to Creativity*. Early humans may have become meat eaters because someone finally became brave enough to leave the cave and find a way to kill the woolly mammoth. Could this have been the birth of creativity in humans, or had it been there all along waiting to be found by a courageous individual who was tired of the plant-eating status quo? Please don't see this as a lesson in conformity to the other extreme. You do you. Seek out the inner creative, playful spirit and discover what woolly mammoth you need to slay.

① Leave the Cave

The creative soul is a visionary within constraints, and each creator's tool is a constraint . . . paint, fabric, metal, a violin, a pen, numbers, the engineering design process. Some of our students will start with the plan, the blueprint; others grab the blocks and start to build. In the end, all result in a product or a performance. When we give students an opportunity to play and collaborate, magic will occur. Sometimes, good science needs a little magic.

## It's OK to Not Have All the Answers

Only in the synthesis of perspectives and talents offered by different students with different approaches can we responsibly tackle the major questions. We are living in a time when global concerns are so large, no one knows all the solutions. Yet, we are still teaching as if we have all the answers. This is a deceptive and dangerous approach.

While developing future teachers, we've had the opportunity to witness lesson planning from the novice sophomore to the more seasoned senior. What shifts is not the cuteness found online that they "plug in" to the procedures, though this does change. The key feature is who in the class is doing the creating. A lesson on symmetry using paint is nice, but only if you allow students to explore with the materials and see how a symmetrical image appears. Paint first, then try manipulating the paper. Have they folded it? What happens? Ooo—do that again. Do you see what Rodney discovered? Rodney, can you share your idea with friends? Letting first graders explore and *discover* symmetry instead of the direct instruction model of "Hold your paper like this. Watch me, friends!" is the key difference we're trying to show you here. Once they *discover* it, challenge them to find symmetry in our world. How can we represent that image on our papers with a few art materials? Only here are students questioning, attempting, designing, restructuring, and creating. Do you see how playful that is? Do you see how much deeper that learning experience is compared to the more traditional approach? It's like Gilbert (2016) said, "Know the world as richly as it longs to be known."

If the teacher gives directions like, "Put your paint here. Now, watch me. Fold just so . . . ," who is doing the thinking? Kids are following directions. There is no creativity here. Our friend John Spencer said once in a keynote speech (2019), "If you give students an assignment and all that's turned in is 25 of the same thing, you didn't give an assignment; you gave a recipe."

When we plan for creativity in our classrooms, we are planning for opportunities. We are planning for scenarios that prompt students to question. We get it: most of us enjoy control. We thrive on color-coding and notebooks stacked just so on our desks. We have a Mason jar for sharpened pencils, another for the fat Sharpies, and another for the Staedler fineliners. But, we have to step back. We have to let go. We have to let them get messy first. We have to let them play.

# Failure

Failure is inevitably a part of every play experience. Someone's block tower will fall, someone will lose the game, someone may spill the paint and ruin the work. In the moments of failure, however, we learn to play better, stronger, and wiser the next time. This word, this experience, this moment of learning known as failure definitely earns its own section in a chapter on creativity. You'll read more on the concept of failure in our section on growth. How many times does one fail when creating? A gazillion, maybe? OK, perhaps not that many, but certainly lots of times. Most everyone knows that Thomas Edison made thousands of unsuccessful attempts at the light bulb before he got it right. The Wright brothers wouldn't have known any success if it wasn't for their repeated and oftentimes painful failures. It took the self-taught engineers years and numerous attempts to get anywhere close to powered flight. We love this quote by Samuel Beckett: "Ever tried? Ever failed? No matter. Try again. Fail again. Fail better." Read some more about historic "failures."

Henry Ford, founder of the Ford Motor Company, failed and went broke five times before he succeeded.

Michael Jordan didn't make his high school basketball team, yet went on to be six-time NBA champ, five-time MVP winner, 14-time All Star, and one of the most celebrated athletes of all time.

R. H. Macy, founder of Macy's department store, failed seven times before his store in New York City caught on.

Oprah Winfrey was publicly fired from her first job as anchor for getting too emotionally attached to her stories, yet this is the very quality that spurred her success.

JayZ was rejected by all record labels for his first album, so he started his own.

Walt Disney was fired by a newspaper editor because "he lacked imagination and had no good ideas."

Twelve publishers rejected J. K. Rowling's book about a boy wizard before a small London house picked up *Harry Potter and the Philosopher's Stone.*

Talk about an impressive list of failures. Sadly, in the education world the most common mention of the word fail, failure, failing has to do with an F on the report card. That F implies that the student is incompetent, not a good worker, not a good test taker, and, worst of all, unintelligent.

Recently, in a room filled with teachers, we showed them a student's work with an F grade on it. We asked them to make critiques of the student solely based on the work seen. Almost every teacher in the room gave negative replies. It makes us *maddern'uh wet hen* when we think about it. Some old men long ago constructed a judgment system comprised of five letters and somehow that is relevant to today's students' intellectual ability. That letter is as useless as a milk bucket under a bull. We long for the day when playful classrooms change that narrative— when the word *failure* is synonymous with bright, intelligent, well educated, and well rounded. We are so tired of an antiquated letter system stifling creativity.

In Robert and Michele Root-Bernstein's book, *Sparks of Genius: The 13 Thinking Tools of the World's Most Creative Thinkers,* a common theme throughout is how school often holds back some of the most brilliant humans. Why? Because they are often the "failures." Trying, failing, trying, failing wasn't an option for them, yet that is how we learn best . . . from our mistakes. It is in those moments of try/fail that most of us find our flow.

If there is any profession where failure and mistakes should be inspected, expected, and respected, it is ours. The very nature of learning comes from trying, messing up, figuring out what went wrong, and trying again. For years we taught students the scientific method. Pose a question, make a hypothesis, test your "logical guess," draw a conclusion to see if your assumptions were correct. If not, no big deal. Why are so many of us afraid of that same approach with play and creativity? Elizabeth Gilbert (2016) tells us that it's because we are afraid . . . but afraid of what, exactly? Who cares if the block tower falls over, if the Play-Doh creation is a hot mess, and the house of cards you tried to build is all woppy-jawed. Being creative with an idea, and playing it into existence only to see it fail, provides education in a way that a traditional textbook lesson never will.

Julie had never heard of "woppy-jawed" before, so we consulted http://onlineslangdictionary.com to confirm its existence. It is 'in fact' common, and we laughed a lot at the coffee shop about one of their sample sentences with the word: "You need to tighten the bolt on that tractor seat. It's all *woppy-jawed*." We even had a play break right in the middle of our work to sketch an illustration of the sentence. It was fun, creative, playful, and got our brains going in a whole new direction. Before we doodled and giggled, our brains were as worthless as a banana left in a hot car, but the moment of play inspired our creativity. See our cute tractors?

(Continued)

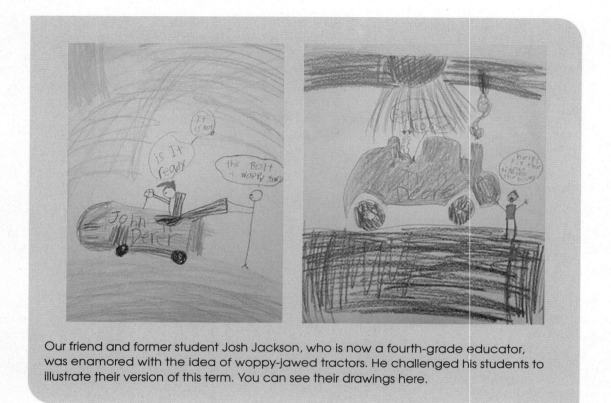

Our friend and former student Josh Jackson, who is now a fourth-grade educator, was enamored with the idea of woppy-jawed tractors. He challenged his students to illustrate their version of this term. You can see their drawings here.

## Play Is for All Ages

The playful classroom is full of flow, choice, and failure. People of all ages are immersed in thinking and working toward goals. If you search "play" on the Internet (and of course we've done that), you'll find more resources than you can shake a stick at . . . if you're looking for it in the context of early childhood education. This gets us all tore up. Play isn't just an early childhood concept. Yes, it's necessary for development, but even more—it's needed to cultivate thinkers—and should be applied to all learners. There is a reason millions of adults worldwide have participated in the *Marshmallow/Spaghetti Tower Challenge*; look it up! Peter Skillman introduced the idea at a TED conference, and ever since, the challenge has continued in classrooms and boardrooms around the world.

It's fun, engaging, and playful, and it inspires critical thinking for all learners. A playful classroom will lead us to a new place of learning, but we must first let go of antiquated ways and embrace new thinking.

Great teachers evolve . . .
. . . even if the process is messy.
. . . even when the planning documentation is notebook
    paper and not a purchased online printout.
. . . even when students disagree.
. . . even when materials aren't available.
. . . even when ideas don't come easily.
. . . even when ___ (fill in your own excuse).

In our work with students, no matter if they are 5 or 55, we value nontraditional materials to invite creativity. Frequently in our courses and presentations, tape, tin foil, sticky notes, straws, yarn, etc., are used to inspire creativity, engage all learners, and develop higher-order thinking skills. Those materials in and of themselves are not often viewed as traditional educational manipulatives, but in the hands of the right teacher, they become powerful learning tools. It is time when we as educators begin to rethink routine, ordinary, "normal" thoughts in education. We should never limit ourselves to the confines of comfort and conformity found inside the safety of the box we are often told to think outside of. Instead, we should be asking why is there a box to begin with, and make every effort to destroy it for the sake of reaching and teaching *all* students.

I (Julie) didn't always teach like this. I should say, *value* this. A little history here: this piece—this creative peace (sic)—is where this book was born. Jed and I would meet in the coffee shop and somehow always end up on this topic. We have spent hours bickering about creativity and its value in the process of teaching. Like two hens over a rooster: truly fussing. Here was my turning point; I used to give daily quizzes in my social studies classes to make sure students were reading the material. This course was taught around the same time as Jed's course. In fact, they were scheduled back-to-back. So, in the time between classes (a 15-minute gap), I saw students reviewing and talking about the reading for Jed's class. Of course, I asked what was up. They didn't know what Jed was going to ask them to do to show their understanding of the reading, and they wanted to be ready.

My reaction? *Nice!* I had already decided I didn't love the structure of my class. Challenged with the way to teach both content and pedagogy for K–6 social studies curriculum in 15 weeks,

I was overwhelmed and feeling ineffective. Fast-forward to a few weeks later, in the car on the way to a professional development event, when I am having an honest conversation with some trusted students. Trusted, because I knew they would tell me the truth and not just what they thought I wanted to hear. I still hear those words:

> *"JJ, we skim the content you give us to read. We do just enough to pass the quiz. We read, really read Jed's stuff."*
>
> *(pause for my shocked, offended face . . . relaxing now . . .)*
> *"OK, why?"*
>
> *"Well, I can't do his assignments unless I understand what I read. Like, how can you make a tin foil representation of your Harry Wong chapter unless you read it and really get it? He's going to ask me about my foil creation. I'll have to justify what I did."*

Well, there you have it. Thank you, Molly Schwarz, for helping me grow to the educator I am. I'm still evolving, you know. We all are.

## Wrapping It Up

Some of you have read this BIG MOMENT for me and wonder, "How was this creative? How is tin foil such a big deal?" You see, it's just that. It's not the tin foil. It's not the Play-Doh. It's not the puppets or the painter's tape. It's the level of thinking you have students engaged in. It's how we challenge them. Mama says, *You plant a butter bean, you get a butter bean.* What are we planting? How are we cultivating the thinking and learning in our classes? Are we giving students information, facts, and content, or are we challenging them to use the information, facts, and content to question, to create, to discern?

When did we get to the point in education where direct instruction (a validated practice, yes) was the *only* way and the *best* way? It is *a* way. It is needed, yes. But not for every lesson, every day. Not for the whole class period. Not one presentation slide after another. Who at this point in our technological trajectory doesn't see a speaker pull up a slide of text and mentally check out? We did it just yesterday (no offense, said speaker). Our kids do it, too. A good rule of thumb for your classroom is to ask yourself this question:

> Would I enjoy sitting through this lesson?

If the answer is no, fix it, change it, or scrap it and start over. (We often throw it away and start over. Just ask the friends who followed us on this writing journey.) There's no shame in admitting that something we've done could be done better. We are already asking ourselves questions about lessons we've mentioned in this chapter. Could they be better? Could they be stronger? Could they be more playful?

Don't get upset with us. Please. We are all on the same team for students here. It's OK to give students a slideshow as a resource and challenge them to think critically about the content. Instead of using the deck as your main presentation, scaffold the thinking process. Make *"I do, We do, You do"* become *"We wonder . . . let's figure out."* This is creative. This is the playful classroom.

This is why Play Inspires **Creativity**, and Creativity Inspires **Play**.

## Playful classrooms
## believe ...

Creativity can happen anytime, anywhere – with lots of materials or none at all.

Play and creativity can be synonymous and often happen simultaneously.

New ideas are born when time, space, and opportunity for play are provided.

Humanity advances when we create.

# Play Builds Trust
## Trust Builds Opportunities for Play

*. . . in ourselves, students, parents, colleagues, and administration. If we constantly doubt one another's abilities, motives, judgments, and qualifications, how can we move forward together?*

# CHAPTER 13

# Play Builds Trust

"Light as a feather. Stiff as board. Light as a feather. Stiff as a board." We hope you chanted that like it was a spooky Halloween night. I (Jed here) can still hear my circle of friends chanting around me as they lifted my middle school body off the ground. There I laid, eye level with my standing peers as they held me using just two fingers each. I was terrified of being dropped flat on my back from 4.5 feet off the ground, but something told me to trust them. I had no choice but to, really. Anything less than trust could have caused my body to jerk, thus causing them to jerk and, bam, splat, there I'd go down to the ground, ending in a concussion or cracked skull.

As an adult reflecting back on that playful moment with my schoolmates, I cannot believe how I trusted them. I am not so trusting as an adult. I only have a few people with whom I would even consider participating in this type of play. Maybe it's because I am a lot heavier than I used to be. Not middle school me, though. I was happy to be the light-as-a-feather example, no matter who was around me. Everyone knew the rules, knew the expectations, and we all trusted everyone in that moment to do the right thing because that's the way we played.

Best not play this game with students. It is more of a slumber party game amongst friends than a school-day event. Julie had never heard of this game. She said, "*We didn't play that in Walhalla.*" The server and I had a blast explaining it to her at our favorite writing spot at The Downtown Deli and Donuts in Spartanburg, South Carolina. It was one of countless playful moments that we had in the writing of this book. If we can make writing a book this playful, imagine what you could do with a room full of children who haven't had their playful spirit crushed by the weight of adulthood. If you've ever played this game we speak of, tweet us about it. Use #ThePlayfulClassroom

Kids are still that way. Observe them while they play tag, give them a ball of yarn, and see what happens. Watch them left to their own devices for inside recess.

I remember another game we used to do called *Trust Fall*. Someone would stand on a platform (table, countertop, stage) and fall backward into a group of outstretched arms of peers promising to catch you. I cannot believe I ever did something like that. I am terrified of heights and falling, to the point of it being somewhat debilitating if I get too high (too high being the fourth rung of a ladder). I guess something about the youth camp setting where this took place—coupled with a group of my friends encouraging me to fall— built up my courage, and my trust in their promised catch outweighed my fears. Funny how a playful moment could do that for me. Has it ever done that for you?

# CHAPTER 14

# Don't Sit and Get

The research is clear: When students are required to remain seated for much of the school day, many negative behaviors occur, which teachers then attribute to bad children instead of a lack of physical activity and cognitive breaks (Sahlberg & Doyle, 2019; Rhea, Rivchun, & Pennings, 2013). It's not the kids—it's the schedule we provide. Have you heard of the LiiNK project? No? Hunnnn-ey! You're going to be more excited than a woodpecker in a lumberyard.

Let us introduce you to Dr. Debbie Rhea. She is a professor and associate dean of research in the Harris College of Nursing and Health Sciences at Texas Christian University. See, she did this cool thing: because kinesiology (the study of human movement) really cranks her tractor, her readings led her to results from schools in Finland, and she was intrigued. So, she did what any of us would dream of: she took a trip. A six-week sabbatical to Helsinki and Jyvaskyla, where she visited, observed, studied, and experienced the beautiful national symphony of children who ran across playgrounds at the 45-minute mark of every hour (Sahlberg & Doyle, 2019). That's right, students in Finland receive at least 15 minutes of recess every hour. Once refreshed, these children return to their lessons renewed and energized. Dr. Rhea was blown away.

When she returned to Texas, where students were getting 15–20 minutes of recess *a day*, she launched an experiment called the LiiNK project (Let's Inspire Innovation in Kids). Piloted with four schools in 2013–2014, this study has grown to have more than 8,000 primary schoolchildren and another 8,000 in the control group (not receiving the LiiNK intervention). Participating schools receive two components of Finnish-style education: (1) recess time is tripled from 20 minutes each day to 15 minutes every hour, and (2) implementation of ethics/character development lessons. See that? They not only honor play as a behavior, they are cultivating a playful mindset in children with positive human qualities we all aspire for: *trust* among them.

The results? Well, in Debbie's words, "Change is hard when numbers don't tell the story—emotions do." Nevertheless, the data looks really good. Not just good, it might be better than a nanner sammich with a sprinkle of pepper. Let me just list of few of the stats here for you. Across all of the LiiNKed schools:

- Students' on-task behaviors improved by at least 30%.
- Writing skills have advanced by at least six months in a single year.
- Classroom misbehavior has dropped.
- Empathy and social skills are dramatically Improved.
- Students are more productive.
- Students are less fidgety.
- Students are more focused.
- Students take initiative to fix problems before seeking teacher intervention.
- Discipline rates, including bullying, have declined.
- Student attention? Double-digit gains.
- Students' listening? Improving.
- Students' decision-making? Improving.
- Students' problem-solving skills? Improving. (Sahlberg & Doyle, 2019; Rhea, 2019)

Early teacher estimates are that the implementation of the LiiNKed components has sped up learning by months. Not minutes, no. No need to add 15 minutes to the school day. No need to start earlier or lessen the time kiddos are at lunch. No. It's simple. We do this rogue thing called *let them play*. Kids already know how to play. They know how to structure their play when we step back and give them the opportunity. They need the time to grow. Let's get out of their way. But . . . to do that, we must trust them. How do we do that? First, let's see what happened in a recent college education class (Figure 14.1).

Often in my college classes (Julie speaking here), I coach students through an experience that challenges them. My goal is to get students thinking about their views; thus, they often reframe their perspectives on a given topic. One day in my math course, students were challenged to think beyond the traditional bell-ringer activity. I introduced them to open middle math problems that invite discussion because of their low entry point and high ceiling. This class experience included both the math conversation as well as the concepts of growth mindset and a tad bit of neuroscience. I rarely ever dictate to my students what they will do with their new understandings. Rather, I challenge them to develop a product they can use as future teachers that

"In a sense, Rokel," replied Dr. Jones. "Mistakes allow our brain to create new pathways and strengthen the pathways that are already in our brain."

**FIGURE 14.1** Children's book on growth mindset by @ROKinTheClass and @MonicaDLandrum.

showcases these concepts. They have the power of choice. They have an authentic audience.

Because of this shift (focusing on what they want to create rather than what the professor wants), student products are varied and unique. Two students, after having experienced open middle mathematics, wrote and illustrated a children's story they can use in their classrooms. The story explains to children how mistakes help our brains grow. In kid words. With emotions from situations kids really encounter. Other students created a hyper-doc lesson. And some others sketched and blogged their way toward understanding. Before each product goes live, students turn it in to get feedback for growth. We want their public product to represent their best work. So, they try, try again until it's ready.

This is a section on trust. Play provides the opportunity for trust to develop. We know now (*we might say we've always known*) that play is needed for learning. That play is inherent to the develop-mental needs of children and our mental health as we grow older. But yet, our systems don't reflect this knowledge. For the most part, our schools focus more on academics (cognition), emo-tions (school counselor classes every 2 weeks), and movement (PE and those few daily minutes of recess) as separate entities. This is an antiquated way of thinking. The compartmentalized paradigm has been proven false with all the research on learning and development conducted in the last 30 years (even longer than that, really). What is true is an integrated paradigm where cognition, emotion, and movement are tied up like a delicious bowl of spaghetti noodles. To learn, to enjoy, to experience, to remember—we need them all. All day long.

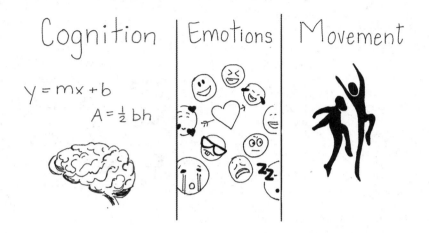

OLD, COMPARTMENTALIZED PARADIGM

NEW INTEGRATED PARADIGM

The students in my math class were in their early 20s. They are the last of the millenial age group to attend college. My approach to their learning is based on my knowledge of what that generation needs for success. They learn and interact differently than previous generations because of the world they have grown up in. I allow them freedom to work, giving them time, space, and opportunity to grow in their learning trajectory. For this to happen, both parties must trust each other.

Teaching in modern classrooms, we must consider the way millennials are impacting our perspectives—specifically in the areas of play and *work*. We mention this here because work is often viewed as the antithesis of play. For our students, play is the work. For adults, a playful mindset is inherent to the work. Consider the results of a Gallup study from 2008 to 2016 (Gallup, 2016).

Millennials:

- Don't just work for a paycheck; they want a purpose.
- Are not pursuing job satisfaction; they want development.
- Don't want bosses; they want a coach.
- Don't want annual reviews; they want conversations.

Why is all this applicable? Because it's not just their job; it's their life. Society has developed a trust in this process for millennials. We've experienced the successes this mindset has launched: ride-sharing applications, social media, dating apps, video production tools, alternatives to hotels, and a wide variety of other technological advances that have shaped our society because of play.

Imagine if we trusted our students like we trust the evolving workforce population. Imagine if we really trusted the research on play. In our experience as play advocates, we don't generally get pushback on the benefits playful mindsets bring to academics or the socioemotional benefits of cooperative learning; rather, the pushback is on the movement piece. We teachers seems to want quiet, orderly classrooms all the time. We get nervous if a student needs to stand at her desk while she writes. Some of us can't imagine laying in the floor and reading. So, let's turn our focus to movement. How does physical play benefit the learner? When we know the benefits, trust will develop and the system will evolve.

# Benefits of Physical Play

## Physical Play Improves Our Intellectual Capacity

Physical play, the kind most adults in the South would stop with a string of promises attached to the end of a hickory switch, is actually fertilizer for our brain. When we engage in physical play, our brain releases a chemical called brain-derived neurotrophic factor (BDNF), which acts in our brains much like Scott's Turf Builder. Neuron growth is stimulated within the cortex and hippocampus regions—these are the parts responsible for memory, learning, language, and logic (Debenedet & Cohen, 2011). In his popular TedX talk (2014), Peter Gray begins with research on animal play. Turns out, animals with the largest brains, with the greatest capacity to learn, are those who play the most.

## Physical Play Builds Emotional Intelligence

When we engage physically with others, we develop a stronger sense of reading body language. *Is he going for my gut? Or is he going to grab me over the head?* We have to see what's happening in the physical world and draw conclusions about intent. Over time, when experiencing repeated play with the same friends, we learn their ways and what their go-to moves are. This skillset transfers to our abilities to navigate the emotional adult world. *Is he asking this because he is concerned? Oh, what I just said clearly upset him.* There are a multitude of settings we can navigate as grownups because we developed the skillset through play.

- Reading a boss's mood
- Knowing how to question a coworker
- Knowing how to challenge a peer
- EVERY. HOLIDAY. WITH. FAMILY.

*Plus also* (as Junie B likes to say) physical play helps kids learn how to regain self-control. You get mad, sad, excited, jealous, afraid . . . and then you get over it. Because you want to play. If you take that emotion into the play, it's no longer *play* for everyone and soon it ends. These social interactions and their complexities in our youth help us build the confidence we need as adults (DeBenedet & Cohen, 2011).

## Physical Play Helps Us Build Friendships

In physical play-encounters, each person develops the ability to discern the intent of other players, distinguishing between innocent play and aggression. You know when someone is playing and when someone clearly intends to inflict harm. It's intuition; you feel it. This skillset transfers to our ability to interact socially and solve problems. Taking turns is another aspect of friendship and sharing we learn through play. If one person is "it" the whole time, the game gets boring. The variability and fairness of turn-taking begins in physical play. The negotiation of these rules and how players interact also develops our leadership skills. We must all agree for play to take place—what wonderful prep for eventual professional success and long-term commitments.

## Physical Play Develops Our Moral Character

What happens when you pair a sixth grader with a third grader at recess? Of course, the older kid will go easy on the younger one. We see this in animals too: when the stronger alpha dog, say a Labrador, plays with a poodle. Tails are just a-waggin', but you know good and well who would go down in a real fight. In play-research, this behavior is called "self-handicapping," when the stronger play partner holds back on strength and force when playing with a weaker or smaller opponent. Why? Because it's the right thing to do. Enter moral development, stage left.

## Physical Play Promotes Physical Wellness

Yeah. We know this seems obvious, but yet we still allow kids to sit most of the day and fuss about how we can't give recess time because *standards, standards, standards . . .* (refer to Section 1, Chapter 5, Excuse 1). Please don't default to thinking about physical wellness as simply your svelte physique (wink, wink). Wellness here includes complex motor skills, concentration, coordination, body control, cardiovascular fitness, and flexibility. We cannot continue to rely on gym class and recess for these benefits. We *must* invite physical play in our classrooms. Now, please don't tackle your students. Think dance, think relay races, think walking while reading, think jazzercise meets vocabulary development. Play with it!

## Physical Play Is a Catalyst for Joy

In anthropological studies of hunter-gatherer cultures (see Section 4, Chapter 20), the children play from dawn until dusk. When asked why, the culture elders reply, "That's how they learn the skills for being an adult." As a species, we humans are hardwired for physical play. Our minds and bodies like it when it happens. *Hello, adrenaline. Hello, endorphins.* Even in neurological studies of mammals, when the play circuits are activated, they feel joy.

Imagine a classroom full of joyful students with enormous intellectual capacity, increased emotional intelligence, who had deep friendships with one another, coupled with strong moral character and developing physical wellness. This scenario shows a playful class culture at heart. We think those students would have incredible trust in one another as they worked through various lessons of inquiry. We think trusting those kids with new learning and new experiences would be a breeze.

# CHAPTER 15

# A Story about Trust

Recently, a first-year teacher reached out to me (Jed) for assistance with strengthening her technology integration skills. She desired to create the best classroom she could during her first year, and I wanted to do everything in my power to help her cultivate relevant, meaningful experiences for her students and make them fun, playful, and memorable at the same time. Based on my experience with Skype in my classroom, I decided to ntroduce her to the incredible world of video conferencing with students and teachers around the world.

I took lots of these amazing trips with my students, and they are almost always playful, and most certainly memorable and engaging. Mystery Skype is a highly engaging 20 questions-type game, where one class races to discover the location of the opposing class first. Never heard of it, you say? Look up our friend Gina Ruffcorn (@gruffcorn13), educator extraordinaire who teaches in Iowa. We've sketched her here for you sitting in her fav reading chair, sporting her GoNoodle ambassador shirt. She has the Mystery Skype game down to a science, and her students can run the game daily without any assistance from her. It is really a fantastic experience to watch. One of the most playful experiences I ever had with Skype involved a global sing-along with Mike Soskil, (@msoskil), Livingstone Kegode, (@lkegode), and Yau-Jau Ku (@yaujauku). Mike was in Pennsylvania, Livingstone was in Nairobi, Kenya, Ku was in Venezuela at the time, and I was in South Carolina. All of our classes shared songs from our local areas, and we learned about local customs and traditions. The refrain of "That was the best day ever" was repeated more than once by my students throughout the year. We also interacted with a bee-keeper harvesting honey, an Antarctic scientist observing Adele penguins, and a marine biologist operating on a sea turtle in Key West, Florida. The awe and wonder of all of these experiences helped us all get lost in the flow of learning. It was as if time stood still for the call as we marveled at never before seen things. I still get chills when I think about the "ooohs and ahhhhs" I heard from students as we watched the rehabilitated sea turtle swim to freedom.

I have trained countless teachers across the country using Skype virtual experiences. In 2012, I was named a Skype Master Teacher and collaborated with teachers across the country to create unique global opportunities for students to engage in meaningful collaboration. I was employed by Microsoft for a year where I helped produce video and written tutorials for teachers around the world. I even wrote a "Skype in the Classroom" jingle. I knew more about connecting Skype into the curriculum than anyone in the entire school where this first-year teacher worked. Full disclaimer here . . . Don't read those last few sentences thinking I am bragging. I am not one of those people. I say all this not to boast about my credentials, but to establish the fact that I was indeed very knowledgeable on the subject. I shared all of this information with the first-year teacher as well in an effort to build trust in our professional relationship. In order for her to fully engage in the learning experience I was bringing to her, I had to provide proof that I wasn't just bringing her a *dog and pony,* but a legitimate learning experience that was invaluable to her students and to her technology integration tool box.

One fear we commonly hear when we talk about being a play-ful teacher in a playful classroom beyond grade two is that an outside observer could possibly see the work as less than rigorous and discourage that "type of learning." It is frustrating to hear educated people devalue the role of playful experiences when the research supports it at every level. No, I am not talking about test score data. I am talking about the real life, every day, feedback from participants, young and old, in a teaching session that clearly shows that death by slideshow is not the preferred method of learning. You've read countless nuggets of research throughout this book that supports a playful approach to learning. Trust us.

It seems I have chased a rabbit a bit here, so let me get back on the trail and refocus us. Ahhh yes . . . Skype. I set up an incredible trip for her class. The world-renowned scientist Jean Pennycook (@jean.pennycook) was studying penguins in Antarctica and partnered with Skype to provide lessons to students around the world as she stood beside nesting penguins in their actual habitats. WOW! Did you just read that sentence and begin to covet? I know we aren't supposed to do that, but how could a great educator not? Regardless of the content standards covered, regardless of the tested material taught, regardless of the amount of time the call took, providing students with a real-live look into the frozen land at the bottom of the globe was priceless. My teacher self was downright giddy as I planned it all out. I notified the first-year teacher of the impending awesomeness that was coming to her class and encouraged her to prep them with some penguin study. The first thing she said when I told her about it was, "Oh no . . . penguins aren't our standards."

- She was so worried about it because she knew the K5 and 2nd grade classes covered birds and habitats.

- She didn't want to step on anyone's lessons.
- She didn't want to go off script from the rest of her grade level.
- She didn't want the admins to question if she was following the scope and sequence of the grade.
- She was afraid to "waste time" doing something that wouldn't increase her science test scores.

Remember, we told you this reaction is common, and it is even more prevalent among new teachers. They have been taught throughout college careers to avoid veering off course one teeny bit from the long-range plan, the scope and sequence, and the district pacing guide. Sadly, it squashes their creativity, and it takes years for them to find it again. We know. We were that teacher, too.

Of course, I was devastated at her response. I could feel her uneasiness with the plan for the lesson, and it cut me to the very core of my teacher being.

- She was too young in the career to have already been misguided by the testing machine.
- She was too fresh to have let the zeal and excitement for engaging learning leave her.
- She was too young not to want to try new things in the curriculum.

But, I quickly realized that she was probably being cautious because of pressure from somewhere else in her building. Admins, instructional coaches, grade level chairs . . . we've all experienced these pressures. The fear of negative reactions from people in our professional circle can end the idea of a playful classroom so quickly. We don't blame them, but again we refer to the system, the culture, the climate of modern-day schooling. It has taught them—and us, if we are honest—that flow and play do not have priority over test scores, numerical data, standards, and of course school status in the district and state as a "high performing."

Was that too much? Did we go too far? Nope . . . we probably didn't go far enough. Students are more than a number attached to a letter. We tried to say that as nice as we could. My great grandma Maudie always said that you could say whatever you wanted if you put a little honey on your lips. We dabbed a smidge on there just now. We don't want to complain about the problems that we face, but we have to acknowledge them so we can grow. The system has such a tight grip on the learning experiences we provide, it sometimes feels like we are lightnin' bugs trapped in a jar with no holes. Help . . . we need air!

Back to the story. I asked her—I begged her—to trust me. Trust that this experience was going to do way more than cover standards, yet it would tackle numerous standards. It was gonna do way more than increase test scores, although it would certainly help them, too. It was gonna do way more than stay on script, but it would indeed fit into the grade level plan. She wasn't too stuck in her "Oh no . . . penguins aren't our standards" fears, because she eagerly agreed to put her trust in me as her "teacher" for the purpose of learning more about technology integration and bringing a playful spirit to her teaching practice.

The experience was incredible. Jean Pennycook is not only a gifted scientist but a true teacher. She used every second of the virtual field trip to integrate all areas of the curriculum. The call was filled with way more than penguins and their habitat. Weather, climate change, conservation, adaptations, survival, and social justice were just a few of the topics that emerged during the experience. Students formulated questions, wrote in their journals, took notes, collaborated with their peers, and actually saw with their own eyes a part of the planet that they will most likely never see again. One student even said, "Wow, that felt like recess more than science." Imagine that! Learning was like playing, playing was like learning.

The first-year teacher was beside herself the entire time that Antarctica was displayed on her 10-year-old "interactive" white-board, which had been used previously to display a wide array of death-by-slideshow thus killing student engagement with the speed of a lightning bolt crashing into an unexpectant head. She was thrilled to learn about the power of Skype in the class-room and all of the possibilities for global collaboration around the world with classrooms who had also participated in the Jean Pennycook Antarctic experience.

As professors in EDU programs, we were sad that she hadn't learned of this during her degree program, but we will save that for another book.

She was even more pleased that one of her building's instructional coaches had wandered into the classroom while the interactive live call with a world-renowned scientist was taking place. Surely, she expressed to me quietly, that this would score her some big points with the admins. Of course it would. Not that one needs *points* to validate engagement and overall student happiness with the learning process, but it doesn't hurt to receive a little praise from the boss, right?

After the virtual field trip ended, the first-year teacher led this class in a terrific closing and began to transition to the next item in her plan book. Secretly, I wanted her to throw the scripted plans her grade level had forced on her into a fiery pit, but I completely understand having to play the game, especially during the first year. So, I applauded her willingness to try this new thing and encouraged her to visit www.skypeintheclassroom.com to register for her next trip, and also showed her some of my tips and tricks on the Skype website so she could do even more with it in her classroom. She couldn't wait to get started. I left the room feeling proud for her . . . proud for me . . . elated for her students!

The pride and elation lasted all of 2.2 seconds after I exited the room. The instructional coach who wandered in the room followed me out the door as I left. As if her very life depended on it, the questioning of what she had witnessed began without a moment of delay. Having read Elena Aguilar's *The Art of Coaching*, I can assure you that this coach had not yet received training in how to appropriately question and guide me nor the first-year teacher. Her approach had nothing to do with her concern for the teacher or me. The first question (read this with a side of arrogance and condescension), "Now, what *standards* does a penguin field trip cover in third-grade science?" It was almost as if she had waited the entire 45 minutes of the call to play "gotcha" with me as I walked out.

That's no coach. A coach is someone who desires growth in their team, not someone who wants to belittle. She then proceeded to tell me that all of the experiences at their school must be "content-based," and they didn't really like to stray from the plan. "We have very high expectations here," she said. "Especially for our first-year teachers. We have to show them right away that there is no time for fluff. If we are going to this 'Skype thing,' it must be aligned with the curriculum. We can't just be all 'willy-nilly' around the world. Besides, second grade does penguins."

Y'all . . . The amount of creative language that was going through my head cannot be put into written form for fear of losing my teacher license. Seriously, I was boiling inside. I had more questions than a coon dog has cockleburs:

- Did the instructional coach not see what had just happened in that room?
- Was she so inept that she couldn't see the value of learning science from a real live scientist in Antarctica?
- Did she really not grasp the student engagement that took place as the students hung on every word of the call?
- Was it possible that she didn't see the relevance in learning about how the way humans treat the environment here in America directly affects the penguins at the bottom of the globe?
- Could she not see the hundreds of possible follow-up experiences that could be integrated into *all* areas of the curriculum?
- Did she miss the part where the students were overjoyed and having so much fun learning (playing) and in the "flow" that they didn't want the call to end?

We realize this list has many examples and may seem redundant, but in the heat of the moment aren't we flooded with emotion? Aren't our brains churning out rebuttal? What you read here is exactly what I was feeling.

I can see why she would think returning to that worksheet about adaptations was much more relevant and engaging. Clearly that textbook with the bold key words was much more engaging. Definitely, the fill-in-the-bubble pretest was much more exciting and pedagogically sound. Absolutely, an hour of close reading on the topic would have been better for collecting student data so that they could move name cards on the data wall in the after-school faculty meeting.

As eloquently and professionally as I could possibly muster, I explained the power of what had just happened in details that I should have never had to use with an educational leader, but I digress. I was a guest in the school. I couldn't be rude to her and tell her all the colorful language I was actually thinking about her misguided pedagogy. As she escorted me to the door, I offered to come back and walk her and the team through the entire Skype process in more detail. Sadly, I have never been invited back to that school. My heart breaks for the kids there that will have to suffer through so many moments of boring, unengaging, irrelevant lessons all because of an instructional coach who is squashing creativity, collaboration, communication, critical-thinking, community, and playful fun from every lesson plan in the building out of fear that it won't "meet the standards" or increase test scores.

That's really what we believe it boils down to: *fear*. People are afraid because, yet again, systems are in place to determine a school's value and worth based on its academic performance alone. They think the only way to improve student performance is through drill and practice and test prep, in a highly rigorous work environment. Flip back a few pages and reread the results of the LiiNK study. Educational practices such as playfulness that can be found in a video call to Antarctica can in fact *increase* academic performance the same if not more than traditional methods. We have to trust—trust the research, trust each other, trust our students. Trust is the catalyst for change.

One dictionary definition of trust reads, "a firm belief in the reliability, truth, ability, or strength of someone or something." In order for education to benefit students, all parties involved must dig deep in their trust of one another. When we are talking about children, regardless of their grade level, we are talking about the most precious cargo on the planet. As educators, we are charged with teaching them, caring for them, and loving them as we prepare them for the future. We have heard so many critics of education claim that teachers should "just stick to teaching;"

but do you really want a school full of educators who don't love the students they are teaching? Is there anything more important, and is there anything where trust is more necessary?

Reread that definition. We would almost bet that you skimmed over it, because it's a word that most of us know and use often, yet probably never looked it up . . . a firm belief in the

- Reliability
- Truth
- Ability
- Strength . . . of someone or something

In the profession of education there are lots of "someones" where trust must reside.

Admins to Teachers
Teachers to Admins
Teachers to Parents
Parents to Teachers
Teachers to Students
Students to Teachers
Community to Teachers
Teachers to Community

(If you haven't read the Community section, you might want to jump ahead and do that now.)

In order for our goal to move the playful classroom mindset from the fairytale land of nighttime slumber into the sunlight of reality, trust must be nurtured, grown, and harvested regularly by everyone involved. In order for that to happen, however, we must take an honest look at areas where the cultivation of trust may need some attention. Educators (administration and teachers), parents, students, and community members all play their own critical role in the dynamic of trust for success to occur. That's four stakeholders. Four. A three-legged cow doesn't stand too well, does it?

# CHAPTER 16

# Administrators Must Trust . . .

Let's start with the trust from the administrators. One of the biggest reasons for my students' success was due to the abundance of professional trust my principal gave me. Dr. Cindy Pridgen at Woodland Heights Elementary was the best at giving me the freedom to do what was most beneficial for my students in regard to planning, learning experiences, classroom setup and routines, parent phone calls, and discipline. There was not one area where she ever made me feel like she doubted me. That's powerful, liberating, and led to a lot of creativity on my part. Her trust in me led me to a level of teaching I never thought possible.

> She didn't hover over my shoulder asking about every detail of my day.
> She didn't require me to submit my lesson plans so she could mark them up with a red pen.
> She didn't require me to post my standards, essential questions, my objective, and my procedures on the board.
> She never once said to me, "Does that cover your standards?"
> She never asked me to rearrange my classroom, to be quiet, or to stop making my classroom so fun and engaging because it upset the other teachers.

Sadly, we know administrators who have done every single one of those things. We know of one district that actually told their teachers what color schemes were allowed in their classrooms. We have seen with our own eyes lesson plans that have been marked up in red pen and handed back to the teacher on Monday when the plans were supposed to begin. We have been in countless schools where the teachers were afraid to begin their day because all of the required info hadn't been properly posted on the board. Quite often I (Jed) provide relevant and engaging professional development in schools across the country only to be told afterward by the teachers that the ideas and strategies I brought them wouldn't be allowed in their buildings because of their fears that my community building, arts-integrated, hands-on, and playful experiential learning would not be well-received. Where is the trust? Where is the fidelity in our profession? Where is the assumption of professional intent? The trust that my principal placed in me solidified my love for teaching, my desire to do it right, and my passion to make sure every moment was filled with engagement. It gave me confidence to be a risk taker. It took away my fears of "messing up" and allowed me to flourish. Anything less than what she gave to me would have trapped me in the tiniest of boxes and limited the incredible experiences I offered to my students. It was because of my principal's trust that I introduced second graders to LEGO Robotics.

> It was because of her trust that I wrote musicals for our entire grade level.
> It was because of her trust that I wrote grants, planned events, and applied for awards.
> I actually won a few too, which led to an even greater trust that I would always do what's best for students.

> Any school leader who does not trust their teachers is killing the playful classroom and hurting the organizations which they lead.

Are there teachers out there who cannot be trusted? *Of course!* Even as I type, Julie and I are reading an article about a teacher who placed packing tape over the mouth of a talkative first grader. We are horrified reading it and hope that swift action is taken to remove her from the profession. What was she even thinking? It is teachers like this who damage the perception of the rest of us, who are genuinely trying to be the best we can at the profession. However, should this one bad teacher cause the rest of us to not be trusted as professionals? The answer should be a resounding no. The faults of the outlier educators, in fact, should move all of us to do even bigger, better things for our students, schools, and communities. That means we—the great teachers—need to be trusted even more.

I have experienced what it's like to have a boss who doesn't trust. It literally sucks all the life out of you. It is like a reverse wind tunnel. . . a black hole where no creativity exists. There are no new ideas. There is no excitement. There is no desire to try what you've never tried before.

Colleagues and bosses who don't trust us in our work hold us back from greatness; and in education, it is the students who suffer the most. If those in our work circle constantly point to minuscule things that bug them rather than praise the good things we are doing, we begin to ignore the good things out of fear of messing up. It attacks the very core of who we are and the work we long to do. If you are an administrator reading this, please. . . Build up your people, encourage them, brag on them, give them the freedom to grow. Believe me, you will see far more fruit in the garden of trust than you will if you micromanage every detail of their day. People who feel valued will go above and beyond what is expected far more than those who cower in fear because of intimidation.

You may notice us using the words *boss* and *leader* often in this section. That is intentional. In our research for this book, we found many charts comparing the two roles. They are very different in their practices. It's true of boss/leader and traditional/playful. You could manipulate the headings to apply to whatever environment you are in where a hierarchy exists, but the point is in the approach. The mindset. We think this chart will resonate with all of you who are at the helm of a playful classroom.

| Traditional practice | Playful practice |
| --- | --- |
| Directs | Shows |
| Knows everything | Always learning |
| Creates followers | Creates leaders |
| Gives orders | Gives guidance |
| Demands respect | Earns respect |
| Gives answers | Gives advice |
| Uses "you and I" | Uses "us and we" |
| Talks first | Listens first |
| Takes credit | Gives credit |
| Criticizes | Coaches |

# CHAPTER 17

# Teachers Can Trust . . .

We started by talking about administrators, but classroom teachers (we feel like we're preaching to the choir here) also play a pivotal role in the trust dynamic. There are folks we have to trust, too.

Let's start with our students. They can do exceedingly above what most of us ask of them. It always amazes us, when we ask students to complete a learning task with robotics, how well they do. The specific robots we use are more geared toward middle schoolers, and many teachers have given pushback on our decision to use them because they were "too advanced" and the students "might get frustrated". Our students have always ended up teaching us something we don't know about the robots.

They are risk takers—never afraid to try something new. They never ask me what a button does. They mash it, toggle it, turn it, click it, you name it; and they discover on their own what its function is and away they go, learning *and* having fun. I enjoy every minute of it. Educational moments like this one only happen when teachers let go of their fears and control and truly trust their students.

Once, I (Jed) was asked to train early childhood teachers on how to integrate more arts and creativity into their classrooms. The workshop I led was focused on using common items like tin foil, sticky notes, yarn, and Play-Doh to invite critical thinking into their work as they created visuals to showcase their learning. Most of the teachers were thrilled with the concepts I brought them, but there was one who didn't get it, didn't want it, and didn't believe her kids could do it. I wasn't surprised. (There's always one, right?) She was concerned that what I taught them was just "too hard for her babies." I think she meant well. . . kind of. She didn't want her "babies" to struggle and get frustrated. She didn't want her "babies" feeling bad about themselves. None of us genuinely want to invite frustration and potential shut down for our students.

This quality is admirable, and many of us share this outlook in the profession.

But . . . reflect with me on your own life. When did you learn the most? Was it when you were driving down the road and everything went well, or was it when your car blew a tire and you had to figure out what to do? Was it when you knew the material so well you didn't have to study, or was it when you really had to buckle down, focus, and dig deep into your brain? Was it when your life was going so well, or when it all fell apart, that the learning was greatest?

I am not turning this into a self-help book or some spiritual guide to enlightenment, but the times I learned the most were the times where I was at my wit's end and had not a clue what to do nor where to start. Once, when I took a new job in education as a professional development leader for schools across the nation, I had to figure things out all on my own. Sometimes I cussed. Sometimes I cried. Sometimes I went home and screamed into my pillows.

All that didn't help grow my skills, although I certainly felt better. I knew I couldn't cry and cuss forever, so I began to seek ways to grow into the job. I read books on professional development, talked with leaders in professional development, listened to podcasts about professional development. Soon I began to grow. I could have quit. I could have told myself I couldn't do it. But I didn't, and now years later I am hosting professional development conferences around the state, leading an online professional development book study, and writing a book about professional development. Had I been a student in the teacher's class I mentioned above, I would have never been given the chance to try because she feared I would fail. Did I fail getting to this point? You bet I did!

I had so many projects derail.
Some never even started.
Some began and crashed into a ball of flames.

Every one of those experiences, however, led to my learning something new, and I grew in my knowledge of the job. We need these kinds of experiences for our students so that we can change their beliefs about failures. Failures are stepping-stones to our goals, not barriers.

Back to the teacher who didn't believe her kids could do it. I had no doubt she loved her students and really wanted them to be successful. But with her mindset, she was depriving her students of many unique learning moments that could have shown them how deep her care and concern for their success was.

Moments where their tin foil would rip and they would have to
    figure out how to mend it.
Moments where the sticky notes wouldn't stand up as they
    built a structure and they had to learn about foundations
    and support.
Moments where their Play-Doh dried up and they had to figure
    out a way to fix it.

These moments can only happen for those children, and
students in all of our classrooms, when playful teachers trust them
enough to let go of our fears and allow them to fail, try again, fail,
learn, and maybe fail again once they thought they had learned.

The teacher came to me after the meeting and asked me to
help her. She needed me to teach a model lesson—one that
showcased the philosophy and belief that her students could do
the task I brought before them. I happily agreed and we planned
a date. Inside I was a nervous wreck. My imposter syndrome flared
up like nobody's business!

What if her kids really couldn't do what I was suggesting?
What if the lesson failed miserably?
What if I was proved to be a fraud to the whole school?
What if the teacher laughed at me as I failed?
What if the principal saw me fail and told other principals?
What if the teachers gossiped about my failure?
What if kids asked me questions I couldn't answer?
What if I was really wrong about her kids' abilities?

Lord . . . all the "what ifs." That's enough to scare anyone half
to death, right? Why would anyone want to dare to be different
and risk all those what-ifs becoming a reality?

As I had all those questions, I was confronted with yet another
person who must be trusted in education: myself. I had to trust
my training, experience, and abilities. I had to trust the process
that I had implemented countless times. In order for me to create
a playful classroom, where students were actively engaged in
the learning process, I had to trust my gut about what's best for
the kids under my care. For this particular lesson, her students
were now mine, and I had to believe that they were capable of
greatness.

The day I went to lead the model lesson, I was still a nervous
wreck inside. As the lesson started, I too had my doubts about
kids' abilities. I was letting the teacher's lack of trust influence
my every step during the lesson. I could see doubt all over her
face. I wasn't very good at hiding my nerves, either. This teacher

had years more experience than me. I was definitely losing my playful mindset and forgetting all of the research support of my instructional methods.

But, in a flash my nerves vanished, thanks to the students who began to create big magic with pieces of tin foil.

> Speaking of *Big Magic*, have y'all read it? It is by *Eat, Pray, Love* author, Elizabeth Gilbert. If you haven't read it, you *must*! Stop right now and order it online or call your favorite indie bookshop. You want your own copy because you will need to take notes. Underline. Highlight. Doodle in it. We cannot write a book and not mention how her words challenged us as educators to stop living in fear. From this one reading experience, we are more empowered to live creatively. Tweet us (#theplayfulclassroom) when you read pages 13–15 and tell us if the fears she lists aren't part of the life of every teacher you know. Fear is real in every aspect of our job. There's a lot at stake, and we don't want to mess it up.
>
> Part of the creative living Gilbert (2016) writes about means recognizing the boogey man that you are afraid of and telling him to buzz off. The times when I did trust my educator instincts were incredible moments of authentic learning that could never be captured in the 10-page lesson plan that some preservice programs often require of education students.

Back to those students and their tin foil. I wish I could tell you that the lesson got off to a blazing start—picture the Daytona 500 here. All the kids' engines raring to go, speeding into their creations, and lapping all the expectations of their teacher. Vroom, vroom.

Nope, that was not the way it started. In fact, it was quite the opposite. Most of the students were afraid to touch the foil because they didn't want to mess it up. They just kept patting it and making it smooth and flat. They were afraid they were making too much noise. As I watched this unfold, I could tell that there was no culture of risk-taking in the classroom. The teacher, whether she meant to or not, had taught these kids to be afraid of trying new things. I should have known this ahead of time. Her lack of trust in what I was doing, her lack of trust in herself, and her lack of trust in her students were the perfect breeding ground for fear.

Eventually, I broke the yoke of *failure fear* in that sweet little classroom of kindergartners, and the students started creating with their foil. Their task was to create a model that represented an answer to my question, "Where do birds go at night?" We read an article from @Wonderopolis about the subject, and their creations needed to reflect their comprehension of the article.

Yes, it was challenging for K5 students, but as an educator who strives to create a classroom where every lesson is relevant and matters, this seemed way more beneficial to students than the reading comprehension worksheets I used to do as a kid. If we are honest with ourselves, some teachers are still using those exact same sheets. Some even have faint purple font.

When the students finally got to work, I became super focused on one student who was at a table all by herself. She had been placed there long before I came to the classroom because of her behavior. When I asked why she was there, I was told that she was *very bad* and never on task. Ironically, the reason I was so keen to watch her was because she was incredibly tuned in to the task. Prior to reading the passage, students were to sculpt their foil answers using only their prior knowledge. As you can imagine, most kids made a bird or a nest, but they struggled to support their creation with details from the text.

The girl I was watching created a nest prior to the reading like most of her classmates, but it was after the reading that her thinking began to really emerge. She appeared to be steadily taking her nest apart and adding something to the side of it. There is no way I can possibly put into words what her final creation looked like. To my eyes it looked like a foil nest with a big lump attached to the side with little balls of foil inside the nest. I had no idea what she had created, so like any playful teacher I said, "Tell me about your creation." A good teacher knows to never ever ask, "What is that?" The little girl, who the teacher said was *always bad* and never had anything to say about lessons, immediately went into a fantastic K5 description of her foil answer. "This part is the nest, and in the nest is a group of birds, and this here (the big lump on the side) is a sentry bird. He is watching out for all the other birds while they sleep."

Y'all, it was the cutest thing as she explained it. Can you see her 5-year-old grin, with the missing teeth?

Like many kindergarten kids, she had a little trouble with the "R" words—part, group, birds, sentry—yep, you know how it sounded. It was adorable, and only added to the pride I felt as she didn't let those "Rs" stop her from explaining herself.

What was more adorable? Her thinking, her answer, her sculpture, her smile as she beamed with pride showing me how she comprehended the reading? I was overwhelmed as I listened to her. Her teacher, who doubted me, doubted the lesson, doubted her students, and most assuredly, doubted the little bad girl at the table all by herself, stood to the side of the room with tears in her eyes. It was at that moment I realized the power of trust in the classroom.

How many times does our lack of trust keep moments like these from happening with our students?

Why don't we trust them? It's because we don't first trust ourselves. We want them to be brave, but trust has to happen first. Without trust, there can be no bravery. Do you see?

If we expect students to dive into learning something new, we have to trust the process. I used to tell my students all the time: "Jump into new learning, and one of two things will happen. You will either fly as you learn something new, or the safety net of love and acceptance that I have built below will catch you as you fail and try again."

Failure should be celebrated in learning, not discouraged. Sadly, scary letter grades on the report card have brainwashed an entire generation of humans into thinking failure is never an option. As I said before, though, the times I failed were the times I learned the most. If the goal of education is learning, then failing must be step one.

We want to try that new science experiment we saw Steve Spangler do on *The Ellen Show*.

We want to try that math game we saw on Twitter.

We want to have a class play to reenact our favorite parts of the book we read.

We want to invite special guests from the community to be a part of our history lesson.

But. . . we doubt ourselves, our abilities, we doubt our training and our knowledge of students. We let our fears take hold, and we fall back on the comfort of the worksheet, the online video, and the basal reader, all the while ignoring the big magic that is just around the corner if we only take a peek. Playful teachers are so eager to peek.

No, not all of those tools—the worksheet, the online video, and the basal—are banned from the playful classroom, but they should never be the core of our work. The world is full of too much awesomeness to be learning about it from a worksheet. We didn't go to a college or university for four years to learn how to photocopy and pass out paper. We are better than that. Trust yourself.

# CHAPTER 18

# Parents Can Trust . . .

As a parent of two perfect children (grin), I (Julie) can tell you that we know very little about what happens in the classroom. Our access into the playful classroom walls only happens as teachers give us opportunities to see. Having taught for many years, I was surprised to find that when my children started school, I had little knowledge of their day.

Now, mind you, my family has been blessed with amazing teachers every year. Several of my girls' teachers have been mentioned in this book as solid examples of what the playful teacher looks like. But as teachers, we know what happens in our rooms every day. When we know it and live it, we assume others have the same knowledge. In reality, when the children hop in the car or cross the threshold of home, their answer to the "How was school today?" question is generally nondescript. Even *our* children, yes. Jed and I have been teaching umpteen years and train preservice teachers for a living. We're in classrooms daily, interacting with children and exploring the world with them. Yet, we are closed off from the classroom story of our own families.

When we, as playful teachers, open the proverbial window to our classrooms, inviting parents to see our learning process, we allow the opportunity for trust to deepen. Parents can trust. How can we develop it? Let's explore some ideas together.

## Newsletters

Yes, you likely already have a class newsletter. It goes home once a week or is posted on the school website for parents to click through. But how interactive is it?

Do we . . .

- include links or QR codes to pictures and videos of the class learning?
- include questions or discussion points for parents to talk to children about?
- create it to be inclusive for non-English-speaking families?
- video ourselves talking to parents about each day?
- create how-to lessons for students in a flipped classroom, sharing those videos with parents as well?
- ask parents for their thoughts, giving them a way to connect with us?

## Positive Phone Calls

With the increase in digital technology (Google Classroom, Dojo, Remind, Bloom, etc.), there is a sharp decline in the timeless phone call. How wonderful is it to get a call just to say, "Mary had the coolest idea today, and I just wanted to tell you about it. She's such a creative thinker!"

What if we made a plan to call several parents on payday? (Let's say five; that's a nice doable number for middle school teachers who have 120 students.) We mean, public schools . . . the parents are paying us with their taxes, no? We've made calls like this before and had parents burst into tears because the affirming words we shared about their children meant so much. We know you have done that, too. Sometimes life got busy for us, and we'd forget the power of these calls. Being intentional about it was the only way we could ever get it done. Yes, it took time. Yes, we had a hundred other things to do, but building trust with parent partners must be at the top of the priority list. If we build trust through positivity and genuine care, parents are much more likely to pick up the phone and listen when we need to have a challenging conversation. Trust eliminates the *us/them* mentality and strengthens the *we*.

## Sneak a Peek

Having parents visit the classroom to see playful learning first hand as active participants allows them to connect with the work we do each day with their kids in a very meaningful, realistic manner. Creating moments that are inviting for parents of *all* students to join their children in the learning process allows parents to have a small glimpse into who we are as educators. Several schools around us offer a week-long event for parents called "Sneak A Peek." It is a time where parents can pop in to visit at various times during the day. The times are plentiful so that parent schedules do not have to conform to the school day. Parents become extra students in the classroom and are actively engaged alongside their child. Yes, that definitely changes the dynamic of the classroom for that week, but it gives parents an open door to be a part of their child's school experience. This event is held over five days so that parents who work may have more opportunity to make time in their busy schedules.

## Parent Play Days

If a week seems a bit daunting for you, try just one day. Scheduling a parent play day can be an effective strategy for building trust. What's a parent play day? In our classroom it is collaborative gingerbread house construction or the great apple pie baking championship. These are special one-day events where parents join their children in the classroom for a unique, and purposefully playful, learning experience. Together, students with their parents design plans for their houses and pies, implement their ideas, and celebrate the fruits or failures of their labor. Then, of course, they get to eat all their hard work! Parents absolutely love this kind of interaction with their children. What could that look like in your classroom? We cannot tell you all the specifics of what amazingness you could offer, but we do have some tips about how to make it a successful day.

- **Plan ahead.** We recommend planning at least 30 school days in advance. Parents need time to make arrangements with work, school, or childcare.
- **Build excitement.** Ask students to design invitations for parents. Guide them in producing video ads to share via email and social media. Challenge them to be creative in additional ways to promote the day with their parents.
- **Be inclusive.** Consider your idea and how it may be welcoming to all families. While we choose to build and design gingerbread houses in our class, we do not focus on traditional Christmas ideals during the process because all of our students do not celebrate the holiday.
- **Have fun.** While these types of days can be stressful as the daily routine is disrupted, remember the purpose: building trust through playful learning and collaboration.

# CHAPTER 19

# Students Already Trust . . .

This chapter title clearly differs from the previous two. That is intentional.

Administrators *must* . . .
Teachers *can* . . .
Parents *can* . . .

. . . but students *already*? Yes. Most students already come to school with a sense of trust. For younger children, depending on their experience with adults, they will transfer that level of trust to the classroom. We owe it to them to provide:

- A physically safe space
- An emotionally stable space
- A mentally supportive space
- A judgment-free space
- An all-inclusive space
- A space filled with possibilities

For older students, it's a little different. You know people talk, right? In the South, there's an unspoken rule: Be careful who you talk to when you start talkin' about people. You have to assume at least three of the ten people around you have a connection to who you are talkin' about (and at least one of them is gonna tell on you).

This is so much more accurate in smaller communities. Yep, a school is a smaller community in this case. If you've been in your school building for more than a year, students have already talked about you. No, not like gossip, but who you are, what you represent, and how you treat others. They've already seen you and told their friends about your hallway interactions, facial expressions, and what happened in the media center. All. The. Things.

Students already trust you will live up to the rumor. Their friends don't lie, do they? So, we have a choice. Either we prove them right or we prove them wrong. We aim to be a playful, engaging teacher who loves students. If that is not how we're known, the first step to getting those messages floating around starts with us. Our actions. Our words.

Students already trust us to be who they think we are. Let's make sure who they think we are is the same as who we want to be. This was a short chapter. It says all you need to know.

# Playful classrooms believe . . .

- Trust is crucial for strong relationships.
- Playful, hands-on learning creates moments that cultivate trust.
- Trust in the classroom will take learning exponentially far.
- Our reaction to failure can build trust across all stakeholders.

# Play Builds Relationships

## Relationships Are Strengthened Through Play

*Our students are humans before they get to us, and they're still humans when they leave. It will do us well to remember that fact more than their test scores, data, and grades.*

# CHAPTER 20

# Our Biological Predilection

## A Conversation

Stuart Brown, one of our favorite play researchers, known for his work on the play histories of murderers, serial killers, and Nobel laureates, has also studied play in animals. We are not comparing any of you to those in this list, don't panic; but the results of his work are worth looking at. He argues that to truly understand what play does for us, we should look at it in the context of biology and evolution. In one part of his book, *Play: How It Shapes the Brain, Opens the Imagination, and Invigorates the Soul*, Brown (2009) recounts a conversation he had with Bob Fagen, another prominent play researcher. Brown was curious, and being new to the field, was trying to learn all he could from Fagen. According to Brown, the conversation went like this:

(watching a pair of juvenile bears playing near juneau, Alaska)

**BROWN**: Bob, why do those bears play?

**FAGEN**: Because it's fun.

**BROWN**: No, Bob, I mean from a scientific point of view, why do they play?

**FAGEN**: Why do they play? Why do birds sing, people dance—for the . . . *pleasure* of it.

**Brown**: Bob, you have degrees from Harvard and MIT, and an in-depth knowledge of bears. You're a student of evolution, you've written *the* definitive work on all mammals at play; I know you have more opinions about this. Tell me, why do animals play?

(long, tolerant silence)

**FAGEN**: In a world continuously presenting unique challenges of ambiguity, play prepares these bears for an evolving planet.

119

I can sense the sarcasm in Fagen's response, can't you? Why do we continually analyze concepts of beauty? Play exists—we all do it. We all enjoy it!

Reading.
Writing.
Running.
Card games.
Tailgating.
Vacays.
Amusement parks.
Sitting on the beach for hours, just chillin'.
All of these are play.

It happens in so many settings, with various groups—large, small, and sometimes even alone. "Let it be," sings Paul McCartney. But, alas, if that were so, you might not have purchased this book. Whether you are an evolutionary play theorist or not, play is found to be pervasive across the animal kingdom. Not just in mammals, but down the evolutionary ladder or tree (pick your metaphor of choice), scientists have found play behaviors. Even the octopus has been observed engaging in "relaxed, idiosyncratic manipulations of objects." And ants are believed to engage in play-fighting (Brown, 2009).

One purpose of play in animals is believed to be the learning process for making sound judgments. Play-fighting among bears teaches them when they can trust another bear, when they need to defend themselves or escape. Biscuit and Bear, Jed's dogs, have multiple romps of frolic and fun daily. Here, play becomes a rehearsal for challenges they may face.

When my brother and I (Julie here) were younger, we often played together. Well . . . not always together, but I was certainly there when he played. He was often outside amongst the neighborhood kids practicing his breakdancing moves on a large piece of remnant, rolled-out linoleum. I wanted to be part of his group so badly. I was that little sister who wouldn't go away. Sometimes, they let me join them, but most times I'm sure he was ready to be rid of me. One particular afternoon that I remember clearly ended with his size-10 Vans hurtling at me followed by a game of chase all around the house. He was quick, and my first grade self wasn't as fast. I did what any sweet 6-year-old girl would do: I bit my arm and screamed bloody murder. Mama came a runnin' and Jeff was grounded for weeks. We fussed and fussed. I'm not sure how that plate of spaghetti ended up all over his bedroom door later. It certainly wasn't because this innocent princess had enough of his complaining. You're probably reading this and thinking, that's not playful. That's fussing and fighting. Nah, it was play. We loved each other. We still do. Even though he lives half a country away, we still look forward to our weekly phone calls to connect with the little stories of life. Do you see what play taught me?

It taught me how to defend myself.
It taught me how to strategize.
It taught me how to keep my head up even though the giants were all around.

Yes, biting myself and lying about it was wrong. We're not condoning the sharing of false information. However, it was the only skill I had in my junior plastic toolbox. I've gathered many more laudable tools since. We're sure many of you can relate to this story. Anyone with a sibling has had a fuss, a moment like this. Reflect: Didn't you also learn?

## Hunter-Gatherers: We're More Alike Than You Think

The concept of play is also present in early human cultures. One particular concept accepted across play research is the notion that humans are biologically wired to play. Some of y'all might be thinking, "Well, aren't we all wired differently?" Well, yes . . . we are, but there are some characteristics we all have in common, and the predisposition to enjoy play, or be playful, is one of them. The manifestation of these traits may look different for each individual, but there is a desire within us all to play. We know this through ethnographic studies of cultural groups across time and place. Hunter-gatherer societies anywhere in the world all have common characteristics. They have common social structures, similar values, and like ways of raising children (Gray, 2013). Two of these similarities are:

- **Autonomy** (personal freedom, sharing, and equality) is a common core social value—not unlike our modern democratic culture. Hunter-gatherer cultures take the concept of autonomy far beyond our common emphasis. Each person, the child included, is free to make independent choices daily, free from opinion, free from advice, free from interference.
- **Sharing** is expected, and no "thank-you note tradition" exists. Instead of being a kindness, sharing is considered a duty; failure to share invites ridicule and disdain.

Sidenote here, thank-you notes are a big part of Southern culture. That's why we said that. The tradition is so entrenched in some areas that you may write a thank-you note thanking the person who sent the original thank-you note. Crazy, right? Not if you are from here; it's just part of who we are.

Sharing and autonomy are concepts intertwined in the larger notions of egalitarianism: everyone's needs are equally important. We see this concept manifest in Debenedet's discussion of playful sociability (2018). Those with high levels of this quality focus on WE, rejecting a THEM versus US mentality (read more about this concept in Section 1). Many hunter-gatherer cultures generally have no one person in a leadership role. There is no chief or "big man" who makes decisions for the group. Instead, those concerns are addressed through group discussions—treating women, men, and children with equal voice.

Speaking of children, you might be surprised to learn of *the high level of trust placed on the decisions of the child*. Children in these cultures are allowed to follow their own will; the reasoning here is that when trusted with their own decisions, when allowed to play and explore freely, children will develop the skills needed to contribute to the group's economy. Children are allowed to play with adult tools, even those we might consider dangerous, because they believe only through playing with these tools will children become skilled at using them.

You can read more about hunter-gatherer cultures in Peter Gray's work, *Free to LEARN* (2013).

You may be thinking right now, OK, that's nice (plastic smile on your face), but it's time for me to run. Good seein' you! (Internal script: What in tarnation do hunter-gatherer cultures have to do with the education of children in our cultures?)

No worries, my friend. We get it: what our kids need to learn is far different from what is needed in hunter-gatherer cultures. Yes, the cultures differ greatly. Yes, the conversation shifts. But you'll see the connection soon. It's like our friend and *New York Times* best-selling author Peter H. Reynolds said once at his bookshop in Dedham, Mass., "The universe is constantly connecting dots. We just have to pay attention." Eventually, we hope to connect the dots for you and show you the how aspects of these cultures are sufficient for today's classrooms. It's coming, but before that, let's look at a little more research.

Across studies of both animals and humans, we see play serving as a way for people to practice skills they will need in the future. Free play allows children to practice decision-making skills, learn to work in groups, share, resolve conflicts, and advocate for themselves. It also allows them to discover what they enjoy at their own pace (Encourage play, 2019). But preparing us for skills of adulthood is not necessarily the focus of this chapter. I mean, yes, we're essentially always being prepared for tomorrow, but . . . bear with us. (See what we did there?)

*We suddenly feel like we need to stop and sketch a bear, growl like a bear, sneak up and scare a friend by acting like a bear, maybe even watch videos of bears playing on the Internet. This seems like a great place for a PLAY BREAK!*

OK, back to free play. The best way to see students experiencing free play within our current educational system structure is during recess. This is because for play to truly be *free*, it has to come about completely from the students—the idea of it and all its components. Sadly, many schools have limited recess time, if they have it at all. During the course of writing this book, we've chatted with several middle school teachers who wish their kids could have recess, but it remains a big no-no in the grades beyond elementary. So, while the example we're about to share is in an elementary setting, the conclusions apply to all ages.

One day during second-grade recess, a group of students came running over to me (Jed) filled with more excitement than I had ever seen. They were all screamin' and carryin' on about an invention they had just created and I just had to see it. Of course, I became just as giddy as they were and began to ask questions about their creation. "It's a cheer," they said, "for our reading club." Goodness, my giddiness turned it up a notch. Here we were at recess, a time to decompress, to run, to be free, to play, and my students were developing cheers about reading. I was as proud as a peacock.

They all fell into their formation, two rows, five in each row, but staggered so I could see each grinning face. Octavia got them all started with a nice "1, 2, ready, go."

"Read, read," they all shouted as they stomped their feet to create a beat. I can still hear it right this minute. It was such an electric moment on the playground. Their collective voices shouting "read, read" was quite loud and rippled across the playground. All three classes that were playing at the time stopped what they were doing to see what was going on. As the crowd huddled around them to watch, the cheer continued. It had lots of words to lead the crowd in a dance, there was a melodic beat, and it was constantly encouraging the audience to "read, read." It didn't take long for the entire grade level to learn it. Next thing I knew, 60-plus kids were then reciting this brand-new reading cheer in unison, all the while trying to create more reading cheers for our reading club. Sadly, I didn't have my phone at recess that day and the moment exists only in my memory, but fear not—We loved the cheer so much that we asked Octavia and her original group to perform it during our grade level musical. We are confident that a mama or two caught the whole thing on camera, and it lives on out there somewhere.

The camera zooms out, up, and over the school building, then focuses in on an afterschool cheer practice. The coach is up front directing girls (and the one guy who is bold enough to break the gender norms) to their positions. "Run through it again!" the coach shouts, and all begin to clap along with the leader—one who was chosen by the coach during tryouts. Mid-cheer, they are paused and redirected on a particular technique for cultivating unity with arm motions. These cheerleaders are working hard, and they all choose to be here. They are playing—having fun with physical exercise and enjoying the feeling of camaraderie offered when one works with others.

In which scenario are we building skills for the future? The one in which a leader gathers her friends, in which conversation and collaboration encourage ideas for cheer moves and chants? The one in which performances are impromptu and feedback from onlookers is authentic? Both cheer scenarios offer opportunities for growth, but only the one instigated by the children on the playground builds independent thinking skills that are more often needed in the workplace to solve problems facing businesses and organizations. Yes, we all need to know how to follow a plan given to us by someone else, a boss, for example. However, what do we do when the plan goes off the rails and we have never had to solve problems on our own?

Cathy Davidson says it well in *The New Education* (2017), "STE(A)M expertise without any grounding in interpretive and critical thinking skills may get you your first job, but it won't get you promoted" (p. 140). We shortchange our students by focusing on narrow specializations. We owe it to their future, and our own, to prepare our students for change—when the jobs as we know them are no longer needed. Thomas Friedman, three-time winner of the Pulitzer, said it best: "My generation had it easy. We just had to find a job. Our kids will have to go out and invent a job." By cultivating a playful spirit in our classrooms, we will empower a new generation of inventors and creators.

## A Story About Cats

Stuart Brown acknowledges preparation for the future self as a major theory of play literature. But, even more interesting for our point here is his story about cats.

(We would like to add that we included this story for our former student, Josh Jackson. He is obsessed with cats and we will forever love him. He is also a fantastic elementary teacher.)

Turns out, cats who are deprived of play-fighting turn out to be just dandy hunters. So, if the play-fighting wasn't preparing them for a future of hunting, what's it for? Listen, meow. Hahahahaha. Too much? OK, moving on. Cats who are deprived of play-fighting in youth actually lack another skill: the ability to socialize successfully. According to Brown (2008), these cats will lack the ability to discern friend from foe, will not catch another cat's social signals, and choose to either act aggressively or retreat—both actions that are out of the norm for a cat's social graces. Talk about white paws after Labor Day! It's this play-fighting and mock-combat that provides our feline friends with emotional intelligence—the ability to perceive another's emotional state and act accordingly.

Remember when we mentioned serial killers before? How does the topic of serial killers get in a book on playful classrooms? We'll tell you, but before we do, we want you to know we are not taking that topic lightly. It is serious, and during our research for this book, we were intrigued by the information we found. When interviewing hundreds of murderers, Brown found a common theme: They all lacked play in their childhoods. Of course, there were other factors present to create the person these murderers became, but knowing that all had a lack of play history is eye opening and should be a call to action for all of us. We need play in our developmental years (and throughout life!) to help us develop the social skills needed to participate in society. It's why that book *All I Really Need to Know I Learned in Kindergarten* is so wildly popular. If we can't communicate and interact socially, like the cats, what good are the other skills?

# CHAPTER 21

# The Impact of the GERM

According to Sahlberg and Doyle (2019), the *war against play* can be explained as a largely unintended consequence of political ambition to "improve education." In the last two decades, as the federal No Child Left Behind law brought a focus on test scores and minimized budgets, play opportunities have been crowded out and in some cases, altogether eliminated. Recess has become viewed as a time that's dispensable in an effort to win a gold ribbon, district accolades, and be featured on state department of education social media as a high-performing school. Coined by Pasi Sahlberg, the Global Education Reform Movement (GERM)—the story of drill and practice—ends with play falling victim. It doesn't stop with play, though; there are numerous manifestations from the GERM (Sahlberg, 2006). If you've been in schools or teaching in schools from 2000 forward, check the following list of effects against your experiences:

- Increased competition among schools for enrollment (rise of charter schools in the United States),
- Standardization of teaching and learning in schools (a shift from focusing on inputs to outputs),
- De-professionalization of the teaching profession (*if you can read a script, you can teach*)
- Large-scale standardized testing, even with children as young as 4 years old
- Market-based privatization of public education (incorporation of school choice and voucher debates) (Sahlberg & Doyle, 2019)

The school year has grown longer, the school day ends later, and time allocated for play has been reduced. In the 1950s, elementary students enjoyed half-hour recesses each morning and afternoon, with an hour dedicated to lunch. As of the writing of this book, the Center for Disease Control (2017) recommends at least 20 minutes of recess daily for elementary-aged children.

Precise data on recess is harder to come by than sweet from a lemon, but as of the 2011–2012 school year, only 22% of American school districts required daily recess, and less than half met the 20 minutes minimum requirement. As we type this, we literally had to pause and discuss. How is that even possible? 78% of American schools didn't require recess just seven years ago? How sad, yet all the more reason for us to write, you to read, and us all to act.

Peek back at that list of five effects from the GERM above. Feel that? Yeah, it's unsettling how it all starts to come together, isn't it? And yet, despite all the hoopla, the pep rallies, the carrot-dangling check to entice compliance, this movement in which play has been shown the back door has not resulted in increased student learning or well-being. You can read the political support, no matter which side of the aisle you sit on. All three of our most recent presidential administrations have championed this *race*, provided billions in grant funding, and ignored root causes for educational problems, such as poverty and inequitable funding (Sahlberg & Doyle, 2019). But, calm down. The focus of this chapter is not to point fingers at anyone. Rather, we'd like to draw attention to the fact that, while play was removed to make time for testing and practice, we've also witnessed a rise in inattention, hyperactivity, psychological disorders in young people, and depression. The rate of suicide among Americans has increased 30% from 2000 to 2016 (Miron, Yu, Wilf-Miron, & Kohane, 2019), especially among older teenage boys.

We know from multiple sources (Gray, 2013; Marano, 2008; Skenazy, 2010; Twenge, 2010) that a child's freedom to play and explore on his or her own—independent of adult interference–has greatly declined in recent decades. Children have fewer opportunities to learn to solve their own problems, control their own lives, develop their own interests, become skilled at the pursuit of what interests them. As a well-intentioned society, we think we are protecting them with supervision, but in fact we may be diminishing their joy, their sense of self-control, and increasing the odds they will suffer from depression and other disorders. Longitudinal data tell us the rates of anxiety and depression among adolescents are higher now than during the Great Depression, World War II, the Cold War, and even the 1960s and 1970s. The shifts in data do not correlate with war, world events, or a fluctuating market. Rather, changes are aligned to the way in which young people perceive the world (Twenge, 2010). In the world of psychology, we call this our locus of control. Those who perceive behavioral control over their lives are less anxious or depressed than those who feel victim to circumstance. We've made all kinds of gains in the world of science—cures for disease, communication, transportation; literacy rates are up; and wealth is more attainable to the average person. Yet, these data tell us that young people are less likely to believe they have control over their lives.

Society has done this. We have removed play from schools. We said it didn't serve a purpose. We put more emphasis on learning as we saw fit, putting what kids needed for a strong developmental foundation on the back burner. We thought—they'll just have to play when they're not in school. We separated play and playfulness from the learning process and treated education like an assembly line. Everyone stand side by side and routinely follow your procedures as prescribed by the manager and do not deviate from the plan in order to achieve maximum performance. Notice the standardization in that thought? Unfortunately, we forgot to remember that all kids aren't the same, and a one-size-fits-all approach just doesn't work in education. Play allows us to step away from the routine of the assembly line and build relationships and connections with those around us.

We have allowed this routine to become a prevalent piece of teaching from kindergarten through higher education, and to fix it we have to start owning it. We begin by knowing our students and giving them what they need. It starts with relationships.

# CHAPTER 22

# Love First, Teach Second

His name was Chad. He was the oldest of four children, all of whom were receiving special education services from my school. Very quickly, Chad became like a son to me (Jed). I looked forward to sitting in the floor reading with him, helping him with math home-work while we waited for the bus after school, and sometimes playing tag at recess. Sometimes he would spend the afternoon in my classroom after school playing the piano. He had never taken a lesson, and it showed, but he felt very empowered to create as he sat behind the keys playing made up songs. I sought ways beyond special education to help Chad get assistance out-side typical services; he struggled with reading. Our district had an individualized summer course from which I knew Chad could benefit. I had sent the signup form home dozens of times, but it was never returned.

Chad came from a line of family members who had similar school services. Maybe it was because of family history with spe-cial services that his mother didn't want him to take the class; I wondered if maybe she needed assistance understanding the form. So, I decided to go visit. One Tuesday afternoon, I rode the bus home with Chad. Are you shocked? My colleagues were. Don't worry, the bus driver came to pick me up after her route. I could have driven, but what means more to a mama? The fact that the teacher was with her son all the way home? The fact that I didn't drive my fancy car (mind you, it was a used 2007 Chevy Equinox) to her house as an intimidation factor? I came in simple terms to meet her where she was. I simply wanted her son to suc-ceed, and that's what I wanted to communicate. It wasn't about me. It was about Chad. It was about going above the status quo to meet his needs. It was about knowing his mama as a human just as much as I knew him. As a result of my bus ride, Chad was enrolled in a summer reading program and began to experience growth. This is love first, teach second.

# LOVE FIRST. TEACH SECOND.

We were writing this chapter over our favorite Southwest Chicken Salad (best doggone salad dressing EVER) at the Downtown Deli and Donuts in Spartanburg. The owner, Elizabeth, gave us free donuts because it was our second day here this week. She is investing in her customers. She is building relationships. We compared how she was investing in the atmosphere of her restaurant with how Jed rode home with Chad. Elizabeth was creating a welcoming atmosphere at her establishment, whereas Jed was investing in the specific needs of an individual. Both are needed, but are different in their approach.

Jed and I agree the playful classroom text needs sections focusing on relationships and community. These topics are almost synonymous though, wouldn't you agree? You cannot have one without the other. How can we have community without relationships? How can we build relationships that don't result in community? To combine them would result in one LONG section, and we really want this book to be digestible – long enough to communicate our message, but short enough to keep it interesting. So, how will we differentiate the content here? We decided halfway through this delicious salad (with extra dressing and love muffins) that community is the learning environment we create for our students, and relationships consider our humanity within that environment.

Building relationships is more than knowing a first and last name, knowing test data, knowing how the child performed in the teachers' class the year before. It is certainly more than knowing that teacher's opinion of the child. But believing these words and showcasing this belief are two different conversations. How do we embody this ideal? How do we really show children we care? How do we do this playfully, in a way that doesn't come off as intrusive?

This is not a complicated maxim. It means that we connect on a human level first and foremost. We recognize that our students come to us as people first, students second. We cannot teach them if we cannot reach them. They will not be reached until they know we care. We're talking to you, dear elementary teacher who gets to school at 7:20 a.m. and escapes to the closed door of your classroom for those last 10 minutes while students sit in the hallway bored to tears and being yelled at for talking. You, who are checking your social media accounts alone as you sip your coffee waiting until the required minute to let students in your classroom from the dreaded hallway seating.

We are not saying that self-preservation and care are not important, and we want educators to have all that, but maybe do that in the car in the parking lot before we enter the building. Think of the building as our stage, and once we enter it, we are "on." The kids who see us walk past know us as Ms./Mr./Mx. So-and-so, not as Tabitha, Todd, and Tracey. We are a part of their school "show," and if they see us run to our room and shut the door, they are gonna wonder why we aren't playing our part.

If we love them first, why don't we invite them in to play strategy games with a group? To chat with their friends in the comfort of our rooms while we all get mentally prepared for the school day? Would you want to be sitting in that hallway? Odds are, it is a cold, hard, germy floor, and just moments before that dastardly concrete met their backside, they were in a cozy, warm car with a parent right nearby. This hallway certainly doesn't sound like a playful experience, and we certainly are not saying every part of the day has to be, but dream with us about what could happen if we turned the dreaded moments of school into playful times that students, and teachers, enjoyed rather than hated. We never once looked forward to morning duty in the cafeteria. It wasn't because we had to arrive early on duty days, but it had everything to do with the disgruntled coworkers who were more concerned about quiet and order than meeting the needs of students.

What better time to get to know students than in this unstructured part of the day? What better time to add playful moments to their day? We can't tell you how many times kids came in our rooms crying and needed some distraction or comfort first thing in the morning. Some were sad about leaving their mom for the day, others may have gotten in trouble on the car ride to school. For those who teach upper grades, your students bring more emotions from home into first period than you may ever know. They need comfy moments, validation, and empowerment as well. Who knows what each of us could be bringing with us emotionally each morning? That goes for teachers, too. Our jobs are so tough. The drain on every part of us is taxing. How much could we benefit from a playful, fun, exciting morning duty rather than wanting to pull our hair out at the start of the day? Who in the world wants to start their day constantly "shushing" a cafeteria, hallway, or gym full of kids? Not us. Not you, we bet.

## Confession

I (Julie) used to be that teacher. I used to leave my students in the hallway in the mornings—that's procedure, it's just what we do. But over lunch one day, I asked students what was the worst part of school. I was curious. I was afraid their answer would be math. No, it was the hallway. You see, many of them had been sitting in the hallway for 30 minutes because they ride an early bus. My tushy would have fallen asleep! I thought to myself, "when I have hallway duty, I'll be nicer." Later that week, I was writing on the board about 15 minutes before time to let students come in, and I could hear the hallway monitor yelling at students who were wiggly, some who were chatty. I don't remember even thinking about it. I just walked to the door, looked at my line of homeroom kiddos, smiled, and motioned for them to come in. They were so happy. After that first day, we established expectations for that time. They had great ideas for how they could use the morning time to activate their brains (checkers, cards, LEGOs, sketching, etc.). Now, I love to get to school early and save my students from the hallway. This doesn't mean they run wild about our classroom, no. They come in and make choices about how to spend their morning. If they choose poorly, we have a conversation. Having to return to the hallway is a natural consequence for abusing the ability to come in our class early. Of course, some have to return to the hallway. But usually only once.

While we're discussing the meaning of *love first*, let's chat for a moment. I'm a teacher, but I'm also a mama. I see and hear many teachers who loudly declare "how many days are left" either in person, on social media, or as a countdown on the board. Imagine that for a moment: you are a student, and your teacher is counting down the days they have left to spend with you. That is not how we mean it, I know, but let's reframe; let's do it in the sadness of parting rather than the excitement of being rid.

The first time I was aware of this was in a conversation with my friend Matt Johnson. We were at a Christmas party, and he was teaching third grade at the time. I asked him, "So, how's it going? Are you ready for a break?" This question is standard around the holiday season, right? We all ask it and expect to be asked as well. Yes, we are all ready for a break. The expected reply is something like, "Whew, we've got 11 days spa left. I'm so ready for the break!" but Matt's response was different. He said, "It's great! We're working on some reader's theatre, and the kids are pumped about the math videos they're creating." Never having heard this response in December, I probed, "Nice. . . sounds fun. Aren't you ready for a break though?" *I mean, how dare he reply in such a non-standard way, right? Let me force him to admit he's tired so that I feel better about my own "tiredness" and avoid any guilt and shame.* Matt simply said, "Nah—it's all good."

Not even a week after this festive evening, I picked my own littles up from school. You must know first: that particular year, my people had two very different teachers. One clearly loved her job and made the learning fun. She loves first, teaches second. The other child's teacher taught, but she clearly didn't love it. The kids knew it too. They knew in the way she spoke to them: her lackluster approach. She taught innovative content, but the sparkle was missing.

Back to the story. So, the girls got in the car and one said, "Mama, I don't like my teacher." (Why?) "She doesn't like us. She's counting down the days until she doesn't have to see us anymore." (Did she say that?) "No, she didn't have to. Why else would she count down?"

How could I argue? I don't type these words to be judgy. I too, have counted down. But, I don't anymore. Not since my eyes have been opened. I think, too, some kids don't want to leave us; school provides the only stability in some of their lives. And we count down happily? Could we instead celebrate each day, dreading the time when we must part? Whether we mean it or not (and I hope we do), we must let them know we love them. That we don't want them to go.

# CHAPTER 23

# Play Personalities

I (Julie) always enjoy the first weeks of school. The smell of newly sharpened pencils and spiced tea.

*(Jed here) Seriously, spiced tea? Who is writing this right now? Crayola crayons, fresh clean notebooks, and crisp new pages of a book are all smells that come to mind. I have no connection to spiced tea and "back to school" time.*
*(Julie rolls her eyes, smiles, and continues)*

The smiles on the faces of children as they make new friends.
The joy of learning their teacher loves them.
Being in a new grade with new friends and a new teacher.

In all the years I've been teaching, I've not taught two students who were completely alike.

- Latonya loved markers and gel pens, but her notebook was a mess.
- Chris put up a solid front, but he was crumbling inside and needed constant, quiet reassurance. Comments on the art in his sketchbook always helped him make it through the day.
- Storm loved numbers and their constancy. His work was always in neat rows, mistakes are erased cleanly and never crossed out. He doesn't like a smudge on his sneakers.
- Autumn's house burned over the weekend, and she lost all her clothes and toys. You can't see it on her face, though. She still smiled and lined up her collection of Littlest Pet Shop friends beside the pencil groove on her desk.
- Jordan can't stand the unstructured time between classes. While waiting on the bell to ring, he kept me company

asking questions he knows the answers to. He helped make monitoring the hallway more interesting.

- Ivan comes running to warn of any planned fights during these class changes. He can't read well, but appreciates the lack of judgment for *all the questions* during our gender-separated health education class. He shows this appreciation with protection in the form of information.
- Blake is on the baseball team. His hat, though against school rules, sits on his head in my class as he receives *supplemental support services*. He is never counted tardy because he can't be seen walking in the "resource" classroom. He leaves just before the bell daily in efforts to preserve the image he has created.
- Shelby smiles and the penciled-in freckles on her face move with her excitement. Her pigtails have wires in them to create the perfect Pippi Longstocking effect. Though she is now a mom, has two degrees, and is a practicing, successful marriage and family therapist, I still see Pippi.

We all have our list. I could keep going forever with all the memories of children who have impacted my life. I illustrate these few to make our next point. Play and playfulness are based on the individual. What is playful to me may confound you. What you enjoy might be what I adamantly avoid.

My discovery of play types or play personalities was one of the most defining moments for me in my play trajectory. I can remember it vividly. We were sitting at a round table at the front of a large room at Clemson University's Madren Center. Jed was sitting beside me, taking up two chairs with his self and his messenger bag. His journals, the carefully placed bag of colored pencils, and rows of Paper Mate InkJoy gel pens were aligned already in rainbow form. "I don't care for the Flair pens," he said, as if he were disgusted by their existence. I was a bit distracted by Jed's preparations, and annoyed at my discombobulated feeling because (I mean. . . THE STUART BROWN was talking!). The lighting was turned down so the audience could see both the presenter (Stuart Brown) and his slides, projected on two screens at either side of the stage. My memory picture is yellowed, but I think it's because of the lighting: a sepia effect. Dr. Brown may never know the impact he had on me that day. He clicked the button and the slide on the screen changed to this image:

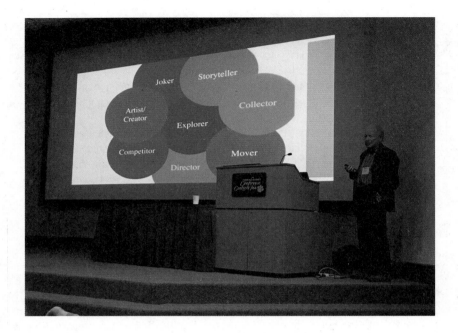

If you consult the Internet with "play personalities" as your search terms, you'll have varied results. But the core eight play personality types Brown discussed in his keynote and in his book are summarized next:

# The Joker

Whether or not you are this person, you no doubt know someone who fits this type. Jokers love practical jokes. They are always pulling pranks. Puns always bring a chuckle.

- What's a pun's favorite movie? It's a PUN-derful life!
- What's a pun's dream job? An acu-PUNcturist!
- Why was the pun a bad comedian? He always got the PUNchline wrong!
- What's a pun's best trait? Her PUNctualtiy.

Have the puns made you laugh? Maybe? Maybe not? (Not me, says Jed. Lame dad jokes, as Julie guffaws in the background.) I bet they've *groan* on you. Hahahahahaha.

Jokers love to make people laugh, and their creativity in doing so is always under construction—growing ever stronger with practice.

# The Kinesthete

Do you know the story of the child dancer told by Sir Ken Robinson? If not, you'll want to pause reading and watch his TEDx talk, "Do Schools Kill Creativity?" The whole thing is *amazingly* good. Here's the transcripted part we're referring to. Sir Ken is talking with Gillian Lynne, a choreographer of *Cats*, *Phantom of the Opera* and other works.

> *Gillian and I had lunch one day and I said, "Gillian, how'd you get to be a dancer?" And she said it was interesting; when she was at school, she was really hopeless. And the school, in the '30s, wrote to her parents and said, "We think Gillian has a learning disorder." She couldn't concentrate; she was fidgeting. I think now they'd say she had ADHD. Wouldn't you? But this was the 1930s, and ADHD hadn't been invented at this point. It wasn't an available condition. People weren't aware they could have that.*
>
> *Anyway, she went to see this specialist. So, this oak-paneled room, and she was there with her mother, and she was led and sat on this chair at the end, and she sat on her hands for 20 minutes while this man talked to her mother about all the problems Gillian was having at school. And at the end of it—because she was disturbing people; her homework was always late; and so on, little kid of eight—in the end, the doctor went and sat next to Gillian and said, "Gillian, I've listened to all these things that your mother's told me, and I need to speak to her privately." He said, "Wait here. We'll be back; we won't be very long," and they went and left her.*
>
> *But as they went out the room, he turned on the radio that was sitting on his desk. And when they got out the room, he said to her mother, "Just stand and watch her." And the minute they left the room, she said, she was on her feet, moving to the music. And they watched for a few minutes and he turned to her mother and said, "Mrs. Lynne, Gillian isn't sick; she's a dancer. Take her to a dance school."*
>
> *I said, "What happened?" She said, "She did. I can't tell you how wonderful it was. We walked in this room and it was full of people like me. People who couldn't sit still. People who had to move to think." Who had to move to think. They did ballet; they did tap; they did jazz; they did modern; they did contemporary. She was eventually auditioned for the Royal Ballet School; she became a soloist; she had a wonderful career at the Royal Ballet. She eventually graduated from the Royal Ballet School and founded her own company—the Gillian Lynne Dance Company—met Andrew Lloyd Weber. She's been responsible for some of the most successful musical theater productions in history; she's given pleasure to millions; and she's a multimillionaire. Somebody else might have put her on medication and told her to calm down.*

(Robinson, 2007)

Some people need to move to think. If you find yourself dancing, hiking, constantly puttering about, this play personality type might be your cup of tea. Caution though—this type is focused on movement, not competition. That's another play personality type. If you're likely to be found outside clearing land, turning the garden, playing football, or any other active situation, you might be a kinesthete.

# The Explorer

Whether you consider this category literally or figuratively, the explorer play personality type uses exploration as a tool for provoking their imagination and growing creatively. You might scroll online to secure your next travel experience, or you might lose yourself in reading a novel set in another place. We aren't definite on this, but we are pretty sure Dora and her fans are a part of this group. If you love the new and different—whether it's music, art, feelings, ideas, beliefs, perspectives, or places—you might be an explorer at heart. Dr. Brown (2009) tells us, "Each of us started our lives by exploring the world around us. Some people never lose their enthusiasm for it."

# The Competitor

If you find comfort in rules—if you love playing games (especially when you win)—this type might describe you. I (Julie) live with one of these people. She's 10 years old. She's my daughter. Every night at dinner, she wants to go around the table playing "Guess my number" or "Would you rather . . ." Being told to brush her teeth before bed turns into a race with her sister. We all know people like this, and maybe you are *won* of them (stop it, Julie; this is not the Joker section). I like games, but this is different. Living with a competitor helps me know this is not my personal play type. It's fun, but not all the time. All. The. Time. She wants to be a PE teacher when she grows up. What a great choice!

The world needs competitors because they develop games that noncompetitors would never think of. Take a moment and look up Walter Camp, the father of American football. No doubt this man was a competitor play type, and look at his impact on our culture. Competitors will work toward mastery of any game that has specific rules—no matter if it's team-based or Solitaire. The skill to invent, create, implement, tweak, and replay those rules is quite a level of intelligence. When given the choice to play for fun or play and keep score, they ALWAYS default to the latter. Why play if you're not keeping score?

## The Director

Directors are the great planners. The ones who love to organize the celebration—baby shower, wedding, class party, field trip, tailgate refreshments, you name it. They love to make order out of chaos. Because this scene always involves people, directors are often charismatic, affable folk to instigate fun. They may not outwardly like titles like, "Director of . . .," but they secretly love the power and control that allows them to improve all kinds of situations.

Do you catch that? The director isn't the loud, bossy one in the room. The real director is the one in the kitchen, working behind the scenes without recognition. The director doesn't need recognition; it's all about the end result—an organized event where all people leave feeling like it was the best day ever.

## The Collector

What's your refrigerator look like? Is it covered in magnets and photos? Do you have a drawer of every letter and card you've ever received? What about your walls? Do you display treasures you've gathered along life's way? You might be a collector. These friends collect memories. These friends collect experiences. But there's some kind of theme, and whatever it is, they can't get enough. You might wonder what the difference between a collector and an explorer is—especially if a person likes to collect experiences. Well, first of all, you can be both. There's nothing that says you have to pigeonhole yourself. But there is a clear distinction. Brown (2009) shares an example: "One person I know travels the world to see solar eclipses—which might seem like the action of an explorer, except that he has to see every single one and methodically collects evidence of each eclipse."

## The Artist/Creator

Painters!
Sculptors! and
Scribblers! oh my.
Potters!
Printmakers! and
Photographers! Say hi.

This is your space. Notice we didn't say "those with their own studio" or "those who are published." Anyone who finds joy in the act of creation is an artist or creator. In starting from scratch or joining disparate materials to build a product. In fixing something that was broken or improving something already made.

Do you know how many years we sat together over hot beverages, typing our ideas and scribbling our thoughts in journals together before we took the leap to send some chapters to Jossey-Bass? The fact that you're holding our finished work in your hands still seems a miracle to us, and it makes us no more of an artist or creator than you. We just kept on in the joy of the work until we were brave enough to share it. "The point is to make something—to make something beautiful, something functional, something goofy. Or just to make something work" (Brown, 2009). This play personality type is clearly where we like to be. We bet many of you feel happy in this space, too.

## The Storyteller

You are a storyteller if you are jotting poems on napkins or writing a novel in your spare time. Do you love to read? Do you love to go to the theater? The movies? Yep. This is your space then. Storytellers often play out scenes in their minds—whether it's daydreaming or their way of improving their afternoon chores. Did you have to slay dragons with your broom while sweeping your porch? Did you have to explain to the books why dusting the shelves was important for their health? Are you making up silly tales to tell those around you? Are you singing, dancing, narrating? You're a storyteller at heart.

In Section seven of this book, *Get Out There and Play!*, we'll explain how to incorporate opportunities for each play personality type in your classroom. For now, consider which type(s) you might be. If you're unsure, we've created a little quiz to help you out. For those techy teachers, check out theplayfulclassroom.com for the digital version.

# Play Personality Type Quiz

Directions: Circle or highlight the response that best represents you.

1. Which of these could you do for hours?
   a. Build a city from LEGOs
   b. Beat your high score
   c. Make party treats
   d. Perform puppet shows
   e. Jump in a leaf pile

2. What's your pick for a hot summer's day?
   a. Water balloon fight
   b. Taking photos
   c. Planning an indoor fun house
   d. Chilling inside watching *I Love Lucy* or an Eddie Murphy marathon
   e. Exploring a new trail, hoping to stumble upon a waterfall

3. What are (were) you like in school?
   a. Class clown
   b. Artistic
   c. Day dreamer
   d. Athletic
   e. Leader of all things

4. Which is one of your favorite toys?
   a. Trampoline
   b. Costume set
   c. Colored pencils
   d. Car collection
   e. Xbox

5. Which of these is your favorite app?
   a. Buzz Feed
   b. Pokemon Go or Wizards Unite
   c. Minecraft
   d. Words with Friends
   e. eBay

6. If you could go on an adventure, which would you choose?
   a. BMX biking
   b. Going to a carnival
   c. Go camping cross country
   d. Competing in The Amazing Race
   e. Getting stamps from all the National Parks

7. What do you enjoy most about sports?
   a. Winning
   b. Playing
   c. Coaching
   d. The jokes about it
   e. The write-up in tomorrow's paper

8. What is your favorite type of movie?
   a. Adventure
   b. Animated
   c. Drama
   d. Comedy
   e. Documentary

9. If you could learn something new, it would be _____.
   a. Party or wedding planning
   b. Painting, pottery, or carpentry
   c. Boxing, surfing, or yoga
   d. Geocaching
   e. Cinematic design

10. Which of the following do (did) you enjoy?
    a. Playing jokes on friends/family
    b. Adding to your collection of cherished items
    c. Exploring local creeks in search of new play places
    d. Organizing group games with friends
    e. Field day, mud runs, or escape rooms

11. When you have a project to procrastinate, you
    a. Flip through your collection of comic books
    b. Relieve the boredom by sending funny memes to friends

c. Imagine you're in a movie and act the part of the scholar

d. Get fidgety and do something active to relieve the wiggles

e. Organize the work, then delegate or tackle each item

12. Which of the following careers would you most enjoy?
   a. Anthropologist exploring new lands
   b. Graphic designer for your favorite magazine
   c. Sales for a gaming company
   d. Antiques dealer
   e. A novelist or news journalist

13. In your social group, do you
   a. Find ways to make every situation a game
   b. Encourage group trips together
   c. All have a common collection—books, journals, coins, jewelry, art
   d. Take lots of pictures to use for the group holiday cards
   e. Make everyone laugh, always lightening the mood

Highlight your answers below:

| | #1 | #2 | #3 | #4 | #5 | #6 | #7 | #8 | #9 | #10 | #11 | #12 | #13 |
|---|---|---|---|---|---|---|---|---|---|---|---|---|---|
| Artist/Creator | A | B | B | C | C | | | B | B | | | B | |
| Joker | | D | A | | A | B | D | D | | A | B | | E |
| Kinesthete | E | A | D | A | | A | B | | C | | D | | |
| Explorer | | E | C | | B | C | | A | | C | | A | B |
| Competitor | B | | | E | D | D | A | | | E | | C | A |
| Director | C | C | E | | | | C | E | A | D | E | | |
| Collector | | | | D | E | E | | | D | B | A | D | C |
| Storyteller | D | | | B | | | E | C | E | | C | E | D |

Which play personality did you choose the most? _____

What's your second highest? _____

Third highest? _____

Do you think this represents who you are? Have a conversation with a friend about your results.

# CHAPTER 24

# The Theme Park Experience

Have you been to Disneyland or Disney World? If you have, I bet you want to go back. Why? Because it was a magical experience. The cast members greeted you happily as you walked in the gates, the eatery, the ride, the everything. If you wore a button that said "First Time Guest," you likely got special treatment—extra fast passes, souvenir mugs, little sursies (that's Southern for "little surprise"). My (Julie's) family went last year—my children's first trip. If the cast members had known my name, I'm sure they would have yelled, "Welcome, Julie!" with big high fives. I mean, who doesn't love to hear their name? Who wouldn't want a fist bump first thing in the morning with eyes that say, "I'm so glad you're here!"

After one trip to Disney, I started to reflect on how I wanted aspects of Disney in my life. If we're in charge of our days, why not make every day like a day at Disney? It's all about perspective. So, I wonder, how do I make my classroom experience like a trip to the most magical place on Earth? Do I welcome my students by name? Do I stand at the door to high five them and say, "Welcome! Get ready to enjoy the ride" as they enter? This is not to say the classroom is a superficial place. We're not "all potatoes and no meat." A lot of thought goes into planning every detail of the Disney experience, down to the number of steps to each trash can (thus cutting down on the litter). We need both. We need the carefully planned learning experience. We also need the research-based instruction. My point is, what good is the careful planning if the delivery isn't done in a spirit of connection? We must communicate that learning is fun, that we love what we do, that this is the *most awesome day ever* if students are to join us on the ride.

One of the most influential books I've read in my lifetime has been *How to Win Friends and Influence People*, by Dale Carnegie. Carnegie makes several points about how to build relationships, and so many of them start with the initial encounter.

## Smile

Ya'll, Carnegie devoted an entire chapter in his book to smiling and the effect of this seemingly small gesture on relationships. In reality, this tiny action has disproportionate impact; it builds rapport, breaks down barriers, and may even inspire those who aren't on their best-of-days. When we smile, endorphins, dopamine and serotonin are released. The endorphins act as natural pain relievers, the dopamine contributes its message of pleasure and satisfaction, and the serotonin sends its antidepressant vibe. All from a smile!

Smiling even causes others to take their harshness down a level. In one study, judges gave those who smiled a lighter penalty; this is known as the smile leniency effect (LaFrance & Hecht, 1995). In fact, much of what we communicate in body language also governs the way we think about the larger world (Carney, Cuddy, & Yap, 2010). We recognize that a smile does not mean the same thing in all countries, but here we give a nod to our culture and the effect of a smile as it warms a room.

There are several videos on social media of teachers taking the initiative to make their morning greeting a unique time of day. Option boards with choices such as high five, fist bump, hug, and dance it out hang beside the classroom door, reminding both teacher and students that interactions can be playful and personal. The coolest part of this is that in every video I've seen, everyone is smiling. When we are playful with each other, smiles happen naturally. If we can begin all interactions with students with a smile, imagine what could transpire.

## Say Their Name

One of Carnegie's (1936) most quoted passages comes from the information about names: "A person's name is to that person the sweetest and most important sound in any language." It's so true, you know. When we're talking with others, we really feel that they are listening to us if they use our names in conversation. Not too many times, ya know—that could get weird. But enough that they communicate they know who we are and are genuinely interested in talking with us. All anyone wants, Carnegie writes, is to feel appreciated. Our names are our greatest connections to our own identity and individuality. Why else would the monogram business be thriving?

If you're a fan of the Responsive Classroom approach, you already know the power of the morning meeting. No matter whether you have a group of 5-year-olds sitting on the carpet criss-cross applesauce or a class of ninth graders sitting in chairs, there are common elements (Kriete & Bechtel, 2002):

1. All involved are sitting in a circle facing in, with no person above the others. This basically means the teacher is with students, not above them. Not standing over them. The physical structure of the group is a key element to communicating equality.
2. All meetings start with a greeting. Think back to your day today. Is it possible that some students came and went through your class without having heard their own name? Morning meeting ensures that never happens. The greeting goes around the circle, varying often in form, but always including student names.

You will read more about names in Section 5.

## Make Others Feel Important—and Do It Sincerely

While this section may seem obvious, let's break it down a bit. Teachers call it engagement, companies call it return on investment, and social media gives it a thumbs up. What is it? Our desire to be liked. We all have it, whether or not we want to admit it. But we're all also keen to the fake response. In the South, we often pass each other and say, "Hey, how ya doin'?" An appropriate response can be anything from a nod and smile to "Good. . . good," to stopping mid-stride to explain all one's medical ailments. Most hope for anything but the latter, but it can happen. Those who use this greeting don't really need to know why Aunt Myrtle is on her fifth treatment for gout; we can tell in the passing what is being asked. All this to say, here's our challenge: Let us stop treating our classroom with a "Hi, how ya doin'?" perspective. Let us approach each person we encounter with a pause, real eye contact, and genuine interest in their response.

When our classrooms are intentionally playful, we show that we have taken each learner in mind when designing instruction. We know the artists and creators. We know the competitors. We know the jokers. We design experiences around who they are and what they need. We trust them with choice. We do it all, playfully and sincerely.

When we take the time to consider our students, smile at them, say their name, and show them a theme park experience every day, we not only have fun, but we strengthen the relationships within our classroom culture.

# CHAPTER 25

# Learning with Them, Alongside Them

## Fire and Brimstone

No shaming here, but (*lean in close, and read this as a whisper*) we know some teachers who won't get in the floor with students. They express shock at the thought of laying down on their tummy to read with a kid. They say the floor is too dirty. How can we say we are good teachers and we love students, but we're too good to sit in the floor and read because (insert your own excuse here), yet we encourage them to lay in that floor and read. Is it not too dirty for them? We can be the adult in the room and a kid at heart at the same time. In fact, that is our job. That is a playful classroom mindset.

In rereading this paragraph, we worry that it comes across as a little negative, but we are *all sinners in the hands of an angry,* errr . . . *administrator?* Sometimes if it walks and quacks like duck, you gotta call it a duck.

> . . . We give you a free pass if you are physically unable to get in the floor. We realize that the floor isn't accessible for all of us and that's OK. You aren't avoiding the floor on purpose while expecting your students to sit there.

When we are playful, we model for our students—the love of reading, the joy of learning, the brain breaks, the . . . everything. Don't think they're not watching when we stand in clusters on the playground and have grownup talk time. What are we modeling then? They are watching, they want to be just like us. Let us show them what is *great* about being a grownup. Let us show them how to be a lead learner in every aspect of their lives.

Sometimes, learning with students requires you to honor them as a person outside the school day. Have you been invited to their birthday parties? Go. We know you have children of your own; why not take them? I know you are busy. Showing up will take 30 minutes of your Saturday. A child will remember those 30 minutes for a lifetime. Your student plays soccer? Go to the game. Cheer them on. Is she getting baptized this Sunday? Go. Sit in the front row with her mama. Is his piano recital this week? Go. Frame the program and give it to his daddy with a photo you took of the evening. Building relationships, true relationships requires more of us than 7 a.m. to 3 p.m. Monday through Friday.

## Authenticity

With every class, I (Jed) tell students about my struggles as a reader and how I have to read things over and over to comprehend. I tell them sometimes reading is boring to me. Sometimes I didn't read my assignments because I didn't think I could. I made a D in Health on my report card in third grade because of a bubble test where I got one row off when answering. I tell my students that my parents are divorced, and I don't have a great relationship with my dad. I am open with them about the bullying I faced for not being like the other boys in my class. I confess to them that I cry, I hurt, I worry, I fear.

One of our favorite speakers and authors is Brené Brown. If you haven't seen her TED talk on vulnerability, go ahead and search for it now. Take a moment to experience that. Brown (2011) says, "Courage starts with showing up and letting ourselves be seen." Our students need to see us being authentic. We can be both authentic and a role model. "Because true belonging only happens when we present our authentic, imperfect selves to the world, our sense of belonging can never be greater than our level of self-acceptance."

I remember how I felt as a child meeting other kids with traditional families. Hearing their stories made me feel like an outsider. The way I see it, the more transparent I am with my students, the more secure they are in their own story. The more included they will feel in our classroom community. I will never forget the look on Susie's face—a student who was abused by her father—when she learned that I, too, had experienced abuse. I saw hope in her eyes—hope that there was a life beyond where she was.

Authenticity in play looks much the same as what I just described. Stuart Brown (2009) describes three essential components of it:

1. Authentic play has an inherent attraction that draws the player in—players always have a choice.
2. Play allows the player to experience a sense of freedom from time and a diminished consciousness of self.
3. The player engages in play for its own sake, without hope of termination.

Let's consider how these three aspects relate to learning experiences. We became teachers because we want to make a difference. Because we love learning and want to communicate that love, we chose a career that allows us to raise citizens who also enjoy learning. So, how does showing up at their football game parallel with repetitive, DOK 1 textbook problems for homework? In our minds, these two are not aligned to the playful classroom. We cannot achieve our goals if we let our homework assignments take time away from the family—if our expectations of student work are separate from reading with someone, playing a game with a brother or sister, or jumping rope in grandma's front yard (yes, you can skip count while doing this and it becomes beautiful math practice). We're not saying we should give no homework (though that is a fabulous idea . . .); what we are saying is that if we must assign work, we should take every opportunity to do so in a way that asks students to read, share, and play with others. How many will go home and sit in front of the television? How many will go in their rooms (assuming they have one) and not speak to another person for hours? How many will stay inside on a beautiful fall afternoon? This past spring (2016), *Dirt Is Good*, a campaign promoting play and experiential learning for children, surveyed around 12,000 parents in 10 countries and released a startling finding: the average child spends less time outside than the average high-security prisoner.

When I (Julie) read that, I was blown away. Not as a teacher, but as a parent. We are guilty too. We sit inside. But, when given perspective for growth, we can change. So, let me ask, how does the work expectation for our students ask them to engage with nature? How can we incorporate play into assignments? How can we show our students that learning can be *fun*?

We hear you, oh homework advocate. You are right—practice is needed to become better at a skill. Some of learning is skills, some of learning requires repeated practice. But, please don't assume that by assigning work, we are requiring students to think deeply. We recently met with an administrator about homework and school policy. Many schools have a policy to limit the time spent on homework, but rarely does that policy dictate the kind of homework teachers give. One such policy we read recently even allowed for grading of homework.

In the box below, we share an email with you. The author of this email gave us permission to share it with you all. Please understand—she *did not send* this email. It's important for you to know that. However, she did meet with the teacher in person about her concerns. Her rant below is authentic, but it doesn't, as Jed's grandma Maudie would say, "spread honey." She opted instead to meet with the teacher spreading sweetness so that she could really *hear* the concern—not our friend's lofty words or criticism. The rant, if emailed, would only have put the teacher on the defensive. However, if we are to be authentic— as teachers, as parents, as humans—we feel you must know the heart of emotion present here. The context? This teacher wrote a note in the child's planner stating that she graded homework because there isn't sufficient time to get social studies grades during class.

Dear (deleted teacher name),

Thank for your note in the parent folder regarding grading homework. I'm disheartened that it took a week to reply to my important questions, therefore, I'm putting my thoughts in the form of an email so the response can be more timely.

If the time allowed for social studies instruction does not allow for authentic formative and summative assessments, I am concerned. As a mother, an educator, and a --- board member, I wonder if the administration should be alerted. Can I assist with the adjustment of schedules so that learning experiences across the curriculum be maximized?

I write you tonight with one main concern, and it is homework: the purpose, load, and use as assessment.

Purpose:

I wonder how a http://superteacher.com worksheet every night grows a reader.

I wonder how a worksheet on bats with scrambled vocabulary helps one want to engage in scientific inquiry.

For any task I ask of students, I question: *Am I assigning work for compliance or engagement?* This guides my decision. I provide it here for mere reflection.

Assessment:

I do wonder how the use of grading (a summative assessment) homework supports the learning journey. If we are to encourage learners to take risks, ask questions, and think deeply, how does a behavioristic approach (providing a grade)

support those goals? In addition, educators must consider the unfair advantage for students who have support and resources in the home. My children have multiple resources in a home: two parents, technology, and loads of books among them. This is not an equitable situation when considering a class full of diverse student backgrounds. As a fellow educator, I implore you to reconsider your choice at grading homework. Assign it if you must, provide feedback on homework for academic growth, but don't grade it.

Load:

At (school), what is the amount of homework expected for a --- grader? Each day, there is homework (worksheets) in every subject. The only break is in science on Tuesdays. We have powered through up until tonight. We have now reached the breaking point. We arrived home at 2:40, had a snack, and began working. (Child's name) did not finish her homework until 5:43. (Child's name) has broken down a few times this fall, usually on a Tuesday when I am working and am not home to coach her. Tonight, she was unable to attend church services because we could not eat and make the 30-minute drive into town before 6 pm.

My child has gone from loving school to hating it. Her comments are negative, when prior to --- grade, she embraced learning. I'm deeply concerned. I welcome your feedback so we can improve the experience of schooling.

The humanity of our profession is honored when we teach from a heart of compassion, not obligation. Students will see quickly when we are not being true in our approach.

We cannot write a section on relationships if we are not authentic in telling of our observations and experiences. We are all educators who strive to provide powerful and inspiring experiences for those in our path. So, we cannot end with this email. Remember: the author opted for a conversation instead of a typed-up vent.

Both listened. Both heard. Both parties have grown together and are better for it.

This is the moral of our story: education and teaching are all about recognizing the humanity before our eyes.

## The Relationship Epilogue

Strong teacher/student relationships don't end after 180 days. They last a lifetime. Take first grader Jamie, for instance. As he moved into second grade and left my classroom, I (Jed) still checked on him almost daily. His great grandparents passed away during that year, and he ended up moving in with his grandparents about half an hour away from our school. I was devastated to see him leave, so I made a commitment to keep in touch. His "Mama Barbara and Papa Wayne" were the best at keeping us connected. They invited me to his birthday parties, his baptism, and his school awards programs. I was there every time he got a new color belt in karate, at his middle school band concert, and cheered loudly the first time he marched onto the field as drum major of his high school marching band. I beamed with pride as he graduated, as he left for basic training, as he returned home to finish college. While I do not have my own children, it is students like Jamie who remind me why I work so hard and care so much. He reminds me every day, whether I see him or not, to keep up the relational work of education. It is priceless to the work, but even more so to the student.

Playful classrooms

believe ...

We MUST advocate for our students' right to play.

A 'We' mindset is strengthened by rejecting any 'Us' vs. 'Them' ideas.

We must love first, teach second.

Play and playful moments are based on the individual-differences make us better.

# Play Builds Community

## Communities Are Strengthened When We Play

*We live and interact with others—locally, regionally, and globally. Play helps us shape a mindset of advocacy, awareness, sensitivity, and compassion for all.*

# CHAPTER 26

# Relevance and the Four-Legged Stool

We have been educators for more years than we haven't, which is what happens to us when we cross the threshold of being 40. By the way, we love this decade so far; it's the best yet! For all the years we have been teaching in public school classrooms, we have felt connected. We knew our students' parents, and they knew us. We sent home newsletters—a paper copy and a digital copy on a Geocities website (remember those?). We have hosted events, where parents were regularly invited in the classroom. Mind you, all of this was in the heyday of the over-head projector. The takeaway from this paragraph is that we were the teacher, and we felt informed. Every day. We knew what was going on.

Segue to present day. Remember in Chapter 18 where I (Julie) told you about my two perfect children? No? Recap: I have two children in elementary school, and I teach in higher education. Same profession, different buildings. I'm not in the public schools every day (though I'm working hard to change that). Our family has been blessed with fabulous teachers thus far, but, as a parent, do I have the same level of "informed" that I did as a classroom teacher? No, of course not. But I did not realize how much I was missing out on until I had walked in the shoes of both roles, independent of each other.

I used to say that education is a three-legged stool, held up and steadied by students, parents, and educators. But that was before the proliferation of technology and the opportunities provided by social media and the plethora of learning platforms we have now (e.g., Google Apps, Twitter, Skype, Flipgrid, Seesaw).

Education is really a *four*-legged stool with students, parents, educators, and the community each playing a vital role. You may remember in Chapter 15 how we mentioned the three legged cow. Well, we drew him with 4 legs sitting on this stool just for your visual enjoyment. You're welcome. We have succeeded when each piece of the stool knows what every other piece is doing so true support can occur. If there are no connections between the legs, the stool cannot stand. So, how do we make that happen? How do we, all stakeholders in education, shift from operating in silos and embrace the team concept?

Like so many aspects of education, we have this thing backward. We start with standards and then think of ways to "hook" children. Pause. This is not a standards rant. We do think we need them. Standards are getting too big for their britches. They are riding around on a high horse and someone needs to knock 'em down a notch. Just last night, my oldest told me, "Mama, I just need to know it for the test. I don't care why." The topic: Europeans and Colonization. What's more important than knowing the truth about the foundation of our country?

Standards are guidelines. They should never be a road-block to the curiosity of children (see the *Trust* section). But let's reframe the view of standards using the words of author Dr. Nathan Lang-Raad (September 14, 2019). He tweeted, "Our job is not to teach the standards. It's to break the standards apart, discover what's interesting about them to students, and then create learning experiences to bridge the two." Talk about building a strong classroom community. Knowing your students like he suggests will no doubt have a dynamic effect on their learning. You've heard the word contextualize, yes? It's the "so what" factor. It's how you make kids care. If they don't care, why bother? They won't retain the information. They certainly won't be motivated to take this new learning and generalize it to think or problem solve. What for? Because of the tests? Hogwash. That's not why you got into education. That's not why you invested between $40,000 and $80,000 in an undergraduate degree. You want to inspire the next generation. You like kids. You like making them think!

To do this, there must be relevance. Like Lang-Raad said, you must, ". . .discover what is interesting about the standards," and make it fit into the worlds where they live. You have to care about what you're teaching, and communicate to kids why it's important. You must convince them. With heat, with passion. With zeal, so it also matters to them.

Every day when I (Jed) entered my 11th grade geometry class with teacher Ms. Angie Jackson (now Mrs. Rampey), the excitement was tangible. I was first and foremost glad to be finished with algebra, but I was also elated to have this brand-new teacher who had all this positive energy and joy for her new career. She always had music playing, fun seating options rather than the traditional rows of desks that hurt my backside, and a sticker chart to celebrate hard work. Her room was cute, cozy, and comfortable, and she had the world's most contagious laugh. Just walking in her classroom made you feel welcomed, and there was a spirit of playful learning that resided there. I often deliver a speech about my top five favorite teachers. I share about how Ms. Jackson made learning so much fun. She was a playful educator before her time, too. My junior year was 1994–1995. Things were still pretty traditional back then, and her new-teacher, first-year spirit broke some of those norms.

I loved it then, and I love it even more now almost two decades into my own teaching career. Whether she knew it or not, Ms. Jackson's playfulness was cultivating a strong sense of community for me within the walls of her classroom. The most amazing thing about this classroom experience was that I didn't have many places in my high school where I felt like that. Other than band class, which by its very nature invited daily playfulness as we created music with breath, there were lots of dark spots in my educational journey as a student. I didn't love school. I was bullied and never felt like I had many friends. Socializing wasn't my thing, and beyond the band, I tried to keep to myself as much as possible.

Ms. Jackson's class changed all that for me. It was during her class that I started to really find myself and engage in the playfulness and creativity that seemed to be hibernating inside me, waiting for the first sign of spring, or a safe community, to come out and be a part of the world. Thanks to the sense of belonging and acceptance I gained from her playful classroom, I sought out new paths in my learning the following year that would continue to build that sense of communal belonging.

During my senior year, I enrolled in an elective class called Media Communications with another playful teacher, Edythe Green. The whole entire course was designed to learn video production, editing, story boarding, etc. Our mission: create a public relations video to highlight all of the greatness of our school. It was such an incredible class. Every meeting felt like recess. Mrs. Greene's class was filled with laughter, learning, and love. While my high school experience as a whole was terrible because of awkward and painful peer interactions, I was so grateful to end my years of high school on such a great note.

Don't we all want to be Ms. Jackson and Mrs. Greene? Don't we want to be the teacher our students remember 20-plus years from high school? I sure do. I didn't go into teaching so my students would "just" learn the quadratic formula and the life cycle of the butterfly. Both of us, and you probably, went into teaching to impact lives. No, not be a savior, don't go that route here. Go the route of impact, and think positively. None of us chose this profession for the pay, the summers off (HAHAHAHAHAHAHAHAHAHA), or the great benefits. We got that degree and meet obstacles head on because nothing is more important to us than positively impacting students. Being an educator who enjoys the work, who cares about his or her students and has fun doing it is the greatest and most direct way to that impact.

While we love our teachers and our personal stories, we know that a book about education and best practices needs research to support the thinking. In a study at the University of Edinburgh (2012), researchers Macleod, MacAllister, and Pirrie have found that the more a teacher cares about her students, the more respect she will receive from them. According to the authors of this study, there is a strong theme emerging in the data suggesting that "young people do what adults ask them when they have a sense that the adult cares for them." The educational standard in most schools often requires students to follow directions, observe classroom norms, and complete assignments that require compliance. Not all students, however, are eager to blindly follow instructions; they need educators who have genuine concern for their well-being at the helm of their classrooms in order for true, authentic learning to take place. They need someone who cares about them and the environment where their learning community resides more than the curriculum and the district's scope and sequence. Maybe that doesn't sit right with you at first because the ultimate goal of many teachers is knowledge and content delivery, but let's take a closer look at the effects of the caring teacher on student learning and its impact on the community at large.

In 2014, a group of researchers (Garza, Alejandro, Blythe, and Fite) interviewed educators, conducted observations, and asked for self-reflections from teachers at suburban institutions in the southern part of the United States. They wanted to know what teacher behaviors were demonstrative of care. Knowing this can help us reflect on our practices: Are our methods aligned with our intentions? They found that participants associated caring teachers with the following behaviors:

- Fostering a sense of belonging
- Getting to know students personally
- Supporting academic success
- Knowing students' names
- Creating interesting and applicable lessons

As we read this research, we couldn't help but view it through the lens of our "play glasses." Yep, play glasses . . . ones with eyeballs attached to springs that fall out of the frames and bounce as we wear them. OK, maybe not those for real, but this is a playful book, and we needed that entertaining visual in our minds as we proceed.

With each behavior listed in the study, there were strong connections between a caring teacher and playful teacher/classroom. Let's break these down like DJ Jazzy Jeff.

*Here it is the groove slightly transformed*
*Just a bit of a break from the norm*
*Just a little somethin' to break the monotony*
*Of all that hardcore dance that has gotten to be*
*A little bit out of control it's cool to dance*
*But what about the groove that soothes that*
*moves romance?*
*Give me a soft subtle mix...*

# CHAPTER 27

# Fostering a Sense of Belonging

Teachers in the playful classroom make learning fun. No, it's not all rainbows and unicorns, sprinkles and cupcakes, but every nook and cranny, including the quiet, reflective, independent working times have a spirit of playfulness about them. Silent reading isn't a time to sit and be bored while staring at words on a page. The playful teacher has modeled, encouraged, and applauded active imaginations so that books have become rockets that launch student minds to never-before-seen places, experiencing dreams among the stars. The playful teacher has helped to instill such great self-worth in each student that his or her times of reflection are viewed as ways to improve the jump shot, the Play-Doh sculpting, or the poetry writing. The independent work assigned by the playful teacher isn't just another mundane task—it's an opportunity to ask questions, seek answers to those questions, and imagine creations that represent our learning.

This is the class we want to be in.
This is the one we want for the children in our families.
This is the teacher we want for all kids.
This is teacher we want to be.

Imagine the sense of belonging that is cultivated in that type of learning community. Just typing it out made us feel safe, empowered, and excited about all of the possibilities. Recalling the 16 types of play (see Chapter 9) and Stuart Brown's play personalities (see Chapter 23), we know that playfulness can strengthen the sense of community and belonging. Team-building experiences, cooperative learning opportunities, and humor-infused lessons are three specific playful methods that can build community and foster a sense of belonging.

Recently, I (Jed) led a workshop for a school that asked me to focus on strengthening the faculty's "team mindset." The school is under new leadership and the principal is working hard to alter the school's culture and climate with her playful personality and intentional focus on fostering a sense of belonging for the entire staff. Included in the workshop were teachers, office staff, parent volunteers, and support staff. There were all kinds of personalities in the room. I knew from personnel interviews prior to the workshop that many staff members were new to the building, many felt like their work was not valued, and many longed to feel included as part of the team. I hoped my study of play would be beneficial for this group, so I chose to implement my self-prescribed plan of Purposeful Learning All Day . . . PLAY. Yep, that's right, I asked a group of teachers to participate in playful activities all day with the desired purpose being that they would learn more about each other, discover their strengths on the team, and increase their feelings of self-worth in hopes that the entire school would benefit from their newfound sense of community.

## Bravery Badges

The day began with building connections between five random objects. I used a ruler, marker, paper clip, copy paper, and a bandage. The bandages were made by a company called Welly. Their marketing on the packaging was great. They called their bandages "Bravery Badges." I chose to include the bandages in this particular experience because community building always requires an extra dose of courage as we find commonality. *Bravery Badges*—didn't your teacher heart just leap? Mine did as soon as I saw the name screaming at me while in the checkout line at Target. Playing and team building takes lots of courage and bravery. Building a safe community is vital to this conversation about playful classrooms. I am wearing a "Bravery Badge" right now to remind me to have courage while writing this book. It is the scariest thing I've ever done.

   Back to the task. Teachers were asked to create a list of common themes using all five of the random objects. It might not sound too difficult at first, but this experience requires unique,"box destroying" thinking (see Section 2, Play Inspires Creativity). It's easy to connect one or two items, but using five items here takes the challenge to the next level. I got this idea from my friend Tanner Christensen's book, The Creativity Challenge. It is one of over a hundred ideas he shares to get the brain thinking in a new direction. I use many of them in my work every day. While their purpose is to strengthen creativity, they also make great team/community building experiences.

Before the teachers began, I explained to them that while the task may feel difficult at first, I wanted them to dig deep into their thinking to make connections. I also used the items as a metaphor comparing the objects to the group in the room. While everyone there had the same job, their goals, their strategies, their purposes, and their histories were all unique with very different purposes. However, just like the objects were all randomly there, they (the people) had been joined together and in order to strengthen their team, they needed to find a common theme amongst themselves.

After the collaboratin time of two Taylor Swift songs, teachers shared out the ideas their teams had formed. As I hoped, they discovered a long list of ways the items were connected. At the same time, they chit-chatted off topic and discovered commonalities among themselves as well. It was almost as if I planned it that way (wink wink). We teachers are fantastic at that, aren't we? Crafting one experience with one outcome that covertly, indirectly leads the learner to a totally different place. Ahhh . . . don't tell me I can't make a horse drink water. Those teachers were laughing, cutting up, (PLAYING) and building community, as I (their facilitator) was fostering their sense of belonging through team building, cooperative learning, and humor. Why? How? Because I cared about them, their work, and their students. Because I gave them the time, space, and opportunity to be playful. Because they were all brave and felt like they belonged.

Teaching is an art.
Building community is an art.
Play is the brush that helps us paint.

Try painting with play in your classroom as soon as possible to show your students you care about their learning community.

Read how you can bring bravery badges and other unique items in your classroom in Section 7, Get Out There and Play!

# CHAPTER 28

# Getting to Know Students Personally

Each year before school begins, we take the time to handwrite letters to students and their families. We want to begin the process of knowing our students as soon as possible. Nothing, and we really mean nothing, is more important in our own playful classrooms than the relationships with our students and their families. We use the word "families" here instead of parents because family encompasses all those who love and care for the students entrusted to us at school. The benefits of the role of relationships in learning have been well-documented, but just in case you haven't read any of it, here're some knowledge sprinkles for you.

According to the analysis, relationships play an essential role in understanding student achievement. The relational process is regarded as an inherent aspect of educational life and the foundation for encouraging performance. By combining these perspectives, the significance of relationships for comprehending student achievement is revealed (Aspelin, 2012).

Nordenbo, Sögaard Larsen, Tiftikci, Wendt, and Östergaard (2008) define teachers' relational competence as a key factor behind student performance.

Grosin (2004) argues that successful schools and pedagogy are characterized by a learner-centered approach and by respectful and trusting teacher-student relationships.

In a series of reports (e.g., 2005, 2009), the Swedish National Agency for Education has demonstrated the importance

of the social competence of teachers and of close,
personal relationships between teacher and student to
school performance (Aspelin, 2012).

The primary aim of education is to enhance the potentials
for participating in relational processes—from the local to
the global (Gergen, 2009 p. 243).

Unlike play research for anyone older than 10, this is an area
where the research and the stories are plentiful. In this book we
wrote an entire section devoted to relationships. The section on
trust is connected to relationships. Cultivating community . . . yep,
you guessed it . . . relationships.

RELATIONSHIPS MATTER MOST.

Reflect with us though back to your certification program. How
many classes did you take learning about the value of connection? How many courses led you to a deeper understanding of
the power of relationships in regard to content delivery and sound
pedagogical practice? Better yet, how many of your professors
modeled this by developing strong teacher–student bonds with
you as they helped craft your philosophy of education? We hope
the answer is lots and lots of classes, courses, and professors provided you with relationship-based learning.

In our experiences as students, teachers, instructional coaches,
professors, and participants in countless professional development meetings, we can affirmatively say that relationship/
community cultivation is usually mentioned as an afterthought
that assumes most people know its value and have the ability to
develop strong relationships and community with students and
professional peers. We have asked more teachers than you can
shake a stick at about their training and their coursework—both
at the preservice level, and at the continuing education level.
Nearly none had ever had any specific training on how to build
community and strengthen relationships with students, parents,
and colleagues. The default answer for most of them is, "I had
a classroom management course." Most everyone we consulted, with the exception of school counselors, said that it was
always implied, yet never the sole focus of their development as
an educator.

We grieve when we read the research about the importance of community and relationships in educating students, yet see so many missing pieces in the system. We believe that becoming a playful teacher will strengthen the relationships and community in our classrooms and fill in some of the holes we might have missed in training to become a teacher. By creating a playful classroom there are three key areas that allow us to increase our knowledge of students on a personal level and cultivate community.

## Play Reveals Thinking

If you ever want to know how your students think, don't give them a standardized fill-in-the-bubble quiz. Give them a can of Play-Doh and ask them to create. Give them a piece of tin foil and ask them to sculpt. Give them a big piece of butcher paper and ask them to design. These playful learning experiences in the classroom show you so much more about students than a bubble test ever will. Watch them as they tackle the task. Talk with them. Ask them questions. Giggle out loud (GOL, as my friend Chara often texts instead of LOL) with them as they learn how to manipulate the media to formulate answers.

We say giggle because these tasks often invite laughter. This type of experience engages students on a physical, mental, emotional, and verbal level. Remember, the only thing bubbles ever did was get me a "D" on a health test in elementary school. Those bubbles didn't reveal one thing about me personally, nor my health knowledge. But, the cardboard cutout of the human body filled with hand-drawn organs glued in their appropriate spots sure did. Maybe you don't want to make that for your project, but the playful classroom is filled with purposeful choices that allow teachers to pull back the curtain and take a peek at students thinking in a way that honors who they are as an individual part of the community.

## Play Strengthens Social Skills

Strong social skills are vital to cultivating the community of your classroom. Playing both reveals the depth of one's social skills and provides opportunities for growing that skill as well. Have you ever watched a group of students (or adults) playing a board game? Cooperation, listening, patience, trust, communication, strategy—the list of attributes visible during play are plentiful. Aren't all of those skills necessary for a strong community both in the classroom and the world? We'd say we need playfulness in our lives now more than ever. UNICEF, in cooperation with The LEGO Foundation, says this about the social interaction of play in its publication *Learning Through Play*:

> *Play sets the foundation for the development of critical social and emotional knowledge and skills. Through play, children learn to forge connections with others, and to share, negotiate and resolve conflicts, as well as learn self-advocacy skills. Play also teaches children leadership as well as group skills. Furthermore, play is a natural tool that children can use to build their resilience and coping skills, as they learn to navigate relationships and deal with social challenges.*

The article goes on to say, "Play allows children to communicate ideas, to understand others through social interaction, paving the way to build deeper understanding and more powerful relationships."

While this article focuses on play at the earlier stages of life, we believe every stage of the human existence needs playful moments throughout daily life so that people strengthen their resilience and coping skills and continue to hone their social skills as they navigate adult relationships in the real world. Don't you believe that too? How many adults do you know who need some social skill development? Bless their hearts. By providing these moments often, and intentionally, beyond the educational norms of K–2 learning, we are strengthening students' learning experiences with the core content, we are learning more and more about them as a learner, and we are creating stronger, more socially-aware humans.

## Play Creates Connections

When I (Jed) was in kindergarten, I LOVED the kitchen center. I vividly remember wearing a kid-sized apron, standing at a wooden stove, cooking a pretend chicken potpie. Not sure why I chose to bake that particular delicacy that day. Maybe it was because my great-grandma Maudie made a mean potpie. My "wife and daughter" joined me in the kitchen that day. Shay Davis and Kim Smith. The teacher assistant, Mrs. Wolfe, walked over to observe what we were doing. She joined us in the kitchen as well and "took a bite" of my creation. "Mmmmmmmm," she said. "This is better than the potpies I cook." I have never forgotten that experience.

I remember Shay and Kim.
I remember the smell of the wooden stove and the cozy
    feeling of the kitchen.
I remember how proud I was that Mrs. Wolfe loved my pie.

I doubt she even remembers it after years and years of educating, but I will never forget it. We are connected forever because she played with me. Still to this day, I think about Mrs. Wolfe when I cook.

# CHAPTER 29

# Supporting Academic Success

Yesterday, I (Jed) participated in an online chat about assessment methodologies. It was a great chat, and lots of fantastic educators are doing amazing things around the world. Twitter chats are highly engaging and a dynamic way to build your own global professional learning community (PLC). I have learned so much from my cultivated online PLC, have had my own ideas challenged and tweaked, and have added incredible humans to my network of online colleagues. If you have never participated in a chat with your professional peers via the interwebs, give it a go ASAP. They are always playful and definitely build community through conversations and connections. It will make you a better teacher and person.

Of course, the topic of formative and summative assessments came up as we chatted. What would a good chat about assessment be without those classic teacher buzzwords? If you are like we were in the first few years of our career, you may have to take a pause here and look up those terms so that you can remember which is which. Confession time . . . We have often struggled to recall the difference, especially when we were around the "good teachers" who knew all the buzzwords. Play makes us vulnerable sometimes as we have to admit what we don't know in order to learn. Playful classroom teachers have to be willing to be vulnerable sometimes, right? It is funny, now that I am on the flip side of almost two decades of education, the qualifiers we once thought were "good teaching" are nowhere close to describing the educator we are now. Does that mean we are not good ones? Nope, it means we have gotten better in our craft over time and see things differently based on our life experiences. It also doesn't mean that if you are where we were then, you aren't a good teacher. We are all on a journey that is a constant ebb and flow of prune, grow, blossom, repeat.

The best way for me to keep the two assessments straight in my head was to tell myself that I gather formative assessments while the learning is still "form"ing and summative assessments are given seeking a "summ"ary of all that students were supposed to have learned during the course of study. If I am being completely honest here, I never really learned those in my teacher ed program. Yes, my professors and instructors "covered" them, but I never put them to memory until I was sitting in a room full of my peers and felt like an idiot because I didn't know the basics. Yes, basics. Assessments are the basics of education. We have to do them. We have to grade. Principals, districts, education departments, colleges, parents, and society as a whole expect them. A,B,C,D,F, and 4.0 GPAs are the only way anyone knows how students are doing, right? I say a big fat wrong. We hope you do, too.

The reason we use tests/assessments is found *where two roads diverge in a yellow wood, and we (choose to) take the road less traveled.* When we make decisions with students' best interests in mind, we may find ourselves alone for a while on the path. That's OK.

We should always avoid using assessments with consequences. When we give penalties based on assessments, we invalidate their purpose. An F can get you benched during the big game or ruffle your mama's feathers and have you scrubbing commodes all weekend. Assessments are tools to assist educators in understanding what paths their students are on and how to help them continue walking down that path, or . . . to turn around and start a new one. Sadly, the results of many tests/assessments are instead used for the following:

- Separating those who can from those who cannot
- Labeling students with letters
- Measuring teacher effectiveness
- Creating public perceptions of "good" schools
- Determining what college you can go to
- Determining how much scholarship money you can get for college
- Showing how qualified you are to do a job (We will chat about this one.)

You may think this is turning into a rant, but let's remember what this book is about . . . *The Playful Classroom*. Does any of that sound playful? Certainly doesn't to us. As we typed the list of possible outcomes from assessments, we started to get really nauseated. We remembered the times we had done those things. We didn't know better at the time. It was the system we grew up in as kids, the culture we learned in as teenagers, it was the training we received as preservice educators, and it was the expectation placed on us as we entered the classroom in the role of teacher. Many of us have forgotten that in order to care for the students in a playful classroom we must relearn and reteach ourselves what assessment is truly for. In a classroom filled with student-centered voice and choice, we will be able to see more clearly who they really are, where they are in their learning, and how we can help them to get where they want to be as a result of the "tests" we have given them.

In the playful classroom, we believe that academic success is supported not by higher test scores and grades but by offering feedback for growth and opportunities for revision. The difference is in the perspective. Tests and assessments are used as information for the next step, not an end result.

## Feedback for Growth, Not Grades

The end game in the college courses that Julie and I teach is for students to grow as a learner. The ideas and strategies in our toolbox to help them do that come from the playful spirits we have developed over the years. Our students sometimes hate it because their previous 12-plus years of schooling have taught them to seek the coveted "A" as the only defining measure of their success. But, after a few weeks of getting feedback regarding their assignments, knowing that the grade is secondary to growth, they come around rather quickly. With some of them, you can literally see the yoke of anxiety releasing itself from their stress-filled bodies as they realize we aren't out to get them, but to help them learn.

Talk about cultivating community! Students who are less stressed are more apt to learn and grow in a space that is safe. Showing them that we truly care about the learning beyond a grade allows for such great experiences that lead to leaps and bounds of growth. Why and how is this playful, you ask? Keep reading.

Julie (Jed typing now . . .) is a master at giving feedback for the purpose of growth. She makes it incredibly fun to be in her class and to meet with her about your work. She has an office with a chalkboard wall where students, along with her guidance, can doodle their way through their conference times. Sometimes she leaves said office and meets students at local coffee shops for their feedback meetings. While there, they may participate in situational role plays that offer loads of insight to the student. Often times they will jump into a Twitter chat about the subject of their discussion so that insight from teachers all around the world make their way into the feedback. She approaches everything she does with a playful mindset. No, not everything she does involves a toy and recess, but remember, there are lots of types of play. The mindset that leads her to work is anything but traditional; it strengthens her classroom community, and her students love her methods.

If I am honest here, she is way better at feedback than me. In fact, she's the one who really challenged me to improve in this area. Whether she knows it or not, I observe how she practices as a teacher often, and there are countless things she does with students that I want to get better at. She is up late at night emailing her students about their assignments, she is constantly allowing them time to try, redo, try, redo again, make a new plan, try that plan, fail again, get up again, etc.

When I was teaching my first college course, I very much had the mentality that my students were grownups and should "know" how to do school. While I was very much a playful teacher with my first and second graders, and gave them countless opportunities for growth, my college students didn't need all that grace and mercy Julie was building into her courses. Learn what I say, give it back to me in your assignments, repeat that over and over throughout the semester, get an A for the course. Anything less than that and your grade would reflect that. Yikes. . . Typing that out made me feel such guilt and shame. I was very much a victim of the ol' nonplayful system. Ugh . . .

When I started watching Julie's practices, I realized that regardless of the age of my students, we all need feedback on our work to grow. Letters and scores aren't feedback. They are antiquated labels that define how students performed at one moment in time. None of us, and I mean none of us should ever be judged for one day of our performance. Especially when learning is the objective. Learning means we are gonna fail time and time again. We don't ever get it right the first time. If we do, we aren't in the right class. If you're the smartest person in the room, you're in the wrong room, right? Maybe you are thinking grades are averaged over several days so maybe it's not as bad as I made it seem with the "one moment in time" performance. Well, I know some teachers who give final grades based on three assessments for the whole semester. Being judged on performance for three days out of a whole semester isn't much better than being judged once.

Because of Julie's try, try, again learning method, I made some significant changes to one of my courses that involved students recording themselves teaching and submitting it to me for their final grade. I saw the benefits her students reaped as a result of this one-on-one community building she implemented through her feedback initiatives. I saw how much fun students thought it was to be able to learn and try, relearn, and try again. I admittedly hated the video part of my class, as it really was the "ultimate label" on the students. It was a pass/fail course, and the video really determined it all regardless of the entire semester. I was an adjunct instructor who was repeatedly reminded by my tenure track "professor" peers that I wasn't qualified to redesign the course because I was not full-time faculty, so creating change for the course was difficult. But, I did make some tweaks that really showed my students I cared about them and wanted them to learn, not just be graded. For weeks and weeks before their video, I modeled best practices during our class time that I hoped to see in their lessons. We had the most fun. Reading in costumes in the commons outside, virtual field trips and mystery Skypes, painting with purpose, writing a class Valentine song to share with college students in Pennsylvania, creating tape art in the drab halls of the very official building where our class was housed, and I even brought in a hula-hoop expert for an entire class period where we actively participated in generating ideas for hula hoops that they could use with students in their practicum class. We built the best community of learners. We played during every class. It was one of my favorite semesters ever!

Normally, the video of their teaching was due as their final, but I managed to change that without anyone of those tenured folks noticing. I wanted my students to receive authentic feedback that would help them become better teachers, not penalize them so that they wouldn't pass the course. After all, I was there to teach them how to become great teachers, not tell them how bad they were at it. And, they were paying lots of money for said learning. They deserved the best instructor they could get.

As part of my course tweaks, I asked that they submit the final video two weeks before it was due so that I could give them feedback before it was "officially" due as their final. I cannot tell you how they freaked out. They panicked like Chicken Little as the sky fell. It was somewhat comical now that I think back, but in the moment they were terrified. I asked them to trust me through the process and know that they would be better for it in the end. Because of the playful, caring community I had built, they began to warm up to the idea. After they calmed down, I created a schedule of meeting times during which we would watch their video together at a local coffee shop and discuss what we saw. Coffee was my treat! It was meant to be more of a collaborative effort than me judging their work.

After watching the first video, I was so glad I had decided to take this approach. The student had been a fantastic pupil in class. She had great ideas, always participated, never missed a session, and always added to the discussions. Her thoughts and practices in our class time were on point. Her video, however, was not so great. Had she turned in her first attempt for her final, she would've failed the class. Nothing from our class time was included in the video. No creativity, collaboration, communication, nor critical thinking. No playfulness. For the first 30 minutes of the 45-minute video, her students sat as she talked. There was no doing, no experimenting, no constructing, no anything fun and exciting, and no community-building at all. Because I had followed Julie's try, try again method, this student learned from the feedback I gave her during our one-on-one meeting. She redid her video, implemented all of the areas of learning we discussed, and the result was brilliant. In the first video, she didn't apply anything learned in class because she was afraid to do what I asked. Her very traditional cooperating teacher at the school where she was placed had told her how focused she must be on standards, scores, and grades. My student was at the early stages of her learning and did what her cooperative teacher told her. Thankfully, in the second video, she put aside her fears and did her thing . . . and she did it well. She passed the class! Imagine if I had just graded her final and moved on without discussion, without feedback. That moment could've impacted her life forever. A playful classroom teacher is eager to support academic success with feedback and not just grades.

## Scores and Career Goals

We said we were coming back to this in our list of assessment results. Read this dialogue we overheard in a coffee shop and you will know why.

> *I calculated what I need in every class to get an A.*
> *Was that smart or not smart?*
> *I need a 90 and a 92.*
> *Oh wait . . . I probably just need to get an 89.*
> *In that other class, all I need is a 65 to get a B+ and an 80 will get me an A.*

The above quote was a direct statement by a medical student sitting beside us at a coffee shop as we typed this very section. It was uncanny that she and her classmate were having this particular conversation as we sat just two feet away at the same table. After we heard her say this, we chatted for a bit. The discussion clearly involved them venting about grades. She went on to ask, "Why would I do my best when I don't have to?"

It shook us to the core, yet it shouldn't have surprised us at all. The system has taught us that the grade is more important than the learning. The system has taught us that the grade is what gets you to the exit step, not the learning, not the experience. Y'all. A medical student. Let that sink in.

We asked this student, "What is the difference between someone who makes a 100 and an 85 on the test in your course?" Her response, "Nothing really, just what school they get into next. It's really more about what you do with the learning other than the score, but right now I have to focus on the grade and not the learning."

As educators, and as humans, that should scare us to death. We have often heard people say, "I want an *A* doctor working on me, not a *C* one." The A earned doesn't necessarily mean they are a better doctor. It means the doctor was a better test taker. Think back to that Western Civ. test you aced in college. Yay, you made an A. Twenty years later, what have you done with that A? What can you tell us about Western civilizations? Our guess is, not a thing. The young woman we spoke with hopes to one day work in an emergency room. I don't care if she makes an A because she's a good test taker and statistician who beat the system by figuring out what number she needed to be "successful." Yes, we asked her. Those tests? Paper/pencil. Memory assessments. I want to know can she apply her learning and save my life. What about you?

This is not her fault. It's the fault of us all. Both the system and those who perpetuate it have created this mindset. You've been there—we know we have. In grad school, we wanted the A. We determined from the syllabus just how much effort was needed to walk out of that classroom into another. . . toward the accomplishment of our goal. We saw classes as a means to an end. This is exactly the view of this young lady down the table from us.

We can tell she is intelligent. We can tell she is passionate. But, even in medical school, her view on learning is tied to the assessment rather than the problem solving and understandings needed for her life's occupation.

# CHAPTER 30

# Knowing Students' Names

We know we discussed the power of names in Section 4: Relationships. It deserves space in a section on community building, too. My second-grade teacher called me John. Everyday. All day. John. I hated it. My name was, is, always will be, Jed. My grandaddy was John. Not me. While my legal name is in fact John Edwin Dearybury III, my mama called me JED (my initials) since the day I came home from the hospital. I asked my teacher to repeatedly call me Jed. I will never forget her response. "Had your mama wanted you to be called Jed, she should've put that on your birth certificate." Yikes. Did you cringe as you read that mid-'80s era teacher voice screeching off the page? It is hard to believe that was once a perfectly acceptable answer to an 8-year-old just asking to be called by his name. Things got so bad with that teacher that my mama eventually had to go up to the school and have a come-to-Jesus meetin' with her. She finally started calling me Jed, but most of the time it was Jeb. I guess "beggars can't be choosers" was a lesson I learned early in life. Jeb was closer to Jed than John, right?

Unfortunately, we both know teachers who don't call students by the name they request. This isn't/wasn't an isolated mid-1980s event. Teachers regularly call students the first name they see on the roll, or even worse, butcher the pronunciation of said name on the role, and even when corrected, never make any attempt to learn and say it correctly. Remember when we mentioned Dale Carnegie's words about the value of our names? It really is one of the most important sounds one can hear, especially in the classroom. Teachers who care about students, who value their classroom communities, and want to create a safe, playful place of learning, will make sure to use names appropriately and correctly.

Just as we must be intentional about knowing our students' names, we must be sure to instill that same value into the students we teach so that in our classroom communities, there are shared values among peers. When they know each others' names, and show that they value one another, safe, playful communities are easily created. Recently, I worked with a school that had merged with another community of learners from a different area of their district. The two buildings merged into one and had created this unique dichotomy of spaces. Many students from school A didn't know anyone from school B and vice versa, yet they were all in classes together as one. The teachers, both from school A and school B, were asking me for tips on how to get students to learn one another's names. One teacher said that his collaborative instruction was suffering because it was taking so long for the kids to learn who each other were. During cooperative learning times, students from school A were finding other students from school A to work with, as were the students from school B. He said, "It's almost as if I have two classes in one. There is no cohesive team feeling. It is still an us-against-them feeling, and I want it to be a we".

I was thrilled this teacher recognized that aspect as a key component to his collaborative, playful space. He is a PE teacher, and what classroom is more playful than that? Also, what classroom needs a strong sense of community more than that? Lots of students have horrible memories of PE classes that aren't so community-minded, but I have some doozies. Being made fun of for not "playing like a boy" and for wearing the wrong shoes to gym class come to mind. Both of those incidents were messages from uncaring, unplayful teachers, not my classmates. Some of the ideas I suggested for this playful-minded PE teacher that wanted a stronger community in his gym are listed below. Give some of these purposefully playful ideas a try and see how they impact your class community.

## Greeting Students

I never needed a big production awaiting me every day as I arrived to school, nor does *any* student really, but as I write about greeting students at the door, I will never forget the one day I wasn't standing at my post to greet Quanisha as she walked into the room. I was busy frantically getting things ready for the day and didn't see her come in. She proudly announced, "Mr. Dearybury, I'm here. Aren't you gonna greet me?" Needless to say, I never missed another greeting. Why? It mattered to her, and it most likely mattered to others. I was greeting my kids at the door with a handshake, high five, or a hug long before that cute little poster made its rounds on the Internet.

I must admit though, I am secretly jealous that I didn't do it like my friend Barry White Jr. (@thatsbwhite). Take a moment to do an Internet search for his classroom greetings. Such excited, engaging energy flows from him as he connects with and greets students using their own personal handshake crafted collaboratively with each individual. We know not everyone likes it. We know that not every kid might want that same kind of greeting in the morning. But, I bet we all could grow from this teacher who took the time to cultivate such a playful community of learning.

## Build a Playful Community

Allow students to be the daily greeter. Ask the greeter to engage each student with a fun question, a riddle, a pun, etc., as they enter the room. The greeter could rotate each day or stay the same for a week. This would get kids talking to each other that otherwise might not ever speak.

## Nicknames

Little Boo, LuLu, T. Lee, Jarvelous, Gracie-Lou, Willy Lee, Katie Bug, `Nisha, Allie Poo, JD, DayDay, Lily Shop, Mr. Clark, AC, JoJo, and Porter are all nicknames I used to call students. Almost every student I ever taught had a nickname if they wanted one. It became a thing with all of my students, and they begged me to give them a nickname. Sometimes the name came easy because it flowed from their name.

Of course, these names were crafted with love and community pride, and I made sure I had permission from all students to call them by this nickname. I would never use a name for someone if they didn't want me to. I am glad the playful banter that comes with nicknames is a part of my classroom history. It always made our classroom feel like home. Families have special names for the people they love, and I love all my students. Nicknames worked for our community.

## Build a Playful Community

If students are comfortable, share nicknames from home, or even let them come up with a nickname for you. My teacher—nickname was Mr. D or Mr. DB. Some people wouldn't "allow" that because they think it's disrespectful. Personally, I think respect is earned by other means than a name or title. That is probably a different book, though. :)

## Cheering for One Another

Have you ever run a road race where the running bib had your name on it? It is one of my favorite things about the *Run Disney Race Series*. Yet another nod to the way Disney make their guests feel—a truly memorable experience. Your name is always printed on the front of the bib for all to see. No, not your full name, but the name you tell them that you want to be called as you run through the most magical place on earth.

Running is hard. Avid runners will tell you it is 99.9% mental. I (Jed) have run seven full marathons and countless other races or varying distances. The races I love the best are the ones where I hear people cheering for me by name as I make my way through the course. No, I don't always know the people, but because my name is on the bib they can shout out encouragement directly for me as I pass by. I cannot tell you what it means to hear complete strangers cheering for you by name. Those mystery people have helped me accomplish some pretty amazing running feats.

Imagine what personal cheers in a classroom setting could do for cultivating your community, and cheers are a blast to create. You can do it, students can do it . . . There's NO wrong way to cheer for someone. There's tons of learning objectives that could be met be creating them, and . . . it's fun and playful. We see this as a "win–win" experience for all classrooms.

## Build a Playful Community

An Internet search of the term *class call-backs* will result in lots of class cheers you can use to gain group attention. We challenge you to start here, but move toward creating your own as your class builds community. Encourage student ideas in this process. While gaining group attention is needed, we can also use this kind of idea as a class celebratory chant. When you celebrate students and their individual accomplishments, ask your class to "shine" on them (code for smiling and wiggling spirit fingers in their direction).

# CHAPTER 31

# Creating Interesting and Applicable Lessons

As an educator, it is very difficult to sit through an uninteresting lesson that has no application to my life. I have been to countless classes where five minutes into the lesson I am questioning my attendance and wondering if I will ever have a need for the speaker's wisdom. In moments like this, there is almost always a disconnect, a shutdown, a checkout, whatever you want to call it. Just know my brain leaves the session faster than the #3 car from pit row.

The interesting thing about this is that I am talking about grownup me. Me with cognitive abilities to process new information, to glean the most valuable information of the presentation and apply it to my life, to learn something new from the teacher, and to walk away from the experience with new knowledge. Yet . . . my mind peels out of there like a #24 Dupont in overdrive.

(Yep, we did it again. We referenced Nascar twice on the same page.)

We did that because we have to over-illustrate how fast the learner will mentally leave your learning experience if you haven't cared enough to make it interesting and applicable. If 41-year-old me does this, what does 10-year-old Timmy do as he sits in his chair, confined for the next hour with only the memories of recess two hours ago. He wants to learn. He's not a bad kid. He knows that being "smart" will help him get a better job than his mom and dad because they tell him every day. But, for the life of him, he just cannot understand why he needs to know about the clothing people wore in the Roaring 20s, or why in fact they were roaring, as he stares at your 30-minute slideshow of pics you found on the Internet from that time period. Our lessons must be interesting, engaging, and relevant. All of these pieces must come together in our classrooms in order to build a strong community of learners who will then make stronger communities in the world at large. We felt a bit downtrodden the first time we were called out for this kind of instruction. To help get those tractor tires rolling, we'd like to give you a few ideas to help you along.

**Idea 1:** If a sweet little student comes to you and says, "My daddy gets cranky when he doesn't get enough sleep," please encourage discussion in your room about the importance of sleep. Please take the opportunity to turn that sentence into a survey on Google Forms shared on your class social media page collecting data on the relationship between hours of sleep and mood. Wait? Scatterplots aren't part of your math standards? (They certainly are in some grades though.) Does that mean they won't understand? And even if they don't, couldn't it make its way into your curriculum because it is student-centered and driven by personal connection? What a great opportunity! This does not take a lot of time, y'all. Look at the image here. Two questions. That's all. The creation of such doesn't even take 20 seconds.

## Sleep Survey

*Required

How many hours of sleep did you get last night?*

Your answer

My Mood Today

0    1    2    3    4    5

Using the picture above, enter the number of how you feel today!

Your answer

**Idea 2:** What about the kid who comes to school in winter asking about why the trucks put salt on the roads? Do we encourage students to hypothesize on the purpose of the salt? Do we grab some Mason jars from the cabinet and the salt shaker off the table at lunch? Are we testing how long it takes saltwater to freeze versus tap water? Are we giving students opportunities to draw conclusions? This is playful. This is relevant. This is real-world application and connection. It not only builds the classroom community but it connects the learning to the bigger community at large—the one beyond the school building. Students won't be in school forever. If the lessons we teach them aren't carrying over into the real world, then what's the point? What good does knowing how "2 plus 2 equals 4" do for me if I don't know when, where, and why?

**Idea 3:** A student is reading in a library book during silent sustained reading about a really unique bird called a cassowary. It is from Australia, and it is quite odd looking. She is supposed to be silently reading but her "ohhs and ahhs" distract her neighbors. Next thing you know, 10 students are huddled around her, all intrigued by the bird. You could stress about it and take away all of the kids' recess because they were not following the instructions for SSR, or . . . you could jump in the floor with them, guide them how to do research online to learn more about the bird, find some cool videos of the bird in action, and maybe even have the original student do some independent work later and present her findings about the bird to her already super-engaged classmates. So what if "birds" aren't in your standards? Public speaking, research, grammar, and more are all on every grade level's long-range plan.

The art of teaching is taking student curiosities about sleeping, snowplows, and cassowaries, and connecting them to our content. Every curiosity can be related to a standard. Without that connection, we end up treating education as a factory model. Kids are not widgets. Once there is relevance, one can consider community.

# CHAPTER 32

# Beyond the Red School Door

One year my (Jed's) class was awarded a grant from a national pet store chain. We were all so excited to get the news that we were getting free money to get a pet for our classroom. The grant provided us with a list of optional pets, and immediately the students went into research mode deciding which pet would be best for our learning space. They looked up basic facts about each animal choice, they watched videos of other classes with kids their age who had adopted one of the pets from the list, and they even tweeted classes who had pet pics online to ask basic care-taking questions. I remember how proud I was to watch the community of learners that we had worked hard to build in room 100 spill over into the real world as students reached beyond our walls.

Students found lots of classes online that were the proud owners of bearded dragons. If you have never seen one, take a moment to look it up. Of course, my class was intrigued by this creature. First off, any creature with the word *dragon* in its name is gonna thrill a Harry Potter–obsessed class. This was also about the time the movie *How to Train Your Dragon* came out. They were sold from that alone. Next, they learned that the *beardie,* as many folks call it, had unique color-changing abilities. This was especially interesting to my kids because we had just finished up an arts integrated unit using Eric Carle's *The Mixed-Up Chameleon.* I admit I was a tad excited about seeing the color change and wondered how noticeable it would be. The final selling point for this particular pet was its spikey exterior. A good amount of my students were interested in WWE wrestling, and they convinced the rest of the class that a spikey creature would be best if we wanted to be like their favorite wrestler, John Cena.

If you have never worked with second graders, let me tell you this: If you mention there is a possibility of a color-changing spikey dragon living in your classroom, there is no way another creature is gonna win out. Sorry to all the hamster, gerbil, turtle, guinea pig loving folks out there. This was a no brainer for my kids.

Once we had decided the animal of choice, we made plans as a class to visit the pet store and pick out our little bundle of bearded bliss. I was shocked at how many students showed up at 10 a.m. on Saturday to shop with me. Needless to say, there was quite a buzz about it. When we all walked into the store, the clerks' faces lit up. I am still not sure if their initial looks were those of excitement or fear as the kiddie-herd, led by this teacher man, made its way through their doors. I explained to one of the workers who we were, where we were from, and what we hoped to purchase. The best laid plans, of course, always have a different outcome, and they aren't always bad.

My students, without hesitation, started telling the clerk all they had learned about bearded dragons. About their diet, sleeping patterns, reptilian nature, and of course the color of their poop. Kids are obsessed with that, aren't they? I stood in awe watching this moment unfold. The clerk begin asking questions back and, next thing I know, 45 minutes had passed and we had done nothing but stand and chit chat by a cage full of bearded dragons on a Saturday morning at our community pet shop. We got to watch the clerk feed them, clean them, tidy their cages, and we all got to hold a few different ones so we could decide which one was best for us. With all the learning that happened, I felt like I deserved overtime for the morning. I wasn't supposed to do it per the company rules, but I tipped the guy. He didn't have to teach my kids, but he did.

I think about that moment every time I pass that pet shop. That's what a playful teacher hopes for from a community. After working so hard to cultivate a space within my four walls, it was thrilling to see that moment spill over into the world beyond our school doors. There are countless ways we can take playful learning beyond the building, that in turn strengthen and cultivate the greater community.

The story about the beardie doesn't end with the pet shop clerk. After we got "Spike" all settled into his new crib in room 100, it was time to adjust our lives to his presence. Trust me, as much as we wanted him to, he did not conform to us. We had to become aware of so much in order for Spike to be happy as a member of our classroom community. He needed:

- Fresh water every morning
- Poop cleaned from the cage twice a day
- Meal worms to eat every afternoon
- Crickets for the two-day weekend

- A pet sitter for three-day weekends
- A watcher during breaks

It was a lot. The kids and I were both a tad overwhelmed with all the responsibility. The first two weeks were tough, and I spent a lot of my own money buying crickets and meal worms.

About the third week into beardie ownership, our class read Stuart J. Murphy's book, *Lemonade for Sale*. This is Amazon's description of the book:

> *Four kids and their sidekick, Petey the Parrot, run a lemonade stand whose patrons include all kinds of wacky neighbors—even a juggler. They create a bar graph to track the rise and fall of their lemonade sales. Author Stuart Murphy and illustrator Tricia Tusa make understanding bar graphs a breeze with lively art and a warm story.*

While we were reading, students shared about ways they have earned money for things they wanted as they built that connection from self to text. It was great, but it got even greater when Willy Lee said, "We should start selling lemonade or working to make money for Spike's food." I admittedly had never even thought to do that. I guess my brain assumed it would be my pet and my responsibility. Nope. immediately, the students took ownership of Spike from that moment on, and I never spent another dime on him. The students, in their own time after school, did chores for neighbors, put coin jars at their parents' businesses, saved their allowances, and one kid even went to the World Famous Beacon Drive-In here in Spartanburg and got permission to refill drinks, clean tables, and ask for donations to the class pet fund. He raised over 60 dollars for crickets and a new, improved, water dish. WOW!

The best part about the entire experience wasn't how much money they raised, which was a lot—$373 in just a few weeks—but it was the way they worked together to make it all happen. They set goals, they made graphs, they brainstormed lists of possible jobs and donors. They wrote letters to relatives who lived far away. They even tweeted the pet store to ask for freebies—which they got! It was awe-inspiring to watch it all play out. Our little classroom community definitely cultivated their sense of belonging and involvement in the community beyond our little red schoolhouse doors.

Strengthening community ties outside of the school building is vital to a successful, playful classroom. Teachers cannot bear the burden of educating every child alone. It truly takes a village, a community of stakeholders involved in the process. I often invited parents, business leaders, legislators, school board members, and local TV personalities into my classroom. We know many of you do this as well. Local meteorologists are a favorite across the country.

Evidence supporting this practice is readily available and should be kept handy so that you can share these little bits of wisdom with your colleagues. The National Education Association (NEA) (2008) cites many researchers who verify parent, family, and community involvement as keys to addressing the school dropout crisis. Strong school–family–community partnerships not only foster higher educational aspirations but also result in more motivated students. It's not surprising to us that when enough stakeholders are present and making an impact, students will want to do well. It's exciting to know that the research holds true for students, young and old, regardless of the parents' education, family income, race, or background (Barton, 2003; Jeynes, 2003).

This list of suggestions from the NEA (2008) can help all of us be more aware of methods for expanding and cultivating the classroom community beyond the school. How can we engage more stakeholders? Take a gander at the following thoughts to jump-start your mule:

- Survey educators and families to determine needs, interests, and ideas about partnering.
- Develop and pass family-friendly policies and laws (i.e., leaves of absence for parents/caregivers to participate in school or education-related activities; flexible scheduling to encourage participation by diverse families).
- Provide professional development on family and community engagement for school faculties.
- Offer training for parents and community stakeholders on effective communications and partnering skills.

- Provide better information on school and school district policies and procedures.
- Ensure timely access to information, using effective communications tools that address various family structures and are translated into languages that parents/families understand.
- Hire and train school-community liaisons who know the community's history, language, and cultural background to contact parents and coordinate activities.
- Collaborate with higher education institutions to infuse parent, family, and community involvement in education into teacher and administrator preparation programs.
- Develop an outreach strategy to inform families, businesses, and the community about school and family involvement opportunities, policies, and programs.
- Regularly evaluate the effectiveness of family involvement programs and activities.

See Section 7 for additional, playful ideas to expand your classroom community beyond the red school door.

# CHAPTER 33

# Across the Country, and Around the World

We have heard countless people say that they don't read the headlines or watch the news anymore because it is depressing. While we agree that there are troubling stories almost daily, that is all the more reason we should strive as educators to intentionally create playful, engaging experiences for the students in our classrooms. By now you have seen the research and hopefully understand its importance in the learning process. The world needs humanity, now more than ever, to develop playful sociability and to reject a *THEM* versus *US* mentality. In this chapter, we want to introduce you to a few of our favorite playful, global learning experiences that are making great gains to develop the *WE* mindset explained in Section 1.

## Global School Play Day

Since its beginning in 2015, Global School Play Day (www. globalschoolplayday.com) has led 1,445,690 students to a full day of play in an educational setting. A playful team of educators began this grassroots movement with two goals in mind—to educate the world about the power of play and to get us all playing! Educators are encouraged to use a regular school day to teach students, parents, colleagues, and administration about the benefits and necessity of play. We may be a tad biased, but this book and the research it contains would be a great resource for all educators to use in support of this fantastic day, and to make it a weekly, even daily, practice that becomes part of our school cultures. On their website, Global School Play Day organizers offer these tips:

- *Don't organize* anything for your students.
- *Don't tell them how to play* with the toys/games.

- *Don't interfere* with your students unless you see something that could get you fired or would physically hurt a child (this does not include something that may be physically uncomfortable for a child).
- *Don't leave them unsupervised*—the day is unstructured by adults, but not unsupervised.

If we were bettin' kind of folks, we would almost guarantee you read those first three tips and had some heart palpitations. Before you catch the vapors, remember back to Section 3 and trust. They can do this. You can do this. The most difficult part of the process for adults during moments of free play is to not interfere. As educators, we often want to jump in and make sure the teachable moments aren't missed. Being aware of those moments makes you a great teacher in our book, but during free play we have to practice the time, space, and opportunity model we have mentioned so often. In this scenario, students need time to figure things out, space without you in it, and the opportunity to learn independently.

Most important, the fourth bullet above reminds us that supervision is always a must in the school setting. Eyes and ears open at all times. Safety is paramount!

Whenever you visit their website and learn more about Global School Play Day, we hope that you add your class, school, or district to the list of players. If it has already passed as you read this, create your own day of play until the next one rolls around! Kudos to the amazing committee of educators who created this opportunity to bring awareness to the power of play and connect it to the global community:

**Global School Play Day Team**
Eric Saibel @ecsaibel
Misty Higgins @mistynorman12
Oliver Schinkten @schink10
Scott Bedley @scotteach
Tim Bedley @tbed63
Bethany Chaffin @bethanychaffin
Jon Samuelson @jonsamuelson
Lindsay Stewart @lindstew

# Global Read Aloud

Reading in and of itself is fun and playful for millions of people around the world. While the body may not be physically active, the mind is running through a rainforest filled with the world's most beautiful foliage as the rainbow or parrots and dart frogs squawk and croak. See what we did there? See how playful reading can be? We are ready to pack our bags and head to the Amazon right now! Reading with a friend can be even more playful. Book clubs, book talks, and book studies are all playful learning experiences with a literacy focus. The Global Read Aloud project (http://theglobalreadaloud.com) is an opportunity to show our students how they are part of the larger world. They are one person, but look at all the connections one person can make! How much more impactful it is to talk with the kids we normally only see in pictures from a social studies textbook. How much smaller the world suddenly becomes, for students to know the book they hold in their hands is being read in classrooms across the globe. With connection comes empathy. And don't we all need a little more of that?

From the Global Read Aloud site:

> The premise is simple; we pick a book to read aloud to our students during a set 6-week period and during that time we try to make as many global connections as possible. Each teacher decides how much time they would like to dedicate and how involved they would like to be. Some people choose to connect with just one class, while others go for as many as possible. The scope and depth of the project is up to you. While there are commonly used platforms such as Skype, Twitter, Padlet, or Flipgrid, you choose the tools that will make the most sense for you. Teachers get a community of other educators to do a global project with, hopefully inspiring them to continue these connections through the year.

This amazing experience was created by Pernille Ripp (@pernilleripp) in 2010, and has grown happily ever since.

## Global Maker Day

If your classroom is playful, your students are creating daily. Do they have an authentic audience for their creations? Maybe so. You might have a classroom Twitter account and your sweet cherubs are a tweetin' their beautiful work all day long. What if we told you there was a way to do more? You can:

- Maximize their audience.
- Find more ideas for creation.
- Increase your ROI with global, yes global feedback.
- PLAY!

Global Maker Day (www.globalmakerday.com) is a one-day event during which classrooms can connect virtually and watch other makers discuss their projects, learning spaces, creations, coding, 3D designs, art lessons, etc. Using YouTube Live, classrooms can tune in all day long. Your students can even sign up to present and be added to the schedule.

In addition to the live broadcast, classrooms and educators are sharing student creations on social media using the hashtag #GlobalMakerDay both during and after the event. Whether today is Global Maker Day or not, you can search the hashtag to see all the past creations.

If you are seeking opportunities for maker challenges, creativity, and good ol' play, check out the website and connect with these amazing creators for the movement:

**Global Maker Day Team**
Amy Storer @techamys
Jaime Donally @JaimeDonally
Katie McNamara @KatieJMcNamara
Sarah Thomas, PhD @sarahdateechur
Marialice B.F.X. Curran, PhD @mbfxc
Michael Drezek @m_drez

Playful classrooms

believe ...

Playful classrooms honor everyone's seat at the table—Y'all means all.

There is power in student names—knowing them, saying them, loving them.

Our calling is to create playful experiences that blend student interest with required content.

Community must extend beyond the walls of our classrooms.

# Play Nurtures Growth

## Growth Shapes Our Play

*We can always be better. Let us help each other be more.*

# CHAPTER 34

# The Truth About Success

One of our favorite learning experiences to use in our playful workshops is the card house challenge. We give each group of teachers a deck of cards and ask them to build a structure that is at least five stories tall. We allow them to have three songs worth of time to get their plan together and begin to build.

Almost instantly, the fail.
The cards fall in a heap and they start again.
And again.
And again.
And again.

Yes . . . we meant to put so many again's there because it really paints a picture of what their card house building experience is like. It is very difficult for them, and there are lots of reasons for that. They discover these difficulties as they fail. The cards are new, the surface of the foundation is too slick, they have no prior skills, they need more tools, they need more time. We love that they arrive to these conclusions on their own, but without the time, space, opportunity to try, fail, and grow their skills they would have never been able to reach such conclusions.

After the three songs are finished, and the frustration level brings them close to the "I quit" point, we share with them a video of the tallest free-standing house of cards. It measured 7.86 m (25 ft, 9-7/16 in.) and was built by Bryan Berg (USA) on October 16, 2007, in Dallas, Texas. Berg is the official Guinness World Record holder for his incredible feat (Guinness World Records, n.d.). Once we show the video, we give participants the time to try again. Watching the *professional* gave them new techniques, new angles, and new approaches. Most importantly, it renewed their spirits; where before they were as fast as a herd of turtles, they move now with new gumption.

There's a sign I (Julie) hang in my classroom that has helped clarify reality for many students. I'm not braggin'—that's not classy, and my guess is that Golden Girl Blanche Devereaux would say, "That's unsouthern." I know it has helped students because they tell me. I've sketched it for you here. More about this image in a minute.

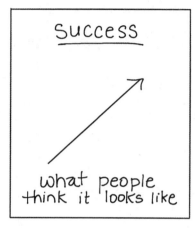

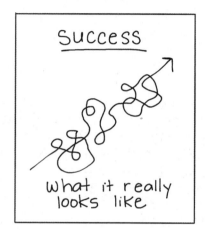

I was born in 1977. My children like to call it "the 19s." If you did not grow up in US schools of the 1980s and 1990s, let me give you a little background. This was an era before state standards were a thing. So, textbooks and teacher experience were depended on for content and knowing what topics to teach. Worksheets were innovative because you could create opportunities for practice on a machine with a crank that rolled out purple-inked paper duplicates. I still remember the ink-stained hands of every teacher in the building. They wore those stains as badges of honor. Teachers were all-knowing—third in command behind Jesus and mama.

Of course, I didn't care about this as a fifth grader in Mrs. Smith's class (pseudonym here to protect those growing in their profession) at Pine Street School in Walhalla, South Carolina. What I do remember is that I had a cool blue Trapper Keeper, complete with new Lisa Frank stickers. It didn't fit in the cubby under my seat, but that was okay because I looked awesome with it propped up on the side of my desk. And, early in the year, I knocked it out of the park with my oral report on Clara Barton (complete with costume). That *knocked it out of the park* phrase? That's my impression. In reality, I earned a "B" on that assignment. Not an 88 or an 82. Just a "B" at the top of my paper. In red. As I write this, I'm eight days away from turning 42 years old. I can still see the B. I'm sure you have a similar story of a school moment you can visualize clearly. Success was defined in my 9-year-old brain as "those who earned A's." I knew this fact because Mrs. Killough, my third grade teacher, taught me the shortest distance between two points is a straight line.

I wanted to be successful. I wanted A's. So, I worked harder. (See that straight line there?)

Mind you, I had no idea what I was doing to earn the B versus the A. I don't remember a rubric or explanation of what makes a good oral report. No, I didn't forget this part of the story. That memory is part of the vividness of this moment—my confusion at how to move that B to an A. My wonder at what I did wrong.

But, heavens—don't dare ask the teacher. In our southern culture, children, especially in my family, do not question authority. It's disrespectful. I, of course, interpreted this as, "Do not ask questions of authority." See what happened in my brain? I could see the "shortest distance," but I was stuck. And I had no way of finding out. I thought that straight line to success was the way. You see, any grade that wasn't an A was a setback for me. It wasn't up-to-par. It wasn't the ideal. So, my line of success takes a turn. Why wasn't I moving forward? No one was there to tell me I really was growing. It may not have happened for my report on Clara, but it was happening in so many other ways. Of course, that's content for another chapter. What I want to explain here is that my perception of growth was so very off. So very incorrect.

Now, back to the picture I mentioned earlier hanging in my classroom. When students see this illustration, they say things like, "Is that really how it happened for you?" Or, "Is that right?" Either way the reaction comes, it's always followed with something like, "Well, that's comforting," or, "maybe add a few more squiggles and you'll have my life." Same, girl. Same. Honestly, I'm usually still reeling from them thinking I'm already successful. Aren't we all still on our journeys?

9 year old Julie

Isn't that truth beautiful? We are who we are because of the experiences we've had. When I look at all the squiggles in that image, I try to imagine life without all the twist and turns. Good gravy, how boring life would be if everything was that straight line from A to B that I grew up thinking was THE WAY to grow. Every up, down, left, right, loop-da-loop, zig and zag provided me, and provides you, with opportunities to grow. Many of those moves were full of moments of laughter and play that led to more laughter and play all as a result of mistakes, try-agains, and lessons learned that led to great understanding. We have to start thinking about schooling with this perspective. We grow because of our mistakes. We grow because of either what we did wrong or because we watched our friends do something wrong. We grow because of ups, downs, lefts, rights, loop-da-loops, zigs, and zags. It's personal. We remember. The learning sticks, and playful moments can be the glue that helps it stay put.

## Blubber and a Little Grit

Have y'all ever tried something brand new in your classroom only to have it fail miserably? Of course you have. We all have. It's what makes us great educators. If you haven't, give it a go. Pick an action item from Section 7, and try it tomorrow. If it fails, figure out why and try it again. It's called reflective practice. It's what keeps us growing.

JED:     *I sure reflected when my blubber lesson collapsed in a heap of, well. . .*

*Here's what happened.*

This was early in my career . . . say 2003. I had found on the interwebs (that's what we called it back then) this lesson that would help students understand how blubber keeps animals warm in the Arctic. The lesson called for two main materials: plastic baggies that snap closed and lard. Think Crisco. If there is one thing we have readily available here in my hometown of Boiling Springs, South Carolina, it is lard (Cowpens, South Carolina, too, says Julie). My granny kept a case of it on hand because you never knew when someone was gonna pass away and you'd need to fry up a mess of chicken to deliver for a family's supper.

This blubber bag lesson is not a new idea. By the time you've read this paragraph, we'd bet it's been done and shared a zillion times on social media. But at *that* time, when we were hearing the first notes of Beyonce being "Crazy in Love," it was new, and I was excited to bring the playful, engaging experience to my firsties.

I got the plastic baggies all prepped and ready with the lard as the plan called for. I had buckets of ice-cold water for each of my five groups. While the kids were at PE, I got everything set up. I invited the principal to come observe the awesomeness so I could earn some extra jewels in my crown.

When the students returned to class, we jumped right into the experience. First, in a nod to B. F. Skinner, I modeled for them the correct way to put their hands inside the bag. The baggies had been doubled so that there was a baggie, lard, then another baggie—the intent was to keep the lard off the hands. What a mess, right? After the students placed their hand inside the bag, they submerged the bag in the bucket of cold water. Make sense?

I S'wanee. The first few rounds went purty as a peach. All our hands were being protected by the "blubber" from the bucket full of ice cold water just like Arctic animals are protected from the cold habitats they live in. It wasn't 'til little Johnathan opened up one of the bags that all of the real fun started. Real fun being that blubber got all over Johnathan, then Dulce . . . then Miriam . . . then Shyquasia . . . then Curtis . . . then . . . .

Y'ALL!!!! HELP!!! WHAT HAPPENED????? OMG!!! There was lard all over that room. Lard. Grease. Like shiny, slippery ewwww. All. Over. The. Room. On the desks, on the floor, on the walls, in their mouths, in their hair, and all over their clothes. If ever I needed Carrie Underwood's "Jesus, Take the Wheel," it was at that moment. Too bad she wouldn't sing that song for two more years.

It was a disaster. Four kids had to call mama for new clothes. One had to get cleaned up by the nurse. One had to just go home and start over. I failed.

But . . . I didn't give up. I continued trying that experience every school year moving forward. Honestly, it got better and better every time I did it. I added different components, I adjusted the parts that didn't work just right, and *most* importantly, I double, triple, quadruple checked to make sure those baggies were sealed. I also made a point to tell the story of my failure each year so that the students would learn that failure is an opportunity for growth, not for quitting when it comes to learning.

This story might lead you to think you have to pick your area and keep practicing until you hone your craft. Start now and keep at it. 10,000 hours of deliberate practice, right? Well, here's a riddle for you.

> What do Roger Federer, Duke Ellington, and Michelangelo have in common?
>
> Answer: They didn't specialize in their known field when they were young. Federer might hold 20 Grand Slam singles titles, but he didn't start out playing tennis. In fact, he played everything from soccer to ping pong. Duke Ellington skipped music lessons to draw and play baseball; and Michaelangelo preferred poetry as a young man (he even wrote about how much he hated painting!) (Epstein, 2019). Why do we bring up these random stories? As just another example that life stories are not straight lines. Those loop-da-loops? They have a purpose. Whatever we're drawn to at the moment holds a lesson for us in our growth trajectory.

This truth is inherent to the nature of play. We bet you missed the first time you aimed a ball at the rim of a basket. Lord knows Jed did. Whenever you see him, ask him about his ball-playing experiences. You may want to take one of Granny's little pills first. He has some doozies to share, and not all of his playful moments are great memories, but they are definitely moments where learning and growth occurred. In one example, he learned the hard way that standing too close to home plate while the pitch is coming will leave a real "purdy" bruise on your love-handle.

All endeavors come with opportunities for failure and growth. In fact, we bet you kneaded that Play-Doh to death before it resulted in your own personal masterpiece. Hopefully, no one tried to crush your sculpting dreams as you worked the dough into what would become your most prized piece of childhood artwork.

# CHAPTER 35

# Encourage a Spirit of Growth

In the world of play and creativity, the benefits come as the adults in our lives nurture and guide, not squash and control. As educators, we must be careful of the language we use with our students. Our words should always encourage and empower students to continue on the path of their learning regardless of the obstacles that may arise.

Be mindful the next time you say or hear:

- No, you can't draw a pumpkin like that.
- Santa is supposed to wear a red suit, not a purple one.
- That LEGO sculpture doesn't look like the Eiffel Tower.
- Turtles don't wear top hats.
- That's not the way you are supposed to do it.
- We've never done it that way.

Sadly, all of those comments above are phrases we've heard from teachers personally or know someone who has. The Santa comment happened to a teacher friend of ours when she was in first grade. Her teacher fussed at her because she "did it wrong." Our question: *How can one color a fictional character wrong?* It is all make-believe. It just so happened that our friend's favorite color was purple and she wanted to put her Santa in a purple suit. How many of my neighbors put out Santas dressed in the colors of their favorite football team? Maybe the student who colored his suit purple would have started that movement of team-colored Santas years before it was a thing, yet her creativity was stifled because "that's not the way you do it."

Sigh. . . What a sad day for our friend's creativity. It was squashed. She told us she never got "out of line" again.

Learning should be fun, and the more engaging it is the better. This is where the grease meets the squeak—invite a playful spirit into everything you do. Play is for everyone, not just the littles. Like our friends at the US Play Coalition say on their t-shirt: "Play is a human right!"

Julie

Jed

I (Julie) can hear the whispering now. You're sitting on your front porch with your glass of sweet tea or wine (no judgment, but I'm Baptist and we don't talk about that), just a blessin' my heart because I clearly am not aware of your carefully planned Vygotsky-approved direct instruction lessons in which you scaffold instruction through the zone of proximal development (ZPD).

Oh, that's cute. See us waving at you from the street? Invite us up on that porch for a chat. We'll rock beside you and comment on your pretty garden, and while we are chitchatting, we'll also share with you that Vygotsky's zone is based on studies of play. Yep, I know. Can you believe it? Lawsy me. Fan, fan, rock, rock.

> *Play is the source of development and creates the zone of proximal development. Action in the imaginary sphere, in an imagined situation, the reaction of voluntary intentions and the formation of real-life plans and volitional motives—all appear in play and makes it the highest level of preschool development.*
>
> (Vygotsky, 1977)

For Vykotsky, play was *imagination in action* (Hakkarainen & Brdikyt, 2014; Vygotsky, 2005)—whether we are kindergartners who become firefighters in the dress-up center or we're eighth graders who insert themselves in a creative work to both build and showcase empathy.

We know that some of you can't fathom a dress-up center in the eighth grade, but just like mama says about spinach, how do you know you don't like it if you haven't tried it? Of course, we have a story about middle schoolers wearing costumes to learn. Get cozy and take a listen.

I (Jed) was invited by a third-year middle school teacher (first year at her current school) to do some model lessons. She wanted her students more engaged in their reading but was struggling to make her lessons fun and inviting. I accepted her invitation and began to think of a playful plan. Now mind you, I have never taught middle school. Julie has, and I have learned a lot from her about the craft; but I do know about engagement, fun, and play in the classroom. My early childhood background has taught me that most people love to learn just like they did when they were little (little as in K–2nd grade). Adults, just like the littles, love to have their hands on their learning, creating, doing, experimenting, playing. As I prepped for the day of learning with her eighth-grade students, I kept that thought in mind throughout the planning and created a lesson that I was pretty proud of. Only time would tell if it was effective with her disengaged students.

I can't lie about it. The morning I drove to her school, I was as nervous as a cat on a porch full of rockers. Middle schoolers intimidate the mess out of me. As a student, I was bullied relentlessly during that time of my life, and I carry it into every middle school I have ever visited to this day. I was doubting myself, my abilities, and most assuredly, my own intellect, for agreeing to such a daunting task. But, in the spirit of growth, I accepted the challenge, and on to the school I went in spite of my anxiety demanding that I turn around.

When I pulled in the parking lot I whispered a little "Lord help me," and unloaded the supplies I brought into my big blue wagon I pull behind wherever I go. It was slam full of two plastic storage bins of costumes. There was a Spider-Man mask, a judge's robe, a blue curly wig, a crab hat, a pig nose, a light-up tie, and a ton of other items that I hoped would be a huge hit with the kids. There was no shortage of possible attire for the class.

Arriving to her classroom during her planning was probably the best and worst thing to my whole day. Best being that no students were in there yet, and worst being that it was just enough time for me to explain to her my plan and see the doubting look on her face that crushed my dreams of a playful lesson. I ignored her lack of confidence and remembered that she had invited *me* to help her, took a deep breath, and waited as the kids started to arrive.

As they began to enter, I greeted them at the door wearing a brown wig and a Napoleon Dynamite T-shirt that said "Vote for Pedro." As I welcomed them, I spoke in character as if I had a pocket full of tots and my uncle was just outside tossing a football beside his RV. It was epic. Immediately students came in engaged, intrigued, and ready to see what class that day was all about. Napoleon instructed students to grab their own dress-up items from the bins and fall into their own character's role. At first they seemed a bit timid, but the more I played into my role, the more they accepted theirs. If nothing else happened beyond that moment, learning had happened, and the classroom that was normally disengaged had become fully focused and ready to learn. It was amazing to see how a small moment of playfulness opened up the class to be ready to engage. Had I taught the entire next hour in lecture format from behind a podium or beside an overhead projector, I am confident the kids would have learned. Just the change in scenery. . . errr attire, had invited a playful spirit into the class, which made the opportunity for learning readily available. But the fun was only just beginning.

As Napoleon, I discussed the novel the students were reading at the time, *Holes* by Louis Sachar. While it was not a traditional eighth-grade level book, the teacher knew the reading level of her class was a bit lower than average and selected this particular text because students had expressed an interest in reading it.

Here's the truth about encouraging a spirit of growth. You need to hear this first. We don't want to beat around the bush.

We must imagine to grow.

We must have the freedom to dream up new ideas.

If you're not asking questions, you're not growing.

We must have the opportunity to play with ideas.

Play includes failure—failure without penalty or judgment.

The intent of this part of the book is to explain how play and playful teaching inspire growth. To do that, we have to make sure we all understand the neuroscience of thinking and what happens when cognition expands. So let's start with some science.

# CHAPTER 36

# Your Brain, an Infomercial

The brain cells we want to focus on here are nerve cells, also called *neurons*. A typical neuron has a *soma* (the cell body), *dendrites*, and one *axon*. When a thought occurs, electromagnetic activity travels down the axon and is transferred to neighboring neurons via a synapse (viewed as the shading). The synapse occurs across a small gap between the neurons. The neighbor neuron receives the action via its dendrites (long feathery filaments that look like tree branches).

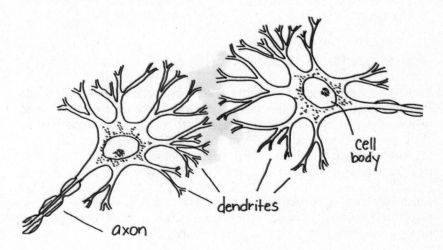

Uh oh, I (Julie) see some glazed-donut eyeballs on our readers. Let's pause for a playful metaphor here. Think of our buddy neurons as kids wearing Spider-Man costumes, tossing a ball back and forth. Each time the ball is tossed, an electrical impulse is emitted. To receive the ball, the kid sends out his spider web, err dendrite, to grab and pull the ball in.

Better? Now speed up this picture in your head 50 times faster. No, that's not an arbitrary number. A typical neuron fires 5–50 times every second. Each link created will then either be strengthened with repeated use or atrophy and fade for lack of use (like that phone number you don't remember anymore). Don't be concerned about the word *atrophy* though—this part is great! It's what makes our brains plastic. No, not milk jugs. Not exactly. *Neuroplasticity:* the ability for nerve systems to change and grow. Each new experience and each remembered event slightly rewires the brain's physical structure. This means that who you are today is not the same as who you were 10 years ago. And, thank heavens for that, right? Our potential is limitless. Remember the days when we determined potential based on an assessment?

Those intellectual quotient (IQ) tests? Obsolete. One score on one day for one test does not define you, friend. Not anymore. Truthfully, they never did.

So that's what happens when we have general thoughts. What happens if those thoughts are incorrect? What if the thought is incomplete? We're getting to the best part. I know, I know. Just get to the punchline already!

## Your Brain Makes an Oops

In 2011, while the space shuttle *Discovery* was launching for the last time and the US Supreme Court was thinking about vouchers in Arizona schools, a group of scientists made some pretty cool discoveries about mistakes. Psychologist Jason Moser of Michigan State University and his team studied the neural activity that occurs when people make mistakes (Moser, Schroder, Heeter, Moran, & Lee, 2011). Y'all ready for this? (No, not C&C Music Factory.) They saw that mistakes cause a synapse to fire. But not just that, because I know . . . this is no different from what you just read. There are two types of error synapses:

1. An error-related negativity (ERN) response is when the brain experiences conflict between a correct answer and an error.
2. A error positivity (Pe) response is when conscious attention is drawn to errors.

OK, I see your eyebrows getting scrunchy. (Yes, says Jed. You lost me at ERN.) It's starting to feel like you need to create flash cards, and some cold sweat might be busting out on your forehead. Relax, though; you don't need to remember the types; just know that there are two ways this can go, but each way is *good*. This cool science means we don't even have to know we made a mistake for the brain to react. The brain sparks and grows either way. Our brains are so cool that they sense a conflict, synapses spark, and growth occurs whether we are consciously aware of it or not. The takeaway here is that mistakes are a good thing.

Not only do mistakes create teaching and learning opportunities, but they create neurological growth!

## Wait, So What About Tests? What About Grades?

I'm starting to wear out my welcome with some of you. I can feel it. You're about to be like my friend, Wendy's daddy when he's had enough of company. He'd turn to her mama and say something like, "Honey, let's you and me go on to bed so these nice folks can go home." Yes, grades are a polarizing topic in school conversation these days, but we'd be remiss if we didn't share with you what's on our hearts. You can bless our hearts later, but we're hoping you don't.

You see, when students know work is going to be graded, most will try their best not to make mistakes. That's not surprising, we know.

But this is a flawed system. If we know from neuroscience that mistakes allow for growth, what we should be doing is creating mistake-rich environments—encouraging students to contribute ideas without fear of being wrong.

Math professor Jo Boaler is doing this very thing with her YouCubed math camp at Stanford University. In this camp, which typically lasts over four weeks, Dr. Boaler and her students work with local school districts to create mindset shifts toward math. Students from local districts, who might be described as underachieving and disillusioned with math, come together to work on difficult, open maths problems in a mistake-rich setting. Errors and discussion are invited. There are no grades, no penalties to the opportunity for critical thinking. Just a pre- and post-test to measure the impact of this type of instruction.

The result? In 2015, with a mere four weeks of open questions, opportunities for deliberation over quadratics and other topics resulted in an average of 50 percent improvement (Boaler, 2015).

They didn't pass out a study guide.

They didn't have a Friday-test.

They didn't tell kids to study or reward them with suckers for daily improvement (why do we do this?!).

Instead (here's the kicker), they let kids experience what it's like to be a mathematician. They encouraged disequilibrium, trusted them to take their learning seriously, and the students learned.

Are you ready to hear more? We'll show you how you can create these kinds of playful, mistake-rich classrooms. Trust us. We're not preaching without any testimony. It's a comin'. Before that, though, let us clarify a little snippet we dropped in a few paragraphs back.

## Learning Thresholds?

We mentioned IQ tests earlier. Alfred Binet, a distinguished looking fella with a pointy mustache, was commissioned by the French government to create an assessment that would identify which students in France might experience difficulty in school. Binet and his buddy, Theodore Simon (both of whom I'm sad to tell you have no playful photo results in any of our searches), thus created the Simon-Binet IQ in 1904. We Americans got interested, and popped in this assessment convo in 1916 when Stanford psychologist Lewis Terman standardized Binet's original tests using a sample of American participants. So, like your FINALfinalFINal3reallythistimeImeanit.docx file, this Stanford-Binet test has gone through multiple revisions over the years. A FINALfinalFINal3reallythistimeImeanit.docx version of the IQ test continues to be used in school districts today.

FinalfinalFINal3rea
llythistimeImeanit.docx

The belief that a person's intelligence can be represented with a score from one paper-pencil test needs so many *bless your heart*s. Y'all. Really? Some of you might know the story I'm about to tell, but I'm gonna tell ya anyway. In 1968 or thereabouts, some sneaky scientists did a thing. They told teachers a few t-waddy tales about their students. They told these tales across six grade levels. See, they were smart: this was no small study. Teachers were led to believe their students had been tested and were grouped specifically according to those intelligence tests. They had the brightest students in the grade! Lies. The students were actually randomly grouped in the classes. There was no IQ sorting hat. So what happened? Those tales made an impact, is what happened! Lawsy, yes. After one year (*one year!*) student IQ scores matched the teacher's false beliefs (Rosenthal & Jacobson, 1968). Yes, the scores on their IQ tests changed according to what their teachers expected. Y'all. This was the late 1960s. We knew then about neuroplasticity, but yet we kept on believin' that test was king to all curricular decisions.

Our expectations are critical to student success. We talk about playful sociability in Chapter 1, but don't go thinking this just applies to recess conversations. Our words impact perceptions; perceptions impact people. We must block any label that comes our way before we have a chat with the children. And we don't mean only grades K–3. That seventh grader and that high school senior appreciate the fact that you want to know them before you read their file.

## The Power of Our Words

Do you need a more recent example? In 2014, we were all watching the World Cup in Brazil. Around that time, researchers at Stanford and the University of Colorado were testing the effects of perception, specifically in the receipt of teacher feedback. Teachers of a high school English course allowed researchers to add one additional sentence to their general student feedback: *I am giving you this feedback because I believe in you*. Only half of their students received this sentence, and the teachers didn't know which students got the extra umph. The result? Those students who got the extra sentence were earning higher marks one year later. There were no other differences in the groups.

That sentence you just read really matters to the research. The fact that there were *no other identifiers* that differentiated these groups helps us draw conclusions and make generalizations about the experiment. That specific quality leads us to this question: How can it be that *one sentence* could change the academic trajectory for these students?!? And even more so for children of color, who often feel less valued by their teachers (Cohen, Garcia, Apfel, & Master, 2006; Cohen, Steele, & Ross, 1999). Clearly, what we say to children makes a difference. Listen, we know you didn't just fall off the turnip truck, but sometimes we do well to have a reminder.

Children, just like the rest of us, need reminders that they matter.
That we care about them.
About their growth.
They need to know we value them.
They need to know they matter.

# CHAPTER 37

# Creating a Culture of Growth Through Play

Julie: My youngest daughter came home today with her weekly papers stapled. She flipped through them just before handing them over for the top paper's signature, and I watched her face fall. She got very quiet, and I noticed the muscles around her forehead and eyebrows move. After a pause, she said, "I got a B. (eyes still on the paper) But Mrs. **** said this paper was just to show what we know. She told us if we didn't know it to skip it. But she graded it. Why did she grade it, mama?"

OK—there are clearly many thoughts here. Why is a 10-year-old putting this amount of pressure on herself for one grade? I can tell you that this mama, who is anti-traditional-grading, did not instill this fear of the feedback alphabet (ABCDF). Why are so many of us educators communicating a growth mindset with our words, but using a grading system that represents the antithesis of growth? This situation focuses on one particular score on a math quiz. Just guess her motivation to complete her math homework (a consumable textbook worksheet—*don't even get me started*) afterward? Null. In fact, she huffed and puffed through it. I share this story not to bash or gossip about my child's teacher. Not at all. In fact, the story is not unique to South Carolina. It happens around the world every day.

Carol Dweck, who coined the term *growth mindset*, tells us that children who learn in a culture where intelligence can be shaped like a muscle enjoy mistakes; they see them as opportunities to learn (1999). We know that mistakes lead to brain growth and opportunities for learning. In the early chapters of Section 6 you read the neurological processes. Are you convinced yet? Are you a believer? It's time we start talking about how to get there. Right now, it might seem like it's over yonder, or take the second left past Aunt Frannie's barn, but it's really not that complicated. How do we take a stand and affect change?

It starts with mindset.

Mindset leads to intentional planning.

Intentional planning leads to experiences.

Experiences lead to confidence.

Confidence leads to spontaneity with experiences.

These experiences beget experiences beget experiences beget . . . you understand.

Playful classrooms aligned with a growth mindset frequently demonstrate the following (Boaler, 2019):

- Develop an inquiry relationship with the subjects you teach. The teacher regularly shares how learners approach the unknown. We **model inquiry with a WISH**: wonder, imagination, spontaneity, and HUZZAH!
- Allow students time for **playful communication and collaboration**. Give them time to talk with each other about their ideas. Why did they choose this particular approach? Where else does it work? As students collaborate, ask them to determine how their methods are similar to/different from each other.
- Invite students to experience **multiple playful paths**. Let them play with concepts or problems that have multiple solutions and/or multiple paths to a solution.
- Make **playful learning accessible** to all students. Classroom experiences begin with an approachable and fun task, which becomes more complicated as students explore. These experiences have a low entry point but a high ceiling, allowing students to work at the highest and most appropriate level for them.
- **Playful curricular integration** should occur frequently, allowing students to work across curricular areas to showcase understanding of real-world tasks through a variety of play personalities.
- **The language of playful teaching** incorporates the philosophy and science of growth mindset through grouping, through their tasks, through the spoken messages, and through the methods of assessment.
- **Play is valued as a way to assess learning**. These assessments inform learning and future instruction, rather than to provide

rank among peers. Students receive regular diagnostic feedback for growth, but this feedback is not punitive or intended as external rewards or punishments.

Let's break it down, shall we? Here you go. Get a refill and pull up a chair.

## Modeling Inquiry with a WISH

While reading one of the popular *Boxcar Children* books, students might become intrigued by the squirrel who is trapped in the main character's attic. They begin to **wonder** how you might get rid of a squirrel in your attic, some even championing the rights of animals when one student says, "Grab your BB gun!" With clean trash and general classroom supplies, the teacher challenges them to design a trap for a squirrel (represented by a tennis ball). For days, these students use their **imaginations** to determine what will both (a) lure and (b) trap the squirrel. They design, test, and redesign their prototypes. The **spontaneity** of ideas from both their own group's collaboration as well as ideas they spy in others' groupwork spurs them on, often altering their ideas and shaping their contributions. The awaited moment comes when groups are given a chance to present and discuss their prototypes. The group questions and feedback. Being the expert, and responding to inquiries from their peers. That moment. That feeling. That's **HUZZAH**!

We had the chance to witness first graders do just this in a local school classroom. The teacher had not written "The student will design. . ." in her plan book. She had not ordered materials, nor had she designed a paper-pencil assessment to determine growth. She simply listened to the ideas of her students and responded to the opportunity. This is playful teaching.

## Playful Communication and Collaboration

You read about play as a cultural phenomenon in Section 4. Just like the hunter-gatherer children, our students need to engage in play for development in personal, social, and cognitive realms. Culture shapes our view of collaboration; therefore, we cannot consider one without the other. If our classroom culture isn't open to alternative viewpoints, we risk tunnel vision. We know we cannot grow if we are not challenged to explain, justify, shape, and reframe thinking. No one wants to exist in an echo chamber. We might still be thinking the world is flat! A mindset of "This is how we've always done it" can lead to harmful and even dangerous attitudes because of our individual cultural limitations. A playful classroom values diversity and works toward understanding culture. A playful classroom is sensitive to the dynamics inherent when people come together.

In a playful classroom, we often see the role of teacher and student shift from person to person. Sometimes, the student is the teacher. Sometimes it's the other way 'round. Playful collaboration allows students to become a teacher in their own domain. This role shifting is important for us to dive deep in problem solving: it helps us better understand problems and more effectively work together to design solutions. The way to enhance collaboration in a playful classroom is to work against becoming dogmatic, rather, striving for pragmatism and holistic thinking.

## Multiple Playful Paths

You've heard how a child at age four has 100 questions and a child in the fourth grade fields 100 questions from the teacher. It may be a cliché in our field, but how sad. Why the steep decline? This is clearly a call to action. We have to shift the culture of the classroom to not only invite questions but also to honor the zig-zig course of seeking the answers. Our educator colleagues John Spencer and AJ Juliani (2016) tout the need for classroom creativity in their book, *Launch*. It was in this text that my attention was brought to the method of thinking by more than 70 creative geniuses in the use of *notebooks and sketches*.

I keep a notebook. I sketch my ideas. I have a running list of projects. I jot notes from books I read. I write down funny phrases I hear. I create lists of my goals. I reflect. I . . .

How many of us have this kind of process? Do you see how many paths there are to follow in this list? If our honored geniuses do this, why not our students? Caution: I do not mean the cutesy interactive journal where worksheets are inserted with a glue stick.

This kind of notebook is a teacher product, not a student product. Which notebook would the student be most proud of?

How many of the assignments we give have a clear solution? Do you find yourself giving feedback with an answer key by your side? Let us challenge all educators, right here (including ourselves): if we can give feedback with an answer key, our assignments need a redesign. Problems with one solution don't invite conversation in the same way as those with multiple possibilities. It seems much easier to create these opportunities in science (design) and social studies (perspectives and source analysis) than in mathematics. Well, it seemed that way for me. But that was before I realized my lens on the subject of mathematics was all wrong. Math is not worksheets. Math is not the even-numbered problems on page 42. Math is the study of patterns. Math is playing, yes *playing*, with numbers. Of course, we want our students to develop number sense. But which of the following math problems does this better (Figures 37.1 and 37.2)?

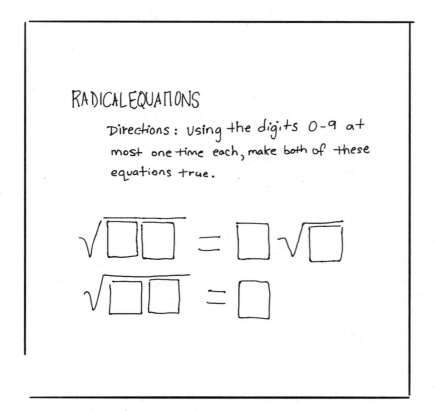

FIGURE 37.1  Open middle radical challenge (Kaplinsky, 2019).

Simplify each radical expression.

1. $4\sqrt{24} - 7\sqrt{150}$

2. $\dfrac{7}{\sqrt{6}}$

3. $\dfrac{12}{8 + \sqrt{5}}$

4. $\sqrt{98x^8 y^5 z^9}$

**FIGURE 37.2** Practice working with radical expressions.

We argue that the opportunities found in open middle math experiences allow more opportunities for students to:

1. Make sense of problems and persevere in solving them.
2. Reason abstractly and quantitatively.
3. Construct viable arguments and critique the reasoning of others.
4. Model with mathematics.
5. Use appropriate tools strategically.
6. Attend to precision.
7. Look for and make use of structure.
8. Look for and express regularity in repeated reasoning.

Does that list look familiar? It should if you've had any encounter with the Common Core Standards for Mathematical Practice (n.d.). This is not a political statement; it's a question of our shared goals. Do we not want each of those eight behaviors for our students? Heavens, for ourselves? Of course we do.

# Accessible Play

We are sure you have realized by now that we are proud to be from the South. Living down here isn't always easy, especially when you step out of the social norms like we often do. If you're not from here, all you might have heard is from your history textbook. Lord, there have been a mess of catastrophic wrongs and incredible injustices against humanity, and we're working to make those right (some more actively than others). In so many parts of our Southern history, accessibility was not available for all people. We must work to change that, and playfulness is an avenue where the good parts of who we are can come together.

We say all this because the next example might throw you for a loop.

Imagine a watermelon seed–spitting contest. Yes, we said it. It is part of our culture. So many of our friends have childhood memories of sitting on porches eating a cold slice of watermelon on a hot July day. 'Cept the seed, you don't swallow the seeds because then you'll grow a watermelon in your belly. So, what do you do with the seeds? You spit them out. One summer we even had a watermelon vine grow next to our front porch because that's where all the seeds landed when we spit them out the summer before. What a playful learning moment that was!

Now, know this, I (Julie) can't stand watermelon seeds. True story: I pick them all out before that red juicy bite goes in my mouth. But in the South, we've got all kinds—watermelons and people. As we start back to school in August in these parts, watermelons are still plentiful, and they make for a great back-to-school playful learning experience. We can easily use this abundant resource as an entry into forces and motion to kick off the year's first science inquiry unit. It's playful. Most everyone can spit, and the reasoning behind strong force and seed distance is clear. This kind of playful approach makes learning accessible. From here, we can

- Measure with nonstandard and standard units.
- Plant the seeds to begin study of a plant's life cycle.
- Study champion spits by age, graphing the data and analyzing its meaning.
- Use sidewalk chalk markers to create a *huge* bar graph.

No watermelons where you live? What if you give everyone plain white copy paper and tape with the challenge to design a costume? Most all students can put paper and tape together. This task has a clear low entry point. But look at the possibilities:

- Visual representation of ideas
- A model to showcase understandings of a reading passage on costumes (comprehension)
- Independent study of how costumes are influenced by culture and politics
- Creation of a pattern for real-life costume design (spatial reasoning and application of nets)

The opportunities are only limited by the size of our imaginations. Start with one experience that all can do, and see where it takes you!

## Playful Curricular Integration

We don't just teach science. We don't just teach social studies or history. We don't just teach math. We all teach literacy, history, math, music, art, community-building, social skills, spelling—all of it. Yes, even you, higher ed philosophy professor.

One of the easiest ways to integrate our curriculum is to start with literature. For every unit we teach, there is a story waiting to be read. When we read to students, we open up new worlds. Those new ideas generally have a setting. Why not take that moment to utilize Google Earth and take the class from where we are to where we're reading about?

Now, instead of a math block, ELA block, and science block, we have a "Here's what we're going to learn" block. Instead of approaching the curriculum as unique, individual compartments, visualize a web made from interconnected pieces of silk. Reading is science is math is chemistry is biology is history is calculus. While each subject has its own methodologies, a playful classroom teacher, like the talented spider, can weave the learning into a beautiful mosaic of discovery and wonder.

Have you ever watched a spider spin a web? They usually do it at night as they are preparing to hunt for the evening. It appears to be the most seamless and effortless process. But, the evolutionary history of the spider has taught each little eight-legged wonder to go back and forth and criss and cross for their survival. Our teacher-world is very similar. We don't have time to teach it all. We cannot cover every standard and reinforce social skills and give feedback and grades and develop character, each in its own allotted time. If we want to survive and for our students to thrive, we must evolve into weavers and tie it all together. That takes time. Time and opportunity for growth.

One of our favorite playful educators, Mike Soskil (@msoskil), often tells teachers to start with the experience. Instead of starting with the standards and seeking learning pathways, let's start with the play—the *fun*—and build connections.

When you're looking for a playful experience, try starting with

- Art materials
- Literature
- Global classroom connections
- Games
- Student questions and ideas

For example: Don't just teach about magnets; gather art materials and have students draw a map of a town with roads. Find a book, enter literacy stage right, and read about how magnets push and pull. Using a magnet on the bottom of a car and one underneath the paper, invite students to playfully move the car around town to connect what they read to the real world. Then, using Skype, have students challenge a class across the country to create a map of their town and learn about a new community. The next day, reconvene online to develop an interactive game about magnetism and invite a new classroom to compete in the magnet madness challenge. A student idea mentioned the day before in their online collaboration has now turned into a student-created website, and classrooms all around the world have been invited via Twitter to join in the student-led initiative to help their peers understand the science of magnets.

WOW! See how that snowballed into something amazing? It all started with a playfully integrated experience.

## The Language of Playful Teaching

The impact of Carol Dweck's (1999) work on growth mindsets has clearly changed education. More than just a new district initiative, we should always be reminded of the *why* behind what we do. Let's look at what we know from her research:

- We now know the brain is malleable.
- Learning causes permanent changes in the brain.

- We now know connectivity between neurons changes over time, especially when we experience failure.
- When we believe our brains can grow, we respond differently.
- Telling students they are smart reinforces a fixed mindset, while feedback on effort and hard work develops a growth mindset.

In 1998, Mueller & Dweck worked with a group of 128 fifth graders in a small midwestern town. These were divided into three groups:

1. Feedback on effort ($n = 41$): "You must have worked hard at these problems."
2. Feedback on intelligence ($n = 41$): "You must be smart no at these problems."
3. A control group ($n = 46$) who received no additional feedback.

After praise, the students were asked if they wanted to continue working. They were given 4 minutes to work on 10 additional problems. After this 10, they were told that they had performed "a lot worse." This negative feedback was crucial to this language experiment. All students received the negative statement of their progress. The results of this study supported the researchers' suspicion that praise for effort versus praise for intelligence leads students to have different work goals after failure.

What happened in the follow-up study is interesting. Here, 51 fifth graders (26 girls and 25 boys) from a public elementary school in a large northeastern city were randomly assigned to the same three praise categories. This time though, students were asked, "How well do you expect to do on another set of problems like these?" The researchers received results here that were consistent with the first study. Except, here we have data to look at the future desires of students—what motivates them. The follow-up study revealed intelligence praise led children to wish to continue looking smart, whereas effort praise led children to want to learn new things. The results of this study can be viewed in this chart (Figure 37.3):

Which do we want for our students: a desire to learn, or a perception of "better than"? If we are to cultivate lifelong learners, our language matters. Our words matter.

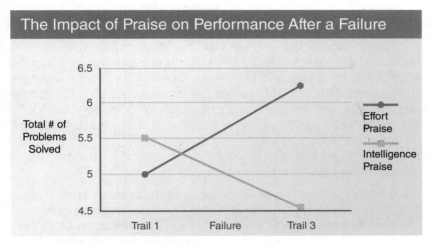

**FIGURE 37.3** The impact of praise on performance after a failure (Mindset-Works, 2017; Mueller & Dweck, 1998).

# Play Is Valued as a Way to Assess Learning

You read about this topic in Section 5, "Community." There's great application here as well. One of our great educator friends, Matt Johnson, now an administrator in Spartanburg School District Two, told us once, "I learn far more about my students when I observe them during a BreakoutEDU session than I ever have from an interest inventory." Isn't this so true? When given an opportunity for play, we see who in a class:

- Is a leader
- Is a quiet thinker
- Is persistent
- Has focus
- Needs to move
- Needs to be still
- Likes to work alone
- Likes to work with others
- Needs teacher or peer support
- Is easily angered
- Has patience

If you've never heard of BreakoutEDU, we will share more about this interactive, gamified learning experience in Section 7.

When children know they are being evaluated, they may behave differently. In fact, I'm pretty sure everyone reading this has studied for a test and known the content, but in the moment of stress-induced anxiety cannot perform as they did during their prep time. When this occurs (and we'd bet it does frequently), do the assessment results really indicate a student's strengths and weaknesses? Of course not.

What if these same skills were embedded in a game? Take a look at these classroom examples:

1.  A high school English class plays *Storyweavers*, a collaborative storytelling game in which students collaborate through play to draft a story. Teachers can craft this in any slidedeck program: Google, PowerPoint, Keynote, etc. Each slide of the game has a set of cards offering choices for plot elements, e.g., setting, conflict. Students spin the wheel and they select cards such as point of view or setting. The student writes a few sentences and the turn shifts to the next player. The teacher is able to observe students during play, ask questions, track their path, and evaluate their choices (Rufo-Tepper, 2015). This game can be expanded to allow practice and assessment of literary devices or types of conflict. The teacher can see clearly how students incorporate these understandings into the work and what topics need more instruction time.

2.  You've heard of the game of charades, where players describe a concept without saying its name? This is easily adapted across the grade levels, allowing the teacher to gather formative assessment about strong or weak conceptual understandings. In a high school geometry class, students might play a game like charades but with a twist. With the incorporation of a coordinate plane, players can use language around the quadrants and axes to create a more complex mental picture.

3.  Michael Matera introduces the concept of three-dimensional note taking on his YouTube channel (@mrmatera). Essentially, students use their class notes to create a 3D model representing these ideas. Materials are varied; in Mr. Matera's video, he utilized blocks, LEGOs, butcher paper, and markers. But you could use anything; some examples are shown here. This idea is clearly a great opportunity for formative assessment (Figure 37.4).

**FIGURE 37.4** 3D Notetaking from @mrmatera's class.

In these examples, students are working in authentic ways, and the teacher can both interact with them (building relationships and community) while offering feedback for growth. All the while, we are playing. The stress is low, and the insight is high. Whether that play takes the form of exploring or directing or creating, the student is in the driver's seat.

For more ideas on play as assessment for learning, see Section 7, *Get Out There and Play!*

# CHAPTER 38

# A Lesson of Play: Nurturing Growth for an Administrator

We have mentioned Matt Johnson, an educator from South Carolina, a few times in this book. Once about how he and Julie chatted at a Christmas party, and another just moments ago as we mentioned how he learns about students through BreakoutEDU. Having seen him in action and being wowed by his work, we thought we'd chat with him as we were writing, so we gave him a call to learn about the role of play in his elementary school, where he is currently an assistant principal with about 650 students. His story fits perfectly in this book, as you will clearly see his growth was nurtured through play.

Matt created a plan for his students called "Guided Recess." After years of watching students at recess, he realized that many of his students just didn't know how to play. For these students, who had experienced years of adult-directed play, the concept of free play was daunting. These were 5- to 10-year-olds—not middle-schoolers sitting like wallflowers at their first coed dance. They should not only know how to play; they should welcome it. But that wasn't what Matt witnessed. Like any great teacher would, he decided to teach them how. Below is an interview we had with him about the process.

**Authors:** **Tell our readers who are you and what you do.**

**Administrator Matt Johnson:** My experience includes 12 years teaching grades 3–6 and 3 years as an elementary assistant principal. My expertise while in the classroom included science, Donors Choose grants, the flipped classroom, and incorporating physical activity during the school day. One of my students' favorite brain breaks was doing burpees to

AC/DC's "Thunderstruck." As a third-grade teacher, I especially loved science labs when we were able to use dry ice, bubbles, and anything that involved making things pop and fizzle. One of my claims to fame, if you ask my former students, was being the quarterback for the students at recess. One of my largest Donors Choose projects was an entire recess package including flag football equipment so that students were safer and had uniforms.

**Authors:** **What questions/concerns did you have about recess? What led you to your questions about recess?**

**Administrator:** I knew I had to find ways to make recess safer, where students made wise choices with their classmates while maintaining fun and engagement. I began collaborating with our PE coach regarding some of the learning experiences I observed in her class, and asked if some of these same games could be transferred to the playground. These needed to be games that were student-led, highly active, and safe for recess.

**Authors:** **What did you hope for/predict would happen as a result of your strategy?**

**Administrator:** What I envisioned were stations where students could play organized games in appropriate spaces with deliberated rules and minimal involvement from their teachers. Long term, I want students to tap into their creativity and begin developing new games or variations of current popular games as well as become introduced to new games and begin practicing skills for sports such as soccer, lacrosse, and others. I also hoped that students would grow in their communication skills and learn to work together when problems arose. I hoped that, when students played games, the fights, injuries, and other problems would decrease and students would be more active. I wanted to collaborate with students to build an environment where recess could be enjoyable again.

**Authors:** **Where'd you get ideas? Who are the stakeholders involved?**

**Administrator:** In addition to the PE coach, I brought my idea to our school's Health and Wellness Committee that is comprised of teachers, students, parents, and local community members. I presented this idea and asked for feedback on whether it could actually produce the results I was hoping for. I shared that our playground used by first through fourth grades would be divided into zones. Each zone would serve a different purpose. Zone 1 would be a partner-style game, zone 2 would be a team game, and then zone 3 would follow the traditional recess we would call "free play." Students were allowed to choose which zone they played in and could rotate as desired without teacher direction.

Our school received a grant for being a part of a healthy schools initiative, allowing us to use money for purchasing water bottles for every student and staff member as well as water-filling stations throughout the school. In addition, we built a fitness and nature trail along with additional PE equipment. The committee suggested we use some of the grant money to purchase game equipment for this new recess initiative. Our PE coach obtained additional funds from miscellaneous grants we were able to use to purchase new play materials.

**Authors:**     **How did you present it to stakeholders? What was stakeholder buy-in initially?**

**Administrator:**     As we began planning the rollout for our new recess model, I anticipated some backlash from students and maybe some parents, especially in the older grades since they were accustomed to our current model of just "go play." I decided on a slow rollout to provide time for teaching new games and provide the time for student buy-in. We called it "Guided Recess," but it was unlike your vision of Guided Reading models. Once a month or so, I would choose a simple game to play with students. My first choice was one students already knew from PE called Frequent Fliers. This rock, paper, scissors game in which the clear "winner" would move from one corner to the next.

I assisted grade levels with a schedule and allowed time, space, and opportunity for practice. Once students saw the fun and experienced the joy of the game's structure, they began to integrate this new game into their recess period on their own. As I anticipated, I began to hear some grumbling from students, so I had to act.

One student, Nathan, did not like guided recess at all. Based on his feedback, I realized that I had actually not given enough voice to the most important stakeholder in the process: the students.

**Authors:** **So, Nathan gave you your first opportunity for reflection. How did you react?**

**Administrator:** I simmered on his idea, and realized that to move forward and see success, I had to honor his voice. I had to put my feelings aside. It didn't happen overnight, but eventually, I mustered up some courage and pulled him aside one day to ask for his thoughts on it all. I have never been so afraid to talk with a third grader. He told me he would rather play games like dodgeball. I asked him about the opinions of his classmates—did they feel the same way? He said he thought so. So, I decided I would survey the students for what games they wanted to play at recess. The survey included games like soccer, dodgeball, football, and then a space for them to add their own ideas. By an overwhelming margin, students selected dodgeball or a game similar.

**Authors:** **So, Nathan was right.**

**Administrator:** Yep. So, I went to our PE coach and asked her thoughts. We settled on a game called Castle Ball where students threw dodgeballs at "castles" made of hula hoops. This quickly became a student favorite—negative comments quickly went away, and the masses were happy.

**Authors:** **Ahh, you had to allow room for growth. What did you learn from this process? What have you learned about play?**

**Administrator:** The biggest lesson through all of this was the importance of student feedback. After Nathan's comments, I developed a recess team with just third and fourth graders. I asked students who I felt would both be honest with me and also those who perhaps do not have the most active lifestyle to give them something to be a part of.

**Authors:**    **So, you considered more than just the kines-thetes. Cool.**

**Administrator:**    Also, without both staff and student buy-in, this approach would have fizzled away and left me frustrated and defeated. My most recent learning is that without student input, no matter how much we enforce rules and regulations, they will also feel frustrated and defeated.

Matt's experience is a story of growth. We've allowed you to watch his process and feel the emotions he felt alongside him. We allowed you to sit and watch his recess movie on the iMAX screen. You've been there, and you're now wearing the T-shirt. But, you don't yet know the beauty of what it means. You might even see opportunities for some fixin' in your own educational world. What do we do about them? How do we move through them? Ah, sweet friends. Like Dorothy, you've had the tools all along. Just click your heels three times. . .

# The Playful Mindset

1. Look for playful moments. They are all around us. (awareness)
2. Provide ourselves and students with time, space, and opportunity. Make a plan to invite playfulness in. (intentionality)
3. Don't be afraid to play, mess up, learn, repeat. Embrace the perceived chaos as part of the learning experience. (process)
4. Keep in mind that the more we play, the more playful we become. On average, it only takes 3–6 weeks to create a routine. (habit)
5. Never forget how playfulness makes us happy. Happy people play. (results)

After we talked with Matt, we could see the playful mindset peeking around the curtain and winking at us throughout his story. Let's unpack, shall we?

First, Matt became aware of the need. He saw kids struggling with their playfulness during the one time of day they should have been enjoying it. The results of their struggles included office referrals and misbehaviors that were leading to lost recess and time away from class. As an administrator with an understanding of the cognitive, social, and emotional relationships inherent to development, it was necessary to craft a plan for time, space, and opportunity to nurture growth through play for his students. Matt was **aware** of the problem, and **intentional** about seeking a solution. He was willing to embrace the **process** to find a solution:

- Talk with teachers.
- Form a committee.
- Write grants for materials.
- Act on phase one of the plan.
- Reflect.
- Invite stakeholders to voice their thoughts.
- Revise.
- Act on phase two.
- Reflect.

Two years into his initiative, the **habits** of playfulness are developing; the school can now celebrate a sharp decrease in the number of recess referrals, kids are actively engaging in the stations without being directed to, and students are taking ownership of the experience by lobbying their administrators for more effective strategies to meet their needs.

In addition to these playful habits, we see **habit** of the cycle. When we are willing to step back and allow for playfulness to occur, we see the cycle be successful, and the cycle itself becomes a habit.

**Results** are not the end of this story. Matt's school is still working through improving their recess times with input from all involved. Results here are the catalyst for cycles' continuation.

Matt's story is one in which he works within the system to inspire change. He is a rogue administrator who believes in the power of play for growth. Don't we all? By now, we hope you see.

Just imagine what could happen if the play revolution grows and we shift the culture of play across the nation. Imagine kids across the globe running outside to play on the 45-minute mark of each hour. Imagine an emphasis on character development that makes students aware of kind choices—less egocentrism and more hearts of citizenship. Imagine the beauty when tent building with blankets and chairs is honored as much as multiplication drills. Imagine a world full of people who trust each other to be playful like the bears in the woods. Imagine the love students will feel when we view them as people first, before their school data. Imagine what can happen when we invite community in our classrooms—local, regional, national, and global.

We can always be better. Let us help each other GROW. . . and be more.

# Playful classrooms
## believe ...

**Everyone has a gift and talent, therefore everyone can experience success.**

**Mistakes are valuable; they encourage brain growth and learning.**

**Problems are solved best when we value diversity and work toward understanding culture.**

**The words we say affect opportunities for growth.**

# Get Out There and Play!

"*She could never go back and make some of the details pretty. All she could do was move forward and make the whole beautiful.*" —Terri St. Cloud

# CHAPTER 39

# The Playful Mindset

We are playful people. The core of our playful spirits comes from the artist background that we both share. Julie is a painter and a writer. Jed is a musician and a creative. Julie's first paintings were born in the back of her Papa's plumbing store on leftover cardboard packaging, and Jed used to bang out Christmas songs on his grandaddy's piano while Alvin sang about a hula hoop on an 8-track tape played nearby. Throughout our professional lives, including the writing of this work together, we have laughed—from chuckles to little tiny accidents—we have spun tales, we have doodled, we have taken notes while walking through the woods, we have made spontaneous calls to members of our community, and we have taken a leap of faith in the work you are holding. However, we need you to know that this work has been a process for us. See that quote under the section header? This work hasn't always been pretty. It has been and continues to be a work in progress. But, as Mary Poppins reminds us, "In every job that must be done, there is an element of fun." So let's get to it.

The arts led both of us to become a different type of learner. Art and the act of creation is our way of playing. We see the world in pictures and hear music in the silence. Julie hears the word stop and immediately spouts out *hammertime, in the name of love*, or *collaborate and listen*. Jed scribbles and doodles his way through every seminar he sits though (while taking up three chairs with all his supplies). As you can tell, we are not limited to one area of the arts. It's like that crafty spider has spun its web and intertwined all the arts inside us.

Over time, the art mindset we shared turned into a playful one. Were they both the same all along? As we close this work, we recall the artist mindset that led us here. The gold nugget is this: we cannot separate the arts and play. Just like the kinesthete and director cannot separate movement and organization from play. No matter the play personality type, all share a process.

# The Playful Mindset

1. Look for playful moments. They are all around us. (awareness)
2. Provide ourselves and students with time, space, and opportunity. Make a plan to invite playfulness in. (intentionality)
3. Don't be afraid to play, mess up, learn, repeat. Embrace the perceived chaos as part of the learning experience. (process)
4. Keep in mind that the more we play, the more playful we become. On average, it only takes 3–6 weeks to create a routine. (habit)
5. Never forget how playfulness makes us happy. Happy people play. (results)

As artists, we have to be aware of our innate desire to create. As playful educators, we must be aware of our students' curiosities. As artists, we have to be intentional to carve out time to create. Playful educators must purposefully incorporate space for play. We all will fail miserably during the process. The more we create and play, the more artful and playful we can became. In the end, play (whatever kind of play) brings results.

After years of reading, researching, and relationship-building in the play community, we came to the conclusion that our artful mindset was really all about play. No matter if we pick up a paintbrush, a ball, a baton, or a book, the process is consistent. It's the path we all walk in our play trajectory. No—not a straight line. A loop-de-loop, a tilt-a-whirl of learning.

We want this book to do three things:

• Provide nuggets of research and best practice so we are confident in our choice to embrace play.
• Challenge us to confront our choices in light of what's best for students.
• Be a resource we can pick up when our playful well runs dry.

Keep this book out; keep it in your line of sight. Grab it for on-the-fly ideas or for inspiration as you create learning experiences. Seek out the people who we've introduced you to. Ask them to be a part of your PLN—your Playful Learning Network. Use the research tidbits to lead you to a deeper understanding of the power of play. Share the brain science with your friends who may need a gentle nudge in their understanding of playful pedagogy.

The playful mindset is a work in progress for us all. In the following chapters, we work through this mindset with several challenges for our readers. As we strive to be more playful—whatever that may mean for each of us—we must follow the play continuum of awareness, intentionality, process, habit, growth.

Piaget helped us understand disequilibrium. Now we use this concept to propel us forward, like a frog flying out of a hot plate. As you read, we challenge you to see where the components of deep play (Section 1, Chapter 2) enter each playful experience. As a reminder, we've noted them again below:

An experience becomes deep play when it . . .

1.  . . . is mentally absorbing, offering challenges and problems to solve.
2.  . . . offers players a new context for using the same skills as work.
3.  . . . offers the same satisfaction as work, but different because the rewards are more clear.
4.  . . . offers a connection to the players' past (childhood memories, home, etc.) (Pang, 2016).

# CHAPTER 40

# Look for Playful Moments (Awareness)

## Challenge #1 Bravery Badges

Being playful makes us vulnerable. It takes courage. Whether we are on the swings all alone or standing at home plate after the winning run on third, we must be brave. A few months ago, we saw a brand of adhesive bandages as we stood in line at Target made by a company called Welly (www.getwelly.com). They had a unique name: Bravery Badges. We instantly knew that we must write about them. Find them. Create your own. Whatever you do, just be sure to remind your students and yourself that play requires courage. Wear them daily as a reminder.

Today, we are gonna be playing a new game. You might not know how to do it at first, but that's OK. You might mess up. You might not win the game. The most important thing I want you to do while we play is to be brave. I have something that you are gonna wear while we play to remind you not to be afraid and to do your very best. It's called a bravery badge.

(any age-appropriate, new game will follow)

Return often to the concept of the badge. Remind students to be brave throughout the day. Notice it happening. Celebrate when it does.

# Challenge #2: Determine the Play Personality Types in My Class. Use That Information to Invite Comfortable Play for All

Use the play personality type assessment in Section 4, Chapter 23, and have a class conversation about the results. We took the test, too. Julie is an artist and a director. Jed is a joker and a collector. He loathes competition. Knowing this about ourselves helps us feel comfort in our decisions. In your conversation with students, develop ideas for each play type and how they can impact your classroom community. The following chart may help get you started. There are additional resources on our website.

| Play personality type | Classroom applications | Additional resources |
| --- | --- | --- |
| Joker | Encourage your jokers to be your door greeters. They will want to make everyone smile or laugh.<br><br>Write a daily funny on the board. Have a submission box for kids to write their own jokes for the board.<br><br>Techy friends might even create a Mr. Johnson's-Joke-A-Day twitter account, managed by students.<br><br>Encourage students to write jokes as part of their curriculum and student choice options.<br><br>Use our laugh cards in your class! | *Humor in School Is Serious Business*, by Dr. Lee Hurren (2010)<br><br>Watch this video and get your chuckle on: www.youtube.com/watch?v=Z4Y4keqTV6w<br><br>Find someone who . . . community builder<br><br>Explore *kid joke generators* online |
| Kinesthete | Have you heard of walking meditation? How about walking thinkers? Design a walking track in your room for kids to walk and brainstorm together. What about walking while listening to an audiobook?<br><br>Create dramatic moves for vocabulary words or concepts.<br><br>Design a tableaux to show meaning.<br><br>Arrange your classroom to encourage/provide space for movement.<br><br>Hello, GoNoodle brain breaks (really, don't we all need this?) | GoNoodle<br>Play challenge cards, see theplayfulclassroom.com (website).<br><br>Destroy the box challenge cards (website).<br><br>*Animal Moves* by Darryl Edwards |

| Play personality type | Classroom applications | Additional resources |
|---|---|---|
| Explorer | Go on a scavenger hunt.<br>    Dissect something—a plant, a sentence, a work of literature. When we do this, we use a new lens.<br>    Go on a nature walk around school to look for connections to your curriculum.<br>    Hello, Genius Hour. Let your explorers choose their own path to learning.<br>    Schedule a call with an expert. Skype for Education has all kinds of free opportunities waiting to happen. | Take a walk art-side (website).<br>    Skype for Education.<br>    Try using our scavenger hunt template to design your own (website).<br>    Free play time with a student-safe search engines. |
| Competitor | Let these friends design their own Kahoot or Quizziz.<br>    If kids need to practice a skill, make a game of it.<br>    Gamify your classroom—students will do far more to earn their point with choice!<br>    Create a curricular twist for classic games such as Taboo, Twister, Scattergories, Outburst, Guesstures . . .<br>    Steam Challenges! There's always a winner in the marshmallow or spaghetti challenge. That may not be your goal, but your competitors will love it. | Kahoot/Quizziz<br>    Math games for number sense (website)<br>*Explore Like a Pirate* by Michael Matera<br>    Traditional games with a twist (in Chapter 42 and on our website) |
| Director | Let kids design a Day of Play, whether it's free play or Field Day.<br>    Let your directors team with your storytellers to create a class play for your unit of study and perform it.<br>    Have a job of "Class manager." This person will make sure other jobs are done.<br>    Allow your director to create a promotional video or iMovie trailer for your class/a concept/a novel— the ideas are endless.<br>    Challenge your directors to design a field trip proposal. Where do they want to go? How will they justify it? Give them a budget and see what can happen. | Global Play Day<br>    Storyboard templates (website)<br>    Movie creation apps (including stop motion video)<br>    Bring TikTok in the classroom<br>    http://www.bullet journal.com |

| Play personality type | Classroom applications | Additional resources |
|---|---|---|
| Collector | Give students space for their own trophy case (in the room or in the hallway)—their collections of favorite book quotes, proud creations, medals/achievements/badges.<br><br>Encourage authentic journaling. Students can collect their learning experiences in a form of their choice.<br><br>Reframe the reading log. Instead of minutes read, the reading log should become a trophy case of books read, and should be a choice, not required.<br><br>Rocks, bugs, leaves . . .collect them all.<br><br>Idea journals. Collect your thoughts throughout the year. | Reading log alternatives (website)<br>Search http://Manueldraws.com for creative idea journals or have students create their own.<br>Pinterest and Wakelet are a collector's dream . . . just done digitally.<br>Scavenger hunts for specific items. See website for details. |
| Artist/Creator | You can integrate the arts in everything!<br><br>Write a children's book explaining your curricular concept to a younger audience.<br><br>Sing song parodies together that incorporate music and your content.<br><br>Illustrate concepts with watercolor, painter's tape on the wall, or sculpted tinfoil.<br><br>Design a tattoo for a particular concept.<br><br>Challenge students to gather five random items from around the room. Combine them to create something new (a new game or an improved gadget). | *Launch,* by John Spencer and AJ Guilliani<br>*A Beautiful Day in the Neighborhood: The Poetry of Mister Rogers*<br>*Show Your Work* by Austin Kleon<br>Quick guide to integrate the arts (website) |

| Play personality type | Classroom applications | Additional resources |
|---|---|---|
| Storyteller | Create a costume for ____ (insert vocabulary, theme, character, idea . . .) Explain the concept theatrically.<br>Create a stop-motion video to tell your story.<br>Give students a microphone that lets them voice record their stories. Publish their work.<br>Skype for Education—connect with an author. Ask about his/her process.<br>All storytellers need an audience. Give your storytellers a purpose with audience and some trust. | Skype for Education<br>Costume/dress-up materials<br>Green screen technology<br>Blogging |

## Challenge #3 Celebrate the Random

On the way back in from recess, or spontaneously during the middle of class—maybe in between bells or during the short walk to lunch. Find a spot on the wall, a piece of student artwork on a bulletin board, a random spider that might be crawling past . . . Engage it. Talk to it. Dream up a story that it shares with you. Ask it questions about its day. Offer it some tea and a biscuit. The giggles will no doubt ensue, the students will most assuredly think you have lost all of your marbles. Then, challenge them to do the same.

This might be a great time to introduce them to the concept of pareidolia. What's that, you ask? In basic terms, *pareidolia* is the term that describes when a face is seen in an object or place where there isn't supposed to be one. We have provided you some samples below. What a fun, engaging way to become aware of the playfulness all around us!

# Challenge #4 Follow and Interact with Playful Educators Online

## Playful educators

| | | |
|---|---|---|
| @juliepjones | @ProfesoraEspaña | @scotteach |
| @mrdearybury | @thatsbwhite | @pintobeanz11 |
| @educaptamerica | @jemellehCoes | @lkegode |
| @mrs_smoke | @Miss_Sugg1st | @ericcrouch |
| @gruffcorn13 | @miss_larkins | @paulsolarz |
| @jmattmiller | @Daniel1Teach | @crumpsclass |
| @mrmatera | @msoskil | @yaujauku |
| @mrpowley | @techamys | @joboaler |
| @tishrich | @Mister_Kelly | @carlaantunesmcp |
| @2017GATOTY | @aaronmaureredu | @yjkimchee |
| @darcygrimesNC | @tonyvincent | |

on Twitter

# CHAPTER 41

# Time, Space, Opportunity (Intentionality)

### Challenge #5 Gather Ye Rosebuds, Errr . . . Tools for Play

Say this in your best Robin Williams, o' captain my captain voice:

*Gather ye rosebuds while ye may*
*Seize the day with tools for play!*

As teachers, we must be intentional about the classroom setting and the opportunities within. Because of this responsibility, we challenge you to gather materials at every opportunity. Visit thrift stores in your area, ask parents for donations, post wish-lists online. When the materials are sitting in plain sight, students will be reminded to use them and be playful. These items may include:

- Costumes
- Keva planks/blocks
- LEGOs
- Hula hoops
- Play-Doh
- Aluminum foil
- Paint
- Rolls of butcher paper
- Buckets of markers and colored pencils
- Musical instruments
- Stuffed animals or plastic characters (from bears to soldiers)

- Clean trash/recycled material
- Pipe cleaners
- Buttons
- Popsicle sticks
- Adhesive: tape, putty, glue . . .
- Makedo
- Lefty Mcgoo (Instagram)

Once you have the tools, challenge your students to use them.

# Challenge #6 Rethink the Rules with Game Adaptations

No matter if you're cleaning out your home closet or gathering new or gently used materials from thrift store and wish-list gatherings in challenge #5, seek out traditional games to add to the classroom resources. Of course, use these games for brain breaks, but also challenge your students to come up with alternatives to the games' original rules. Some ideas to get you started are below:

- Hedbanz
  - Use the cards as concepts you've been studying. Students can create these cards and use them instead of the packaged game cards.
- Twister
  - Use wet-erase markers to write numbers, letters, or questions on the colored circles. Think:
    - Sight words
    - Math facts
    - Spelling words
  - Use the Twister mat as a graphic organizer:
    - Group concepts
    - Sort events into eras
    - Create a timeline
  - Multi game mashup
    - Blend beanbag toss with the rules of Connect Four incorporating questions to earn your toss.
    - Twister meets Jeopardy! Assign points and answers to each color. Use beanbags or let the students choose.
- Scattergories
  - Create lists about random classroom subjects. See sample below and find more lists at our website.

Scattergorie-"ish"

Verb _____

Adjective _____

Book you love _____

Book you didn't _____

Part of speech _____

Gerund _____

Punctuation _____

Book Character _____

Author's Name _____

Literacy Edition

- Catch Phrase
  - This game is a word association game where the players try to guess a word described by their teammate. It may be fun to play this game first as is, then have students create their own version. Students could write their own lists of content-related words and play the game in the exact same manner.

## Challenge #7 Take a Walk "Art"side

Whether you are in an urban or rural school setting, the outdoors is a free space that often invites play. Take your students on a walk "art"side (outside) for a unique learning experience where art and play can work together. If near a wooded area, have students collect natural materials to create artwork that represents their thinking on a specific topic. For example, if you are in California, you may ask students to create images to depict their understanding of the goldrush. If you are in Maine, have them build a lobster trap. Don't feel like you have to wait until the end of your traditional teaching unit to lead students through this experience.

Use it as a preassessment to see what they know in the beginning of a unit. Right in the middle of the unit, take them outside and see where they are in the process of learning new material. The idea here is to connect art, play, the outdoors, and the content. The image doesn't have to be super spectacular. The goal is to see student thinking through playful interactions with their peers.

## Challenge #8 Musical Chair Mashup

How long have your students been sitting down? Why not get them up and moving with a musical chair mashup? No, not the same musical chairs we played as kids. This is a new improved game. Let us explain.

Arrange your chairs in a circle where every student has a seat. In each chair, place a card with new content that you need students to learn. If you are studying ancient Egypt, the cards may contain information about clothing, jobs, inventions. etc., regarding their way of life. Once the cards are in place, have students dance their way around the chairs. We like to use various genres of music that bring different types of dance to the circle around the chairs; however, it may be fun to let students create the playlist used for this game.

After students have had a moment to dance, stop the music and everyone sits in a chair. They then take turns acting out the information on their card for a partner beside them. Once they have figured out each other's cards, the music resumes and they must take a new seat the next time the music stops. There are countless variations of this game and even more uses in the curriculum. After you play for the first time with students, we challenge you to create your own version.

# CHAPTER 42

# Play, Mess Up, Learn, Repeat (Process)

## Challenge #9 Breakout EDU

Escape rooms are all the rage, but you will want to hit the pause button before you lock kids alone in a room. Instead of breaking out, allow students to *break in* by unlocking a box that holds an unknown prize. BreakoutEDU offers boxes that come with a variety of locks along with a treasure trove of online resources —breakout experiences that are preplanned and organized by curricular area. The kit online can be a little pricey if you have a limited budget, but this resource could be the focus of your yearly teacher expenditure or a Donors Choose project.

You already spent that money? Don't let that limit your creativity. We have friends like @techtiesthomas who create free online digital breakout experiences using Google Forms. Search the hashtag #digitalbreakout for examples online.

## Challenge #10 Play-Doh Elephant Challenge

If you or your students need a reminder of the challenge inherent to the creative process, try building this elephant out of Play-Doh. The task: Make your elephant look just like the one in the picture below, or as close as possible.

Inform students that they will only be allowed one minute to observe the picture. At the conclusion of that minute. They will have roughly five minutes of work time to recreate it. In reality, most of the first attempts will not be all that great. Encourage collaboration with a small group so students can brainstorm ways to improve. Connect this to curriculum by discussing a moment of history where there was a failed attempt, by reading about a character who didn't succeed on the first try, by examining a science experiment that went awry. After discussions have ended, allow students to work in teams with the same amount of time. Almost every student will improve during the second round. The process of try, try again becomes evident as they improve on each attempt and provide a playful, visual reminder that is connected to the content discussion.

## Challenge #11 Card House Challenge

Have you ever attempted to build a house of cards? It is a bit frustrating, especially if the cards are brand new and the foundation of the house is a super-smooth desktop with no tiny ridges to hold the cards still. The difficulty of this challenge is what makes it a perfect fit for fifth grade and above. Engineering and design skills are very much needed to accomplish this feat.

The task: Build a card house at least five stories tall. Ready, set, go! As the task begins, you may see students sketching their house and a prethinking strategy. They may immediately build one story only to see it collapse in a heap. They may fasten the cards together using a nearby adhesive once they start to fail over and over. The playful teacher gives very limited instructions during a task like this so as to not influence student creativity. If you want a content connection here beyond cultivating the Cs we have often mentioned, affix mathematical equations to each card. Once the equation has been solved, then they can use that card. Using this strategy honors the need for some skill-and-drill practice in math, while making the task playful and fun.

# Challenge #12 Awesome Squiggles/ Virtual Valentines/Gingerbread Communities

Our friends Dyanne Smokorowski (@mrs_smoke) and Micah Brown (@MBrownEdTech), both playful educators, have created several online experiences that honor and celebrate the process of the playful classroom. There are seasonal challenges that run during specific times of the year, so be sure to look up these incredible educators online so you can get the timeline of each event on your school calendar as soon as possible.

## Gingerbread Communities

http://gingerbreadstemcommunity.weebly.com
What's awesome about where you live? What goods and services, historical buildings, attractions, or other notable places do you find the most interesting in your community? We'd love to see those places in our STEM/STEAM graham cracker gingerbread engineering challenge. The gingerbread communities global collaboration asks your students to design and construct their own communities, then share online: #GingerbreadSTEM.

## Awesome Squiggles

Awesome Squiggles is a global art challenge project where PreK–12th grade classrooms create original art based on four squiggly lines and then share their artwork with new friends around the world. The best part? Art translates into all languages. Come join in the fun!

## Virtual Valentine Exchange

The Virtual Valentines Project is an easy, free project designed to teach students geographical awareness and cultural understanding while connecting classrooms all around the world for Valentine's Day. Through this experience, our goal is to circumnavigate the globe with virtual Valentines greetings and cultural exchanges in order to spread a little happiness to children everywhere. Whether your students are in kindergarten or are seniors in high school, this project will help them learn something new.

We cannot wait to see y'all jump in on these challenges and collaborate with classrooms around the world through interactive play!

# CHAPTER 43

# The More We Play, the More Playful We Become (Habit)

## Challenge #13 Reflect on the Language in Your Classroom

We learned in Section 6 that growth as lifelong learners is greatly impacted by the language we use as teachers. We need more, "I love your effort here," and less "Look how smart you are!"

1.  Start with ourselves.
    Instead of, "This student just won't behave," reframe these thoughts with something like, "I wonder what's going on with this student to make them act out?" or, "I wonder what I can do to encourage this student."
2.  The addition of "yet."
    We need to be intentional about the use of this word in our classroom conversations.
    I can't draw a pumpkin, *yet.*
    I'm not fast at multiplication facts, *yet.*
    I'm not . . . *yet.*
3.  Remind ourselves with sentence stems.
    I love a sticky note. They are great for quiet reminders—pick up creamer. Dentist 3 p.m. Call Verizon—these are just a few notes on my desk right now. Why not put growth mindset sentence starters where we can be reminded to use them in our language? After all, intentional practice can lead to habits.

    > *I like how you chose . . .*
    > *I notice when . . .*
    > *I wonder if you've thought about . . .*

*Have you considered . . .*
*Look how much progress you've made!*
*Which of these are you most proud of?*

4. Have a contagious mindset.
   When we work on our own language, we will change. But, don't we want to help students shape their thinking toward positivity? Why not encourage students to create signage that reminds them of science behind mistakes? Of the power of intention and words? We've listed a few here to get you started:
   - *Nothing is impossible. The word itself says I'm possible!* —Audrey Hepburn
   - *It is hard to fail but it is worse never to have tried to succeed.* —Theodore Roosevelt

   - *I can accept failure. Everyone fails at something. But I can't accept not trying.* —Michael Jordan

   - *If you don't give anything, don't expect anything. Success is not coming to you. You must come to it.* —Marva Collins
   - *Work hard now. Don't wait. If you work hard enough, you'll be given what you deserve.* —Shaquille O'Neal
   - *Twenty years from now you'll be more disappointed by the things you didn't do than the ones you did do. So sail away from the safe harbor. Explore. Dream. Discover.* —Mark Twain
   - *Don't be too timid and squeamish about your actions. All life is an experiment.* —Ralph Wado Emerson
   - *There's no such thing as failure. Only results.* —Tony Robbins
   - *I like criticism. It makes you stronger.* —Lebron James
   - *Failure is so important. We speak about success all the time, but it is the ability to resist or reuse failure that often leads to greater success.* —JK Rowling
   - *It's not that I'm so smart. It's just that I stay with problems longer.* —Albert Einstein
   - *Great works are performed not by strength but by perseverance.* —Samuel Jackson
   - *Success is the ability to go from one failure to another with no loss of enthusiasm.* —Winston Churchill

5. Praise the process instead of the product.
   You might want to review the research behind teacher language in Section 6: Play Nurtures Growth. Shifting our words from phrases like, "Wow, your penmanship is perfect!" to "I love how you've been working so hard on your penmanship!" will make a great difference in the long run.

## Challenge #14 Sculpt and Scoot!!!!

In this challenge, each student needs a can of Play-Doh, a piece of paper to sculpt on, and a piece of literature/an article/a passage from one of the worksheets you used to use. Ask students to read the passage and then begin a sculpture with their dough that represents what they took away from the reading. After a moment of sculpting, have them write one sentence beside their creation, then scoot (move over) to their neighbor's chair. Once they are in front of the new sculpture, they will read what their neighbor wrote and add to the sculpture. They would also write a sentence to clarify their addition. When they finish, scoot again and repeat the process as often as time allows. Once everyone has sculpted for the last time, take pictures for social media and share the learning process with the world. Ask students whose sculptures are interconnected to meet together to discuss their learning from the literature.

The purpose for the scooting in this challenge is so that students become less engaged with their final masterpiece and more engrossed in their thinking. By developing this habit, students will begin to value the work's process rather than only focusing on the outcome. The outcome is very important, especially when, say, writing a book, but the book cannot be written without a full toolbox of writing habits that support the process.

## Challenge #15 How Did You Play to Learn Today?

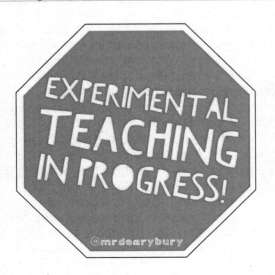

Invite parents and stakeholders to hold you accountable as you build your playful mindset.

- Post a sign outside your classroom door to ask visitors to ask about play in your lessons.
- Include this question as part of your interactive newsletter home to parents, so they will ask students how they played to learn today.
- At the end of every class or school day, ask students to give you a *high five*—that is, five concepts they learned through play.
- Set a goal to tweet ideas to accountability partners (your PLN) online #theplayfulclassroom.

# Challenge #16 Play History Analysis

Grab a piece of paper, poster board, or a big ol' piece of butcher paper and your favorite color marker. Yes, it has to be a marker because life is too short to always use a number 2 pencil. Write down every memory you have about play from childhood. As many as you can. Don't set a timer. Don't feel like the list has to have a certain number of items. It may take you an hour or a few days. If you are like us, we worked on our list for over a year. Once you feel your list is complete, look for the highlights, the commonalities, the connected dots that link your past to the present.

1. Where was the place where play occurred most often?
2. What toys, items, or supplies did you play with most?
3. Who did you play with?
4. When did play happen the most for you?
5. How did you feel when you played alone? With a friend? In a group?
6. Did your family play together?
7. What did you learn from play?

Feel free to add to this list of questions as you look back over your play history. Once you have recalled as much as you can, and you have read through the list, bring as much of your past playfulness into the present as you possibly can. Reflecting in this way will help strengthen your current play path.

# CHAPTER 44

# Play Makes You Happy. Happy People Play. (Results)

## Challenge #17 Host a Tiny Art Show

Everybody loves a miniature. Tiny houses. Tiny puppies. Tiny Tim. *God bless us, every one.*

Why not host a tiny art show? Give your students a Post-It note or a fraction of a stick of clay. Just make sure all start with the same amount of materials.

If you are at the beginning of your instruction, ask students to create art to showcase what they know or what they wonder.

If you are in the middle, use the tiny art show as a way to gather formative assessment.

Near the end? Why not use the tiny art show as a springboard for new ideas and new curiosities?

The beauty is in the process, not the product. The process is discussion when they tour the art show and ask questions about each others' work.

## Challenge #18 Tape Art Museum

Using colored masking tape, or plain masking tape filled with colorful student designs, divide your class into groups of three to four and have them create illustrations on the walls, floors, windows, etc., to communicate their learning and/or comprehension of a specific learning objective. We often ask for the artwork to be at least 3' × 3' so that it will be large enough to view from across the learning space. This is a great experience for bare hallway spots or in the gym or cafeteria. As student groups complete their creation, welcome everyone to the official *tape art museum*. Encourage groups to mix and mingle around the room, in silence at first, and make observations about the art of their peers. Provide each student with sticky notes for the purpose of writing down questions they may have, and then they stick it to the art. After ample time to review all of the artwork, students then return to their original creations to discover the questions of their classmates. The questions that were asked are then used to add more details to the artwork and deepen the learning experience.

# Challenge #19 Destination Learning

Create a scavenger hunt in the building. Have groups of students visit stations to decipher clues that will lead them to specific locations throughout the campus. Upon their arrival, you will have posted/hidden questions that will guide them in communicating, creating, collaborating, and critical-thinking. As the clues of the hunt lead them to various spots, the students will engage in authentic, relevant learning.

- While they are at the cafeteria, they may brainstorm ideas to reduce food waste.
- When passing through the common area, they may create a list of ways to make the space more conducive for playful learning.
- As they gather outside near the playground/field/breezeway, this would be a great time to work collaboratively on the school's anti-bullying initiative and make sure all students have equitable access to learning in a safe space.
- At their last stop, the school gym, students might think critically about the social aspects of sports in high school.

These ideas can be broad, as you see here, or more focused on your curricular goals. Once students have experienced these kinds of destination learning spaces, challenge them to design one for the class!

# Challenge #20 Make a Mark

Students will need one piece of white copy paper and one marker. It is ideal that each student have a different color if possible. The teacher will need a copy of Peter H. Reynolds's *The Dot*. Begin reading the story, even if students have heard it before, and at the moment Vashti makes her mark, ask students to do the same. Big dot, little dot, fat dot, skinny dot, or even a polka-dotted dot. The mark's size isn't relevant to the lesson. Then, as Vashti signs her name in the book, ask students to sign their names to their own paper. Next, they will pass it to a neighbor.

Upon receiving the friend's dot, ask students to add to the dot with some sort of doodle. It can touch the dot, be near the dot, or be completely separated from the original dot. Continue the process of reading two pages and passing the papers to add new illustrations. At the end of the story, each paper will be filled with a new, never-before-seen piece of artwork created by the collaborative efforts of your students. You now have a class full of visual art writing prompts, a unique class children's book ready for illustration, or new items to proudly display on a bulletin board. What's the content connection here? It could be whatever you want it to be.

- You could ask that each doodle added be connected to the class's current area of study.
- You could ask a question and allow student collaborative art to be the answer.
- You could limit the timeline of the art to include only ideas from a particular era.
- You could challenge students to include polygons or particular angles, or to add rules about coordinates to their task.
- You could add a rule each time the paper is passed.
- *The only limit here is our imaginations.*

Regardless of what you do with this challenge, follow the words of Vashti's teacher, "Make a mark and see where it goes."

# CHAPTER 45

# Get Out There and Play

One day while we were working on this book at our favorite coffee shop, an 89-year-old man who had just purchased a large hot chocolate with whipped cream stopped by our table as he waited for his beverage to cool enough to drink. He asked us what kind of work we did. Both of us replied that we were educators. He immediately began talking about education back in his day. He mentioned that they didn't have calculators and computers then. They had to use their minds. "Kids nowadays just don't learn like we did," he said. "They don't want to read or do math. It's just all 'bout the devices and such." Of course, we didn't dare challenge the man. His spirit was so sweet and his heart was in the right place. While we disagreed with him about kids and their desire to learn, we do acknowledge that times have changed since his grade-school days.

As he chatted on about his childhood with a smile on his face, we reminisced about the days of education yesteryear. It was so fun to chat with this man—someone who had seen the world evolve in the most incredible of ways. After he left, we brought the conversations to present day and began to reflect on his words. We concluded that while many things had changed, there were still some constants: Kids still want to learn. Kids still love to play. Kids still have a sense of wonder and awe. Kids are still kids.

And we as educators must intentionally discover their playful personalities (and ours too!) to bring out and celebrate all that they are. Thinking about all the things he said about his own learning experiences, we were also left with this thought: The playful classroom does not have a thing to do with materials, books, technology, or store-bought pizzazz. Instead, what creates a playful classroom are key concepts that transcend the timeline of schooling:

- creativity
- trust

- relationships
- community
- a spirit of growth

Regardless of your school's notoriety, regardless of the number of degrees in your classroom or building, these core principles are available to all of us who bear the name of educator/teacher. We can cultivate them as Livingstone Kegode does in Kenya, as Ann Mirtschin does in Australia, as Yao Ku does in his classrooms all around the world. These teachers and thousands more just like them strive every day to make learning meaningful, relevant, and fun through play, no matter how young or old.

Are you with us yet?
Do you want to be more playful?
Are you ready?
Let's play and learn together.

# Southernisms and Their Meanings

## Introduction

- Are you ears burning?: If you someone asks you this, it means they were talking about you. Only good things, of course.
- Bee's knees: Fantastic
- Best thing since sliced bread: Incredible
- Butter on my biscuit: You're special
- Fine as frog hair: Very awesome
- Fired up: Excited
- 'Bout to boil over: Really excited ('bout = about)
- Cranks my tractor: Really, really excited.
- Comin' a gully washer: Lots of rain
- Lonely as a pine tree in a parking lot: That's really lonely, because you rarely see a pine tree in a parking lot
- Running around like a chicken with it's head chopped off: To act or work in a manner that has no organization or direction.
- Negative Nellies: People who always have something negative to say
- Cow horns will hook: A phrase someone uses when they really mean what they say
- This dog will hunt: A phrase someone uses when what they are saying is really true
- Pull up a chair, and sit a spell: An invitation to join us, to hang out, to spend time with us
- Good Lord willin' and the creek don't rise: Phrase commonly used when speaking of what possibly happen in the future
- Fixin' to: About to
- Play purdy now: Be nice to each other.

# Section 1

- Ya'll: A pronoun that means *you all*
- Just so: Exactly right as it should be
- Sweet potatoes and yams: Kinda the same, but not really
- Waffle House sittin' close: Waffle House, a major restaurant chain in the Southeast, has booths that are really close together. This phrase is used when talking about something, usually a person, that is very close by.
- How it's goin' down: What is going to happen
- Cranks your tractor: Really, really excited
- High-brow: Well educated, very intelligent, almost to a fault
- Bushel and a peck and a hug around the neck: Common phrase used to describe how much you love someone. Grandparents used to use the phrase often when talking to their grandchildren.
- Silly-headed: Can't make up our mind
- Bad rap: Bad reputation
- Let's have a word of prayer: We need to chat; we don't really mean *pray* with you
- Red Rover: Not sure if this is a Southernism, but it was a recess game commonly played by children when we were in school. It is pretty much outlawed now because it's kind of dangerous.
- A sermon is a comin': Someone is about to tell you something really important.
- dog -it: This one is a slang term for "by gosh" or "by golly."
- Same ol, same ol: Referring to doing something the way it has always been done.
- Little heady: If something is a "little heady" it is often difficult to comprehend.
- cuttin' up: Absolutely nothing to do with scissors. We often say this when we are playing, acting silly, having a good time. However, if an adult says, "Stop cuttin' up," you best do that right away because she means that you are misbehaving.
- Where Jesus lost his slipper**: This is NOT a Southernism. We had never heard til my friend Teri from Utah said it one day on the phone. It means something is lost, and really far away.
- All bent out of sorts: Upset
- Off the rails: Not as planned
- Let it roll off you like water on a duck's back: Don't let something negative bother you. Ignore it.
- There's more than one way to skin a cat: This phrase, while we have no idea where it came from, or why anyone would be skinning cats, simply means that there is often more than one way to do things.

- Ruffle our feathers: Make us upset
- Long story short: Just the important details to the story
- Nooks and crannies: Every space available
- Nervous as a cat on a porch full of rockers: Just a colorful expression to describe the depth of one's nervousness
- In the floor: Some parts of the country say "sit on the floor" but we say "sit in the floor." Means the same thing, I reckon.
- Reckon: guess
- Come to Jesus meeting: If someone says this to you, they mean they are about to clarify something for you, or help you understand something very important. Often, it means they are gonna tell you very sternly.
- Hickory switch: Small twig that is sometimes used for discipline
- Got docked: Points taken off
- Sittin' with you: If something isn't "sitting with you," that means its probably making you uncomfortable or uneasy. Not in a bad way, but maybe a challenging, convicting way.
- Take a gander: Take a peek
- Boat load: A lot
- Shook: Surprised
- Y'all best sit down: We don't really mean sit down. We mean get ready for what's about to come.

# Section 2

- Throwin' a hissy fit: Getting upset, usually over something unimportant.
- Solve the world's problems: Have a chat with a friend about things that are bothering you and how you can fix them.
- Feeling antsy: Kinda nervous
- Heavens: No, not the place. This is a word like gosh, goodness, or by no means.
- Bless his/her/your/our/their heart(s): There have been countless questions about this phrase from people outside of the South. We could probably write a whole book on correct uses. In this chapter it means to show pity on us.
- They'll come 'round: Eventually, they will agree.
- Gather to say: Assume.
- Tick on a dog's ear: Ticks are very common in the South and they like to get on dogs' ears.
- Mosey: A slow walk without a real purpose or destination
- Mason jar: Glass jar often used in canning vegetables, but we use them for everything from vases full of flowers, to candle holders, to drinking sweet tea.

- Maddern'uh wet hen: An expression used to describe some-one's level of anger.
- Useless as milk bucket under a bull: This phrase is used to describe how worthless something is.
- Woppy-jawed: Crooked, leaning, not correct in its posture, appearance, purpose
- All tore up: Upset
- Two hens over a rooster: A way to describe how someone is fighting.
- You plant a butter bean, you get a butter bean: This means you get out of something what you put into it.
- Scrap it: Throw away the idea and start fresh.

## Section 3

- Hunney: A term of endearment for a friend
- Happier than a woodpecker in a lumberyard: Really, really happy
- Duke's Mayonnaise: Southern's are proud of our mayo. Don't ever try to tell us there is another kind.
- Nanner sammich: A sandwich with sliced bananas, Duke's Mayo, salt and pepper, on white loaf bread.
- Hickory switch: Small twig that is sometimes used for discipline
- Dog and pony show: Go above and beyond your normal best to perform your job/duty when the boss comes to visit.
- Chased a rabbit: Got off topic while telling a story
- Lightning bug: A firefly
- Downright giddy: Really really excited
- Preaching to the choir: Telling someone/group information that they already know and agree with
- Flared up: Started suddenly
- Like nobody's business: Came out of nowhere.
- Lord: Not like we are praying or referring to nobility; this is more like a term that means "goodness" or "gosh." Sometimes spelled "Lawd," always pronounced this way.
- Scare half to death: It scared you really bad.
- Boogey man: This vague character is used to describe things that you are afraid of.
- Daytona 500: Nascar race. First race of racing season.

## Section 4

- What in tarnation: An expression used to express utter disbelief
- Carryin' on: Making noise
- Proud as a peacock: Very, very proud

- Just dandy: Really good
- White paws after Labor Day: This phrase is just a play on words and a nod to the outdated fashion faux pas of not wearing white shoes/pants after Labor Day.
- Harder to come by than sweet from a lemon: Phrase used to illustrate the difficulty of obtaining something
- Pigeonhole: Label yourself as something very specific in a manner that makes it hard to label you as anything else.
- Sursy/sursies: A small little gift/token(s) of thanks and thoughtfulness
- Spread honey: Say something negative/critical but in a way that seems positive/helpful nice. The allusion here is referencing honey because it is sweet. If you "spread honey" you are attempting to say nice things about a tough topic.

## Section 5

- Too big for their breeches: Something you say when someone is feeling a bit too proud of themselves and acting a little more important than they should be.
- Ridin' around a high horse: A phrase talking about what someone who thinks they are super important does.
- Knock 'em down a notch: Help someone be humble and not too proud
- Hogwash: Something that is not true
- More than you can shake a stick at: A lot
- Bless their hearts: Here the phrase means that you feel sorry for them because they don't have social skills and you are wishing they did.
- Mean pot pie: A really tasty, delicious chicken pot pie
- Commode: Toilet
- Beggars can't be choosers: A phrase said to someone who isn't grateful when someone gives them something they asked for or needed because the thing they received just isn't quite what they wanted. "Take it or leave it."
- Doozie: Something really big or noteworthy
- Faster than the #3 car in pit row: Lots of Southerners love Dale Earnhardt, and Nascar. #3 was his car. Many people view Dale as one of the greatest racers of all time.
- #24 Dupont: Another Nascar reference, this time to driver Jeff Gordon
- Bettin' kind of folks: People who like to gamble
- Catch the vapors: Become short of breath and possibly faint
- Sweet Cherubs: Little angels, or in context of this sentence, students
- "A tweetin'": Sending tweets via Twitter

# Section 6

- Granny's little pills: In our region, it seems everyone's grandma has a pill for everything. Got a headache? Pill. Constipated? Pill. Nervous? Pill. Pulled a muscle? Granny's got a pill for that.
- Crisco: A brand of shortening often used to fry food
- A mess a: A lot of
- Brownie points: Compliments from a superior
- Went swimmingly: Went very well
- Purdy: Pretty
- Love handle: A term used to refer to extra body fat around the waist
- Fussed her out: Chastized or berated
- The grease meets the squeak: The point in time where a solution meets a problem
- Lawsy me: My goodness, good grief
- Fan, fan, rock, rock: A parenthetical phrase to imply that it's hot and someone is fanning themselves as they sit in a rocking chair on a front porch
- Bless our hearts later: Feel sorry for us some other time
- Yonder: Another word for *there*
- Take the second left past Aunt Frannie's barn: We Southerners are very specific when giving directions on how to get to a specific place.
- Other way 'round: Vice versa
- These parts: A term used when referencing the area where you are from

# Section 7

- Lost your marbles: Not thinking correctly
- Like a frog flying out of a hot plate: Frogs are cold blooded and unaware of the slow heat of a frying pan. They jump out rather quickly once they realize its getting hot.

# APPENDIX B

# The Playful Classroom Teacher's Reading Guide

Abeles, Vicki. *Beyond Measure: The Big Impact of Small Changes*. Simon & Schuster, 2016.

Aguilar, Elena. *The Art of Coaching: Effective Strategies for School Transformation*. Jossey-Bass/Wiley, 2013.

Barry, Lynda. *Syllabus: Notes from an Accidental Professor*. Drawn & Quarterly Publications, 2014.

Berkun, Scott. *The Dance of the Possible: The Mostly Honest Completely Irreverent Guide to Creativity*. Berkun Media, 2017.

Brown, Stuart M.D., with Christopher Vaughn. *Play: How It Shapes the Brain, Opens the Imagination, and Invigorates the Soul*. Avery (Penguin Random House), 2010.

Cameron, Julia. *The Artist's Way: A Spiritual Path to Higher Creativity*. Jeremy P. Tarcher/Perigee, 1992.

Carey, Benedict. *How We Learn: The Surprising Truth About When, Where, and Why It Happens*. Random House, 2015.

Christensen, Tanner. *The Creativity Challenge: Design, Experiment, Test, Innovate, Build, Create, Inspire, and Unleash Your Genius*. Adams Media, 2015.

Daniels, Harvey. *The Curious Classroom: 10 Structures for Teaching with Student-directed Inquiry*. Heinemann, 2017.

DeBenedet, Anthony. *Playful Intelligence: The Power of Living Lightly in a Serious World*. Santa Monica Press, 2018.

Gilbert, Elizabet. *Big Magic: Creative Living Beyond Fear*. Riverhead Books, 2016.

Gray, Peter. *Free to Learn: Why Unleashing the Instinct to Play Will Make Our Children Happier, More Self-Reliant, and Better Students for Life*. Basic Books, 2013.

Grazer, Brian. *A Curious Mind: The Secret to a Bigger Life*. Simon & Schuster, 2015.

Henry, Todd. *Louder Than Words: Harness the Power of Your Authentic Voice*. Portfolio, 2015.

Henry, Todd. *The Accidental Creative: How to Be Brilliant at a Moment's Notice*. Portfolio, 2013.

Hurren, B. Lee. *Humor in School Is Serious Business*. Incentive Publications, 2010.

King, Maxwell. *The Good Neighbor: The Life and Work of Fred Rogers*. Abrams, 2018.

Kleon, Austin. *Keep Going: 10 Ways to Stay Creative in Good Times and Bad*. Workman Publishing, 2019.

Kleon, Austin. *Show Your Work! 10 Ways to Share Your Creativity and Get Discovered*. Workman Publishing, 2014.

Kleon, Austin. *Steal Like an Artist: 10 Things Nobody Told You About Being Creative*. Workman Publishing, 2012.

Luna, Elle. *The Crossroads of Should and Must: Find and Follow Your Passion*. Workman Publishing 2015.

MacLeod, Hugh. *Ignore Everybody and 39 Other Keys to Creativity*. Portfolio (Penguin Random House), 2009.

Miller, Matt. *Ditch That Textbook: Free Your Teaching and Revolutionize Your Classroom*. Dave Burgess Consulting, 2015.

Pressfield, Steven. *The War of Art: Break Through the Blocks and Win Your Inner Creative Battles*. Black Irish Books, 2002.

Robinson, John Elder. *Look Me in the Eye: My Life with Asperger's*. Three Rivers Press, 2007.

Root-Bernstein, Robert, and Michele Root-Bernstein. *Sparks of Genius: The 13 Thinking Tools of the World's Most Creative People*. Mariner Books, 1999.

Sahlberg, Pasi, and William Doyle. *Let the Children Play: How More Play Will Save Our Schools and Help Children Thrive*. Oxford University Press, 2019.

SARK (*Susan Ariel Rainbow Kennedy*). *A Creative Companion: How to Free Your Creative Spirit*. Celestial Arts, 2004.

SARK (*Susan Ariel Rainbow Kennedy*). *Inspiration Sandwich:* Stories to Inspire Our Creative Freedom. Celestial Arts, 1992.

SARK (*Susan Ariel Rainbow Kennedy*). Juicy Pens Thirsty Paper*: Gifting the World with Your Words and Stories, and Creating the Time and Energy to Actually Do It*. Harmony Books, 2008.

Seelig, Tina. *inGenius: A Crash Course on Creativity*. HarperOne, 2012.

Tharp, Twyla. *The Creative Habit: Learn It and Use It for Life*. Simon & Schuster, 2003.

# REFERENCES

Ackerman, D. (2000). *Deep play*. New York: Vintage Publishing.

Aspelin, J. (2012). How do relationships influence student achievement? *International Studies of Sociology in Education, 22*(1), 41–56. doi:10.1080/0962 0214.2012.680327

Barton, P. E. (2003). *Parsing the achievement gap: Baselines for tracking progress*. Princeton, NJ: Policy Information Report, Educational Testing Service.

Bateson, G. (1955). A theory of play and fantasy; a report on theoretical aspects of the project of study of the role of the paradoxes of abstraction in communication. *Psychiatric Research Reports, 2*, 39–51.

Berridge, K. C., & Kringelbach, M. L. (2015). Pleasure systems in the brain. *Neuron, 86*(3), 646–664. doi:10.1016/j.neuron.2015.02.018

Bjorkland, D., & Pellegrini, A. (2000). Child development and evolutionary psychology. *Child Development, 71*, 1687–1708.

Boaler, J. (2015, September). *Youcubed summer math camp 2015*. Retrieved from https://www.youcubed.org/resources/youcubed-summer-math-camp-2015.

Boaler, J. (2019). *When you believe in your students they do better*. Retrieved from https://www.youcubed.org/wp-content/uploads/2017/05/When-You-Believe-in-Your-Students-They-Do-Better.pdf.

Brown, B. (2011). *The power of vulnerability*. Retrieved from https://www.youtube.com/watch?v=iCvmsMzlF7o.

Brown, B. (2019). *Daring classrooms*. Retrieved from https://brenebrown.com/daringclassrooms.

Brown, S. (2009). *Play: How it shapes the brain, opens the imagination, and invigorates the soul*. New York: Penguin Group.

Brown, S. (2010). *Play: How it shapes the brain, opens the imagination, and invigorates the soul*. New York: Penguin.

Carey, B. (2015). *How we learn: The surprising truth about when, where, and why it happens*. New York: Random House.

Carnegie, D. (1936). *How to win friends and influence people*. New York: Pocket Books.

Carney, D. R., Cuddy, A. J., & Yap, A. J. (2010). Power posing: Brief nonverbal displays affect neuroendocrine levels and risk tolerance. *Psychological Science, 21*(10), 1363–1368. doi:10.1177/0956797610 383437

Centers for Disease Control. (2017). *Physical activity during school: Providing recess to all students*. Retrieved from https://www.cdc.gov/healthy schools/physicalactivity/pdf/Recess_All_Students.pdf.

Chaouloff, F. (1989). Physical exercise and brain monoamines: A review. *Acta Physiologica Scandinavica, 137*, 1–13.

Christensen, T. (2014). *Why play is essential for creativity*. Retrieved from https://creativesomething.net/post/84134598535/why-play-is-essential-for-creativity.

Christensen, T. (2015). *The creativity challenge: Design, experiment, test, innovate, build, create, inspire, and unleash your genius*. Avon, MA: Adams Media.

Cohen, G. L., Garcia, J., Apfel, N., & Master, A. (2006). Reducing the racial achievement gap: A social-psychological intervention. *Science, 313*, 1307–1310.

Cohen, G. L., Steele, C. M., & Ross, L. D. (1999). The mentor's dilemma: Providing critical feedback across the racial divide. *Personality and Social Psychology Bulletin, 25*(10), 1302–1318.

Common Core Standards Initiative. (n.d.). *Standards for mathematical practice*. Retrieved from http://www.corestandards.org/Math/Practice.

Davidson, C. (2017). *The new education*. New York: Basic Books.

DeBenedet, A., & Cohen, L. (2011). *The art of rough-housing: Good old-fashioned horseplay and why every kid needs it*. Philadelphia, PA: Quirk Books.

DeBenedet, A. T. (2018). *Playful intelligence: The power of living lightly in a serious world*. Solana Beach, CA: Santa Monica Press LLC.

Dewer, G. (2014). *The cognitive benefits of play: Effects on the learning brain*. Retrieved from https://www.parentingscience.com/benefits-of-play.html.

Dweck, C. S. (1999). *Self-theories: Their role in motivation, personality and development*. Philadelphia, PA: Psychology Press.

Elkind, D. (2007). *The power of play: Learning what comes naturally*. Philadelphia, PA: Da Capo Press.

Empatico. (n.d.). *Help us spark empathy*. Retrieved from https://why.empatico.org.

Encourage Play. (2019). *Teach through play*. Retrieved from https://www.encourageplay.com/teach-through-play.

Epstein, D. (2019). *Range: Why generalists triumph in a specialized world*. New York, NY: Riverhead Books.

Finkelhor, D., Turner, H. A., Shattuck, A., & Hamby, S. L. (2015). Prevalence of childhood exposure to violence, crime, and abuse: Results from the national survey of children's exposure to violence. *JAMA Pediatrics, 169*(8), 746–754.

Fisher, E. P. (1992). The impact of play on development: A meta-analysis. *Play and Culture, 5*(2), 159–181.

Fordyce, D. E., & Wehner, J. M. (1993). Physical activity enhances spatial learning performance with an associated alteration in hippocampalprotein kinase C activity in C57BL/6 and DBA/2 mice. *Brain Research, 61*(1–2), 111–119.

Frank, S. J. (1978). Just imagine how I feel: How to improve empathy through training in imagination. In J. Singer & K. Pope (Eds.), *The power of human imagination: New methods in psychotherapy (pages of chapter)*. New York: Springer.

Gallup. (2016). *How millennials want to work and live*. Retrieved from https://enviableworkplace.com/wp-content/uploads/Gallup-How-Millennials-Want-To-Work.pdf.

Garza, R., Alejandro, E. A., Blythe, T., & Fite, K. (2014). Caring for students: What teachers have to say. *ISRN Education, 2014*, Article ID 425856, 7. doi:10.1155/2014/425856

Geertz, C. (1973). *The interpretation of cultures*. New York: Basic Books.

Geirland, J. (1996). *Go with the flow*. Retrieved from https://www.wired.com/1996/09/czik.

Gergen, K. (2009). *Relational being. Beyond self and community*. Oxford: Oxford University Press.

Gibbs, A., & Bryer, T. (2017). *Award-winning "Hamilton" musical was "no overnight success", says creator Lin-Manuel Miranda*. Retrieved from https://www.cnbc.com/2017/12/28/hamilton-creator-lin-manuel-miranda-on-the-making-of-the-musical.html.

Gilbert, E. (2016). *Big magic: Creative living beyond fear*. New York: Riverhead Books.

Ginsburg, K. R. (2007). The importance of play in promoting healthy child development and maintaining strong parent-child bonds. *Pediatrics, 119*(1), 182–191. Retrieved from https://pediatrics.aappublications.org/content/119/1/182.short.

Gordon, N., Burke, S., Akil, H., Watson, S., & Panskepp, J. (2003). Socially induced brain "fertilization": Play promotes brain derived neurotrophic factor transcription in the amygdala and dorsolateral frontal cortex in juvenile rats. *Neuroscience Letters, 341*(1), 17–20.

Gray, P. (2013). *Free to LEARN*. New York: Basic Books.

Gray, P. (2014). *The decline of play*. Retrieved from https://www.youtube.com/watch?v=Bg-GEz M7iTk.

Greenough, W. T., & Black, J. E. (1992). Induction of brain structure by experience: Substrates for cognitive development. *Developmental Neuroscience, 24*.

Grosin, L. (2004). *Skolklimat, prestation och anpassning i 21 mellan- och 20 högstadieskolor.* (School climate, achievement and adjustment in between 21 and 20 high schools, in Swedish). Stockholm: Pedagogiska institutionen.

Guinness World Records. (n.d.). *Tallest house of cards*. Retrieved from https://www.guinnessworld records.com/world-records/tallest-house-of-cards?fb_comment_id=963675110327047_18540 66534621229.

Hakkarainen, P., & Brdikyt, M. (2014). How play creates the zone of proximal development. In *The routledge international handbook of young children's thinking and understanding* (pp. 65–76). UK: Routledge.

High Scope. (n.d.). *Curriculum*. Retrieved from https://highscope.org/our-practice/curriculum.

Hughes, B. (2002). *A playworker's taxonomy of play types* (2nd ed.). London: PlayLink.

Hurren, L. (2010). *Humor in school is serious business*. Nashville, TN: Incentive Publications.

Jenson, E. (2005). *Teaching with the brain in mind*. Alexandria, VA: ASCD.

Jeynes, W. H. (2003). A meta-analysis: The effects of parental involvement on minority children's academic achievement. *Education and Urban Society*, *35*(2), 202–218.

Kahenman, D. (2013). *Thinking fast and slow*. New York: Farrar, Straus, and Giroux.

Kaplinsky, R. (2019). *Open middle radical challenge*. Retrieved from https://www.openmiddle.com.

Kesslak, J., Patrick, V., So, J., Cotman, C., & Gomez-Pinilla, F. (1998). Learning upregulates brain-derived neurotrophic factor messenger ribonucleic acid: A mechanism to facilitate encoding and circuite maintenance. *Behavioral Neuroscience*, *112*(4), 1012–1019.

Kriete, R., & Bechtel, L. (2002). *The morning meeting book* (2nd ed.). Greenfield, MA: Northeast Foundation for Children.

Kriete, R., & Davis, C. (1999). *The morning meeting book*. Turners Falls, MA: Northeast Foundation for Children.

LaFrance, M., & Hecht, M. A. (1995). Why smiles generate leniency. *Personality and Social Psychology Bulletin*, *21*, 207–214.

Lang-Raad, N. (2019, September 14). *Our job is not to teach the standards*. It's to break the standards apart, discover what's interesting about them to students, and then create learning experiences to bridge the two. (Twitter post). Retrieved from https://twitter.com/drlangraad/status/1173053905942536192.

Lewis, P., Boucher, J., Lupton, L., & Watson, S. (2000). Relationships between symbolic play, functional play, verbal and non-verbal ability in young children. *International Journal of Language & Communication Disorders*, *35*(1), 117–127.

Macleod, G., MacAllister, J., & Pirrie, A. (2012). Towards a broader understanding of authority in student–teacher relationships. *Oxford Review of Education*, *38*(4), 493–508.

MacLeod, H. (2009). *Ignore everybody and 39 other keys to creativity*. New York, NY: Portfolio.

Marano, H. P. (2008). *A nation of wimps: The high cost of invasive parenting*. New York: Crown Archetype.

Martin, R. A. (2006). *The psychology of humor: An integrative approach*. Waltham, MA: Academic Press.

MindsetWorks. (2017). *Teacher practices: How praise and feedback impact student outcomes*. Retrieved from https://www.mindsetworks.com/science/Teacher-Practices.

Miron, Y., Wilf-Miron, R., & Kohane, I. S. (2019). Suicide rates among adolescents and young adults in the United States, 2000-2017. *Journal of the American Medical Association*, *321*(23), 2362–2364. doi:10.1001/jama.2019.5054

Moser, J. S., Schroder, H. S., Heeter, C., Moran, T. P., & Lee, Y. H. (2011). Mind your errors evidence for a neural mechanism linking growth mind-set to adaptive posterror adjustments. *Psychological Science*. 0956797611419520

Mueller, C., & Dweck, C. (1998). Praise for intelligence can undermine children's motivation and performance. *Journal of Personality and Social Psychology*, *75*(1), 33–52.

NEA. (2008). *Parent, family, and community involvement in education*. Retrieved from http://www.nea.org/assets/docs/PB11_ParentInvolvement08.pdf.

Nordenbo, S.-E., Sögaard Larsen, M., Tiftikci, N., Wendt, R. E., & Östergaard, S. (2008). *Laererkompetenser og elevers laering i förskole og skole. Et systematisk review utfört for kunnskapsdepartementet, Oslo*. (Teacher competences and pupil achievement in pre-school and school). Danish Clearinghouse for Educational Research. Copenhagen: Danmarks Paedagogiske Universitetsskole.

Pang, A. (2016). *Rest: Why you get more done when you work less*. New York: Basic Books.

Pelligrini, A. D., & Holmes, R. M. (2006). The role of recess in primary school. In D. Singer, R. Golinkoff, & K. Hirsh-Pasek (Eds.), *Play=learning: How play motivates and enhances children's cognitive and socio-emotional growth*. New York: Oxford University Press.

Pepler, D. J., & Ross, H. S. (1981). The effects of play on convergent and divergent problem solving. *Child Development, 52*(4), 1202–1210.

Play and Playground Encyclopedia. (2019). *US Play Coalition*. Retrieved from https://www.pgpedia.com/u/us-play-coalition.

Rhea, D. (2019). *The LiiNK project: Results*. Retrieved from https://liinkproject.tcu.edu/results.

Rhea, D., Rivchen, A., & Pennings, J. (2013). The LiiNk Project: Implementation of a recess and character development pilot study with grades K & 1 children. *Texas Association for Health, Physical Education, Recreation and Dance Journal (TAHPERD), 84*(Summer, 2), 14–35.

Robinson, K. (2007, January). *Do schools kill creativity?* Retrieved from https://www.youtube.com/watch?v=iG9CE55wbtY&t=1077s.

Rosenthal, R., & Jacobson, L. (1968). Pygmalion in the classroom. *The Urban Review, 3*(1), 16–20.

Rufo-Tepper, R. (2015). *Assessing students as they play*. Retrieved from https://www.edutopia.org/blog/using-games-for-assessment-rebecca-rufo-tepper.

Sacks, O. (2015). *On the move: A life*. New York: Vintage Books.

Sahlberg, P. (2006). Education reform for raising economic competitiveness. *Journal of Educational Change, 7*(4), 259–287.

Sahlberg, P., & Doyle, W. (2019). *Let the children play: How more play will save our schools and help children thrive*. New York: Oxford University Press.

SCDOE. (2019). *Profile of the South Carolina graduate*. Retrieved from https://ed.sc.gov/about/profile-of-sc-graduate.

Silverman, S. (1993). Student characteristics, practice, and achievement in physical education. *Journal of Educational Research, 21*(2), 141–157.

Skenazy, L. (2010). *Free range kids: How to raise safe, self-reliant children*. San Francisco, CA: Jossey-Bass.

Spariosu, M. (1989). *Dionysus reborn: Play and the aesthetic dimension in modern philosophical and scientific discourse*. Cornell University Press.

Spencer, J. (2019). *Keynote address at the Innovation Exchange Conference*. Fishers, IN: Innovation Exchange.

Spencer, J., & Juliani, A. J. (2016). *Launch: Using design thinking to boost creativity and bring out the maker in every student*. San Diego, CA: Dave Burgess Publishing.

Stevenson, H. W., & Lee, S. Y. (1990). Contexts of achievement: A study of American, Chinese, and Japanese children. *Monographs of the Society for Research in Child Development, 55*(1–2), 1–123.

Turner, V. (1969). *The ritual process*. New York: Aldine.

Tversky, A., & Kahneman, D. (1974). Judgement under uncertainty: Heuristics and biases. *Science, 9*(5), 340–346.

Twenge, J., Gentile, B., DeWall, C. N., Ma, D., Lacefield, K., & Schurtz, D. R. (2010). Birth cohort increases in psychopathology among young Americans, 1938-2007: A cross-temporal meta-analysis of the MMPI. *Clinical Psychology Review, 30*, 145–154.

UN Human Rights Office of the High Commissioner. (1989). Convention on the rights of the child, New York, 20 November. *United Nations Treaty Series, 44*(25). Available from https://www.ohchr.org/en/professionalinterest/pages/crc.aspx.

Vygotsky, L. S. (1977). Play and its role in the mental development of the child. In M. Cole (Ed.), *Soviet developmental psychology* (pp. 76–99). White Plains, NY: M.E. Sharpe.

Vygotsky, L. S. (2005). Appendix: From the notes of L.S. Vygotsky for lectures on the psychology of preschool children. *Journal of Russian and East Europena Psychology, 43*(2), 90–97.

Winerman, L. (2015). The mind's mirror. *Monitor on Psychology, 36*(9). Retrieved from https://www.apa.org/monitor/oct05/mirror.

Wyver, S. R., & Spence, S. H. (1999). Play and divergent problem solving: Evidence supporting a reciprocal relationship. *Early Education and Development, 10*(4), 419–444.

# INDEX